Tom Cabaniss
10/23/23

THE VOICE ABOVE THE NOISE

Pursuing God In Ordinary and Anxious Times

Dr. Tom Cabaniss

WestBow Press
A DIVISION OF THOMAS NELSON
& ZONDERVAN

Copyright © 2023 Dr. Tom Cabaniss.

All rights reserved. No part of this book may be used or reproduced by any means, graphic, electronic, or mechanical, including photocopying, recording, taping or by any information storage retrieval system without the written permission of the author except in the case of brief quotations embodied in critical articles and reviews.

This book is a work of non-fiction. Unless otherwise noted, the author and the publisher make no explicit guarantees as to the accuracy of the information contained in this book and in some cases, names of people and places have been altered to protect their privacy.

WestBow Press books may be ordered through booksellers or by contacting:

WestBow Press
A Division of Thomas Nelson & Zondervan
1663 Liberty Drive
Bloomington, IN 47403
www.westbowpress.com
844-714-3454

Because of the dynamic nature of the Internet, any web addresses or links contained in this book may have changed since publication and may no longer be valid. The views expressed in this work are solely those of the author and do not necessarily reflect the views of the publisher, and the publisher hereby disclaims any responsibility for them.

Any people depicted in stock imagery provided by Getty Images are models, and such images are being used for illustrative purposes only.
Certain stock imagery © Getty Images.

Unless marked otherwise, all scripture quotations are taken from The Holy Bible, New International Version®, NIV® Copyright © 1973, 1978, 1984, 2011 by Biblica, Inc.® Used by permission. All rights reserved worldwide.

Scripture quotations marked KJV are taken from the King James Version.

ISBN: 979-8-3850-0404-1 (sc)
ISBN: 979-8-3850-0405-8 (hc)
ISBN: 979-8-3850-0403-4 (e)

Library of Congress Control Number: 2023914127

Print information available on the last page.

WestBow Press rev. date: 08/08/2023

This manuscript leads readers on the pursuit of God and His unfolding work in all sixty-six books of the Bible. God is real. God is at work. And God works in history for His glory and the good of those who belong to Him.

INTRODUCTION

Most people paid little attention to the early evidence of a new and emerging upper respiratory infection in parts of China. But soon, the world would take notice. The early days of March 2020 marked the beginning of an experience that quickly began to redefine our lives and days. This rapidly spreading infection was named COVID-19, and it began to invade everywhere and interrupt everything. As our community and church were impacted by this novel virus, we began to grapple with things like social distancing and staying at home. As most of us began to adapt to more time at home, I looked for ways to hold our church together. I began by writing brief daily devotions that were emailed to our church family and posted on our church's Facebook page. COVID came and went. But I continued to write daily devotions that were shared, reshared, posted, and reposted. This writing continues even now.

I enjoyed writing the devotions so much that I decided to write at least one devotion based on every book of the Bible. This book is the result of what began as an effort to keep a church together that could not gather and to keep a church family united that was divided by distance and disease. This book is designed to be read as a daily supplement to one's Bible reading and ongoing faith-building efforts. You could read it all the way through from cover to cover, but it might be better to savor a devotion a day and let God speak to you through the faithfulness of His Word over 135 days. It was written primarily with individuals in mind and from an average pastor to his members. As the title suggests, this book was written with the hope and prayer that readers will hear one consistent and faithful Voice above a world filled with noise.

Thank you for reading these words and for opening your life to hear that faithful and enduring Voice. Whether your days are anxious or ordinary, there is still a Voice that can speak to you with clarity and conviction. May this book help you hear Him!

DAY 1

We find four powerful words in the opening of the Bible. "In the beginning God ..." is the way the Bible starts (Genesis 1:1a). Those four words represent some profound theology. You also have a profound worldview that is based on scripture. You could easily close the Bible for a moment and simply meditate on these first four words, and you would have much to reflect on. First, we are told that there was a beginning. This world or this universe or your life did not randomly happen one afternoon. Likewise, creation has not always existed. There was a definite beginning point in time. And this beginning had a grand Designer behind it. God orchestrated the beginning of the universe and everything in it. Just as He sent forth His Son to be born in Bethlehem in the fullness of time, He also chose to begin the universe on His timetable. God even created time itself. Simply, He gave the beginning its beginning.

Second, we are told that God was present in the beginning. He was not created. He did not suddenly pop into existence. He did not come from a neighboring universe to take over the management of this one. He was in the beginning. He has always existed and will always exist. We call this truth "the eternality of God." He is without beginning and without end. The Bible did not begin with an exhaustive effort to prove or convince readers that God is real. Rather, Genesis simply asserts the existence of God and declares it to be true.

Third, God was the agent of creation. A bit later in Genesis 1, we read that He spoke the universe into existence. Nine different times in Genesis 1 we are told that "God said." He spoke. His words gave rise to the creation that we inhabit today. There is incredible and infinite power in God's Word. Consider in Genesis 1 all that He spoke into existence.

Likewise, consider the power that we find in scripture (also rightly known as and called God's Word). We can place our full trust in whatever God has said or declared.

Fourth, the opening words of Genesis suggest to us that God has a destination in mind. From this beginning, God will navigate His creation to the conclusion that He has chosen for it. The universe is not spinning out of control. Creation has not gone off the rails. The Almighty knows exactly when, where, and how to bring His creation to the final destination. Because the creation belongs to God, He has the right to take it to the end that He wills for it. The Bible says, "The earth is the Lord's, and everything in it, the world, and all who live in it; for He founded it on the seas and established it on the waters" (Psalm 24:1–2). The earth is the Lord's. And God's people are His too. If we know Christ as Savior and Lord, we belong to Him.

At the end of Genesis 1, God weighed and considered all that He had created and all that He saw. We read, "God saw all that He had made, and it was very good. And there was evening, and there was morning—the sixth day" (Genesis 1:31). God's creative powers never fail. They are never second-rate. They are always perfect. And we can always take great comfort in knowing that He is real, dynamic, vibrant, and alive. He is on the throne and has been there even from the beginning.

DAY 2

Genesis 12 features the call of Abram to go to a new land. God's call came this way: "Leave your country, your people and your father's household and go to the land I will show you" (Genesis 12:1). Imagine receiving such a call—to leave behind all that is familiar and everything you know. And even more, to go to an undefined place for possibly the rest of your life. Now Abram did go with a promise—a promise from God that God would bless and honor him. We read, "I will make you into a great nation and I will bless you; I will make your name great and you will be a blessing" (Genesis 12:2). How does this ancient story connect with us today? What can we take away from this call and promise that God issued to Abram?

One lesson we learn is that we often have to trust God for a blessing. God gives us a pathway to follow or a road to pursue, and we have to take some initial steps of faith before we proceed. We may see only the beginning of the road and not the middle or the end. But God has seen the whole road. And we trust God to get us from the starting line to the finish line. We trust God to care for us, to protect us, and to direct us to where He would have us be. Often, God blesses us freely. God can bless us even unexpectedly. But at times, God's blessings come after we have trusted Him and acted as His call has directed us to act.

Another lesson stands out from Abram. God always acts with purpose. When God called Abram, the plan was to build the nation of Israel out of Abram's line and descendants. Of course, from Abram, Jesus would emerge years later as the Savior of both Israel and the world. God has a reason for His actions and the calls that He extends to people like Abram or you and me. It is not in God's character to bounce people around aimlessly like a basketball. God calls, leads, moves, and guides because He is working out His purposes and uses us to do so. We may never know when our obedience to the Lord sets the stage for a major event taking place years or even generations later.

There is a third lesson. We do not always see the outcome of our obedience. Abram could not see the rise of a great nation, the rise of Moses, the Exodus, or the coming of Jesus to save the world. He was simply faithful and obedient to God in his times and ways. God expects the same of us. We can be faithful without necessarily seeing all that God will bring to pass. The future belongs to Him. Obedience for obedience's sake is perfectly good. We obey God and listen to Him because He is God. Often the joy comes from obedience itself and believing that God can use and bless our obedience to Him.

Finally, God can work through our faithfulness and trust to bless others. God promised to build a great nation in and through Abram—people Abram would never know or meet. You could well be a channel God uses to bless others. Perhaps God directs blessings through you to change and encourage others. Blessings do not always remain in our possession alone. Quite often, we are conduits or pass-throughs whereby blessings reach their final destination. Sure, God could have used someone other than Abram or you or me for that matter. But we miss the blessing that could be ours and the favor that God seeks to bestow on us when we look the other way and let a blessing slide through our fingers. Obedience is often step one if we wish to be a vessel or channel through whom God passes along His blessings. Perhaps God will work through you today just as He did Abram long ago. Be ready, be willing, and be surrendered to Him.

DAY 3

Genesis has a number of colorful and fascinating figures. We read the riveting stories of Abraham, Isaac, and Jacob and see God at work to build a nation and from that nation to bring forth His Son Jesus. The life of Joseph, son of Jacob, was one example in which we clearly saw evidence of God at work. Though hated and envied by his brothers, Joseph was the favorite son of his father, Jacob. The dysfunctional nature of this family provides an enduring example of how favoritism can wreak havoc in any home. Even after being sold by his brothers and tossed in an Egyptian prison on trumped-up charges, Joseph never lost his faith and trust in God. He also never lost his character. He refused the sexual advances of Potiphar's wife and refused to bring shame to his boss Potiphar.

Indeed, God used Joseph even while he was a prisoner—locked away and all but forgotten in a dingy Egyptian prison cell. The Bible says, "But while Joseph was there in the prison, the Lord was with him; He showed him kindness and granted him favor in the eyes of the prison warden. So, the warden put Joseph in charge of all those held in the prison, and he was made responsible for all that was done there" (Genesis 39:20b–22). These verses remind us that God can use us even in the most unlikely times or places. We should never be quick to say that God cannot or will not do something or use someone. God took notice of Joseph in a prison cell and showed him favor. A few lessons stand out for us to see.

First, God is always aware of where we stand. We do not and cannot hide from Him. The psalmist wrote, "If I go up to the heavens, you are there; if I make my bed in the depths, you are there. If I rise on the wings of the dawn, if I settle on the far side of the sea, even there your hand will guide me, your right hand will hold me fast" (Psalm 139:8–10). It is a comfort to know that He does not forget about us, and others cannot rob us of or hide us away from His presence and vision.

Second, God can bestow His favor and kindness on us in any circumstance. He is not inhibited or prohibited in the least by anything at all. We might be ready to think that He has written us off or that we are beyond anything He could do to help us. But divine favor is His to show or give as He wills and pleases. When we face challenges, we can and should pray for His favor to be with us and to rest upon us.

Third, God often elevates us in proportion to our faithfulness. If we are faithful in small ways and with small things, He often increases the responsibilities entrusted to us. Because Joseph had been a good prisoner and had kept his character intact, the Lord raised him up to a new level of leadership and service. Joseph was given charge over all the prisoners. Be faithful and trustworthy with whatever God gives you. If we desire to do great things, we may first have to be content with doing small and simple things.

Fourth, God often prepares us for events that we have not yet seen. We know the rest of Joseph's story. He was eventually second only to Pharaoh in all of Egypt and was in charge of the nation's food supply during a time of hunger and famine. He was in the right position to save his brothers and thus keep alive the building of this family into the people of Israel. The training that Joseph received while being in charge of the prison population likely prepared him for greater roles and duties. It could be that God is preparing you now for something that you do not yet know or recognize. There could be some role or place of service that God has in mind. The work or responsibilities you are performing now may well prepare you for what lies ahead. That one thing you might be tempted to write off as boring or mundane just might be some crucial spiritual lesson or truth that God wishes to teach you. Rather than dreaming of more to do or lamenting that you do not have what you want, stay trained and laser-like focused on what God has given to you.

DAY 4

About a third of the way into Genesis, God spoke to Abram (who would later be called Abraham). At the time, the Bible says that Abram was ninety-nine years old. He had lived a long time. The Bible says, "The Lord appeared to him and said, 'I am God Almighty; walk before me faithfully and be blameless'" (Genesis 17:1). In this message from the Lord to Abram, we find three lessons that stand out for us today. Even though the message was directed to a single man who lived a long, long time ago, there is still something for us to see today. First, God revealed Himself. He said, "I am God Almighty." The Hebrew is "El-Shaddai." God is the One who possesses perfect power and all power. A few chapters earlier in Genesis, we learned that God had spoken the creation into existence. And now, with Abram, God was beginning to unfold His plan for redemption and salvation. From this one man, Abram, God will build the nation of Israel; and from Israel will come Jesus, our one and only Savior. As the Almighty, God knows where He wants to take history. He has a plan in place, and He has patiently executed that plan beginning with Abram.

Second, God called Abram to walk before Him "faithfully." Walk refers to one's life, conduct, or behavior. The walk is who we are and how we have chosen to live. The word *faithfully* means to walk in a way that is upright and sincere. The standard really is nothing less than perfection. Jesus said essentially the same thing in Matthew 5:48, "Be perfect, therefore, as your heavenly Father is perfect." God does not relax His standards or holiness. He does not lower the bar. We are always to strive for a sincere and upright walk with the Lord in the way we live. Romans 6:1 teaches us that we are not to continue in sin or to turn the grace of God into a "get out of jail free" card. Jesus lived the perfect life that we did not live so His righteousness is credited to us. But still, the standard does not change, and the bar is not lowered. You would never tell your child just to obey you three days a week and to forget the other four. Likewise, God does not expect or accept partial obedience or occasional obedience. The standard is always to live faithfully and uprightly. Delayed obedience or partial obedience is really disobedience.

Third, God called Abram to "be blameless." The word is *tamin* in Hebrew. It means to walk in truth. It means to walk and to live without blemish in entirety—that is to say throughout your life. Examine your motivations, actions, thoughts, inclinations, and convictions. Let the truth of scripture correct the ones that are wrong or false. When the Holy Spirit convicts us of sin, we are to respond in confession, repentance, and humility. We are to receive the forgiveness that God offers as we place ourselves on bended knees before Him. This call to be blameless carried with it a promise that we find in Genesis 17:2. God promised a covenant with Abram and to "increase His numbers greatly."

So God was going to use Abram to bring His salvation plans into action. When we seek to live blamelessly, God can work through us. We are open to Him, and we desire His will above and more than the things of this world. The depth and joys of our walk with God are often connected with the choices we make about how we will live. His favor rests upon those who walk rightly before Him. We would never expect to experience God's favor or blessing if we lie or commit adultery. For example, Noah's blameless conduct received a blessing—safe passage in the ark when God (literally) rained judgment upon the surface of the earth. Scripture often speaks of God rewarding and blessing His people when they obey Him and walk rightly and blamelessly with Him. His favor does rest upon those who seek Him, honor Him, obey Him, and worship Him. There is a tendency in our world to compartmentalize our lives and think that God belongs on the calendar for Sunday while the other six days belong to us to do as we wish. Dangerous thinking and unbiblical thinking! Every day is the day the Lord has made. Let us rejoice and be glad in each one as we dedicate ourselves to Him.

DAY 5

We often speak about God's promises. And even more often, we have to claim them and rely on them. One aspect of faith is taking God at His Word and placing trust in His promises. In Genesis 21:1–2, we find the fulfillment of one of His promises. As you likely know, God had promised a son to Abraham and Sarah. The idea that a married couple the age of these two would just be starting a family is hard to imagine. And indeed, Sarah laughed at the thought that she could conceive and deliver a child. But nothing is too hard for God. Producing a child is less difficult for God to do than blinking our eyes is for us.

The Bible says, "Now the Lord was gracious to Sarah as he had said, and the Lord did for Sarah what he had promised. Sarah became pregnant and bore a son to Abraham in his old age, at the very time God had promised him" (Genesis 21:1–2). Imagine the joy that Abraham and Sarah must have experienced. Imagine their awe over what God had done when they first saw their son. As we marvel over this miracle, we find three lessons about God's promises that we can consider.

First, God kept His Word. He did what He had promised to do. God is the original and greatest promise keeper. And the fact that God acted graciously would suggest that He kept His promise to people who in no way deserved the wonderful act that He had performed for them. Grace is always a gift and never earned or deserved. If grace were earned, it would cease to be grace. When we prove unfaithful, God remains faithful. When we doubt His Word or promises, He keeps them and blesses us through them. We learn to trust God and to take His promises at face value. You may recall how many times Charlie Brown failed to kick the football when Lucy was his holder. Invariably, Lucy would convince Charlie Brown that she would hold the ball for him, only to pull it away at the last possible second. God does not tease us or break a promise just to see us flounder and fall. He does not dangle a promise and then pull it away to see us fail.

Second, God did exactly what He promised to do. He gave this couple a son whom they named Isaac. There was no bait and switch. God did not overpromise and underdeliver. God did not have to lower expectations. God did not overcommit. We can trust God's promises to be with us, to forgive us, to keep us in His care, and to work all things for the good of those who love Him and who have been called according to His purposes. God does not force us to settle for something second-rate or second-best. He knows what we need, and He supplies that need. Or as Jesus put it, "Which of you, if your son asks for bread, will give him a stone? Or if he asks for a fish, will give him a snake? If you, then, though you are evil, know how to give good gifts to your children, how much more will your Father in heaven give good gifts to those who ask him!" (Matthew 7:9–11).

Third, God kept His promise at the right time. Often, we struggle with matters of timing and when or where God is at work. Our time is not His time any more than our thoughts are His thoughts. God knew the right time to bring a son to Abraham and Sarah, and He did so. And God knows when the timing is right to work in your life or mine. God knows just when to bless, correct, train, act, or work. God sees the past, present, and future all at once and all at the same time. We occasionally have to wait for God to work. Waiting time is not wasted time. Waiting time is not downtime. Waiting gives us a chance to seek the Lord, to draw near to Him, and to lean on Him. And frankly, waiting for God to work is an expression of faith. When we wait, we acknowledge that God is going to bring His will and promises to completion. So we trust not only God's promises, but we trust His timing too.

The promise that God kept with Abraham and Sarah continues to bless them even to this day. From Isaac would come Jacob and eventually the tribes of Israel. From Israel would come Jesus—our Savior and Lord. God may keep a promise in your life today that impacts generations to follow or even your children and grandchildren. Do not grow weary in waiting for God to work. He sees you just as He saw an elderly and childless couple who relied on Him to send the son He had promised. As you see evidence and reports of revival and renewal springing up across American college campuses, pray that God would bring revival and renewal to you as well. Get into His Word and pray, seek Him, and confess your sins.

DAY 6

In Genesis 22, God tested Abraham. And wow, what a test! The test came in the form of commanding Abraham to sacrifice his son—his one and only son—Isaac. Keep in mind that Abraham had waited a long, long time for this son. And Isaac was to be the son through whom God had promised to multiply the descendants of Abraham (as numerous as grains of sand or stars in the sky) and to build a great nation that would ultimately bless the whole world. And now, it would appear that all of those promises were in question. And even the life and survival of Isaac were in question. Obviously, a sacrifice would die and no longer live. A sacrifice as an end—the end! But that was the test in Genesis 22:2, "Then God said, 'Take your son, your only son, whom you love—Isaac—and go to the region of Moriah. Sacrifice him there as a burnt offering on a mountain I will show you.'"

The Bible says that "early the next morning," Abraham began to do what God had commanded. As he made his way to the sacrifice, Abraham did not waver. But in Genesis 22:8, we find this amazing statement of faith from this aged father: "Abraham answered, 'God himself will provide the lamb for the burnt offering, my son.' And the two of them went on together." Six powerful words—God Himself will provide the lamb. Abraham seemed to have this sense or conviction that God would not allow the death or sacrifice of Isaac to go forward. This test was to see how much Abraham loved God and whether Abraham loved God for who God is rather than simply loving God because of what God could give or do. That might seem a little unclear or convoluted, but it connects with us today.

Often, we fall prey to loving God or seeking God for what we can gain or receive in return. We can desire the gifts more than the giver, the blessings more than the One who blesses. So God's test was rather simple. "Do you love me more for who I am than what I can give you or do for you?" Job courageously promised his love and loyalty to God even if God slayed him (Job 13:15). We are abundantly blessed people, and it can be easy not to see past the mass of blessings we find in our lives. May we love the Giver more than the gifts and the Provider more than the provisions.

And God did provide a lamb for sacrifice. This provision of the lamb foreshadows the ultimate Lamb that God provided—His Son Jesus. Just as God spared Isaac's life by providing a lamb, He has spared our lives as well. He sent His Son to be the innocent and sacrificial Lamb that we could not be and did not deserve. Through the blood of the Lamb, we are made clean and our sins are washed away fully and completely. In the most trying of circumstances and on the most gut-wrenching occasion, Abraham knew that God would provide and that God would make a way. That is faith! Today, we hold on to the Lord even when circumstances might suggest otherwise or situations might tempt us to turn from the Lord. Even when we may not see a way forward, like Abraham, we can declare that God will provide a way. God will make a way even when a way may not humanly exist that we can see with human eyes.

Trust God. Those two words may seem trite or even overly simple, but they affirm incredible faith. That was Abraham's position—trust God because He will provide the lamb. And God still provides. Often, His provisions surprise us and amaze us. You will never falter if you trust God and His Word. Trust Him with your life, your trials, your uncertainties, and your situations. Trust Him with your life and your next breath. And one day, you will find yourself breathing celestial air as you see Him face-to-face.

DAY 7

The second book of the Bible is Exodus. And part of this book chronicles the deliverance of Israel from captivity and slavery in Egypt. We learn how God moved in a mighty way to set His people free from Pharaoh's clutches. We read in Exodus 2:24, "God heard their groaning and he remembered his covenant with Abraham, with Isaac and with Jacob." And just a few verses later, God spoke to Moses from a burning bush and chose Moses as his servant to bring Israel out of Egypt. We pause for a moment at the expression "God heard." The God who hears is one way for us to know or to acknowledge God. The name "Ishmael," for instance, means "God hears." God hears us and answers us based on His righteousness and goodness and not ours. We do not win or earn the right to be heard because of something we do or because we have had a really successful day. Rather, God hears us because of who He is and His righteousness.

Followers of Jesus who have come to faith and trust in Him are blessed with the assurance that God hears them. God takes note of their situation or condition. In the case of the Exodus, God heard the cries and groans of His people. God saw their chains, bindings, and slavery. He had not forgotten His covenant with them or promises to them. There can certainly be times when we feel or even think that God does not see or hear us. There can be occasions where situations and battles have worn us down so badly that we think God has moved on from us and left us to ourselves. Life can be hard, and daily battles can take a devastating toll.

But a story like the Exodus challenges our thinking and feelings. We learn that we have not been abandoned or forgotten, ignored, or dismissed. God remembers His promises to us and keeps His covenant with us through His Son Jesus. In 1 Peter 4:7, we read, "The end of all things is near. Therefore, be clear-minded and self-controlled so you can pray." Peter wrote at a time when many Christians believed that the Lord could and would return in their lifetime. These first-century believers expected to see Jesus return at any moment. While Peter did not set a day or time for Jesus to come back, he did command us to be clear-minded and self-controlled. The idea is to hold on to the Lord's promises and His Word while we wait for Him to come for us. We are not to allow anything to rob us of the peace and clarity that we find in His promises and plans. The Lord will bring such things to pass; we need only to be still and wait upon Him.

Today, the enemy can easily flood our faces, eyes, and ears with an onslaught of trials and temptations that can leave us dazed and staggering. The enemy can be so ruthless that we wonder where the Lord is and whether He hears us or cares for us. The enemy is a master at casting doubt and confusion upon God's Word. Go back to the story of Adam and Eve in the Garden of Eden and consider the doubt and confusion that the serpent threw at them. Doubt and confusion still work today. The enemy may not be very innovative, but he is very good at recycling and reusing the same old schemes, again and again, to deceive us into doubting God, God's compassion, and the reality that God hears His people.

We can rest assured today that God hears us. Our situations may not be as dire as what Israel faced on the eve of the Exodus, but He still hears us. He hears our loneliness, confusion, worry, fear, confusion, and dread. He hears the small whimpers and the loud cries. He is and always will be the God who hears. His ears are never too weak or too small.

DAY 8

Soon after arriving safely on the other side of the Red Sea, Moses led the people of Israel in a song of celebration and praise (found in Exodus 15:1–18). God had just safely delivered Israel out of Egypt (what we know as the Exodus) and through the Red Sea on dry ground. Once again, dry ground! God parted the waters, and Israel safely reached the other side. God made a way when there was no way. The song we find in Exodus 15 told of the Lord's greatness and glory. He was Israel's Champion and Deliverer. Exodus 15:18 says, "The LORD reigns for ever and ever." Those seven words are a fitting end to a song of praise. And those words form a period or even an exclamation point on what God had just done. It was a drop-the-mic moment. We can easily imagine the people of Israel were in utter awe of what they had just witnessed and even participated in as they passed safe and dry through walls of water on either side of them.

Even today, we need to be reminded that the Lord God reigns—not just for a term or season like an elected official. No, God reigns—now, tomorrow, and always. Surprisingly, only a few verses later in Exodus, the people are grumbling and complaining to Moses about the lack of water to drink. It seems that collectively, the memories of the people had grown awfully short and frail. We would think that Israel would have no trouble trusting the Lord to provide them with water after what the people had just witnessed Him do. But human memory often fades and fails—and certainly so in remembering the Lord and His deeds. Faith is tragically reduced to "what have you done for me lately, Lord?"

We often need to be reminded that the Lord reigns—forever and ever! When days are long and battles rage, we would do well to remember that the Lord reigns. His throne is as secure as ever. His authority has not diminished in any way. Heaven still rules the affairs of earth and the universe. God gave Israel water to drink (Exodus 15:25). In fact, God turned bitter water into drinkable water. The bitter and undrinkable water of Marah was turned into refreshing, clean, and sustaining water. So in a relatively brief span of time, God performed two amazing miracles. He divided the waters of the Red Sea for Israel to pass through, and He changed bitter water into refreshing water for the people to drink. But, and we know there must be a "but," a few verses later in Exodus 16, the people are grumbling again.

This latest grumbling concerned the lack of food. The people even went as far as to say, "If only we had died by the Lord's hand in Egypt! There we sat around pots of meat and ate all the food we wanted, but you, Moses, have brought us out into this desert to starve this entire assembly to death" (Exodus 16:3). Some lessons are never learned. Israel had watched the power of God on display twice yet still grumbled and murmured against Moses and the Lord (Exodus 16:8). Once again, God provided for the people. He sent them meat and manna. This third miracle reminded the people once again that God reigns. He can do anything He wishes anywhere and at any time.

Maybe you tend to doubt the Lord. Remember that He reigns. He is on the throne of the universe and presiding over the affairs of this earth and providing for us. Think of the times and ways that God has provided for you, answered prayers, blessed you, or met your needs in some special way. The enemy would love to confuse us and rob us of the memories we have of God working in our lives. God is a debtor to no one. He provides. He reigns. He rules. He makes a way when we cannot see or find a way forward by ourselves. Like Israel, we often have to learn, relearn, and continue to learn important lessons about who God is and what He does. One critical lesson we must learn is the message of the Exodus—God reigns! He always has, and He always will!

DAY 9

In Exodus 20, God delivered the Ten Commandments to Moses. The moral law of God is captured in these commandments. The first four concern our relationship with the Lord. The last six concern and govern our relationships with other people. Exodus 20:1 says, "And God spoke all these words." Moses made it clear that it was God who was speaking. We remember that God spoke the creation into existence. And God spoke His law or moral standards into existence as well. Scripture made it clear that the commandments did not come from Moses or by a majority vote of the newly freed Israelites. God declared the commandments. And because God declared them, they were and are good and right. We are reminded that when God has spoken, we are to pay attention. When God has declared His expectations for how we are to live, we are to pay attention. God's ways are designed to protect us from sin and the terrible consequences of sin. God's standards are not burdensome or onerous. Indeed, they are the only way to enjoy freedom, life, and fulfillment. The enemy is the one who oppresses us and imprisons us. The freedom that Satan offers is nothing less than slavery in disguise. God's ways bring freedom. God's Word and ways always set us free and lead us to abundant life.

In Exodus 20:2, the Bible says, "I am the LORD your God, who brought you out of Egypt, out of the land of slavery." God made it clear to Moses and the people of Israel that He was the reason for their freedom and release. No one else had set the people free from captivity. Israel did not win release by overwhelming power on the battlefield or by cunning negotiation and diplomacy. God acted in history to set the people free and to fulfill the promises made to Abraham, Isaac, and Jacob. Reading these words in Exodus reminds us of the promises that God has kept for us. Perhaps you have experienced His promise of forgiveness, peace, contentment, and strength. Maybe you have experienced His healing power. Maybe He has set you free from the awful shame or guilt that kept you enslaved and humiliated.

Exodus 20:3 says, "You shall have no other gods before me." God does not share His glory, majesty, or throne. No one is to take a higher or greater place in our lives than the Lord Himself. There is only one God—revealed as Father, Son, and Holy Spirit. He reigns without an equal or comparison. The word *before* can occasionally be translated as "besides." We are to have no gods besides the Lord God. We can easily find ourselves giving great attention and devotion to lesser gods—the habits, hobbies, noise, and tugs that can easily lead us away from the Lord and to devotion to something lesser than Him. We may not be quite so brazen or cavalier as to build an idol from stone, wood, or gold and worship it. But we can easily allow something (or anything) to capture our thoughts, wishes, ambitions, and motivations. We can trade our lives for very common things that are not worthy of such dedication and devotion.

This first commandment calls for us to surrender ourselves to the Lord—wholly, completely, and willingly. A friend of mine shared a devotion recently where he challenged those of us who listened not to be committed to the Lord but surrendered to Him. He further noted there is a difference between commitment and surrender. A commitment can easily shift, shape, and shuffle into something less than devotion and dedication. Some commitments hold on only as long as there is not something better to do or if something different has not surfaced. But surrender is to live for nothing less than the Lord while putting away any desire to pursue or chase after other things. We may have to ask ourselves if we are surrendered to the Lord or committed. May we surrender to Him—each and every day! There is nothing greater or grander than the Lord and knowing and walking with Him.

DAY 10

Leviticus is one book of the Bible that many believers often skip past. Not many Christians read it or study what it says. It is routinely overlooked and dismissed. I have never heard anyone say that their favorite book in the Bible is Leviticus. And for sure, Leviticus does not have the exciting stories of Genesis or Acts, the miracles of the Gospels or the lovely poetry that we find in Psalms. However, Leviticus is part of the canon of the Bible. It is holy scripture so it does matter, and it does have a message for us even in 2023. The overarching theme is a compelling one. How do we approach God? How do we come before a holy, perfect, majestic, and glorious God?

Did you know that the word *holy* is found more than eighty different times in Leviticus? Holiness before the Lord is a theme. And the holiness of God is plainly taught. God cannot be in the presence of sin and will not permit it to come before Him. So, Leviticus was given to Israel to help the nation and individuals understand how to approach the Lord God in worship and obedience. Remember, God is the LORD—the Great I AM revealed to Moses at the burning bush. God considers our actions but also the intentions and motivations behind how we act. All aspects are to be holy in our approach to Him.

We might even point to Leviticus 19:2 as a summary of the entire book. The Bible says, "Speak to the entire assembly of Israel and say to them: 'Be holy because I, the Lord your God, am holy.'" The basis for our holiness is the holiness of God. Because God is holy, we are to live in holy ways. *Holy* means to be distinct or to be set apart. We do not live as we please because such behavior is offensive to our Lord. We are to be distinctly different people. Paul said we are to shine like stars in the sky (Philippians 2:15). God does not call us to make a few cosmetic changes here and there or to spend some weekly time on self-improvement. We are to be holy—set apart and living in a distinctly different way.

Early in Leviticus, in chapter 3, God instructs the people to bring animal offerings and sacrifices that are without blemish or defect. The reason for this command was to guide the people to understand that they were to bring their best to God—not the leftovers, the discards, or the things they can live without. Even today, we are to offer the Lord our best. We are to give the first 10 percent of our income to Him as an act of worship and obedience. We are to give Him our time, worship, service, and trust. We give to the Lord from the first and best that we have and not just whatever we can find at the end of the day, week, or month. God is without blemish or defect and calls for us not to compromise what we bring to Him.

In Leviticus 3:16, we read, "All the fat is the LORD'S." God made it clear what first and always belonged to Him when an offering was made. When we bring our first and best to God, we do not struggle in deciding what to give or what to bring or what we can spare. Indeed, we learn that when God is glorified by what we bring to Him in faith and surrender; then we will be satisfied in the way that He cares for us in response. When it comes to giving to God what is rightfully His, Leviticus ends in this way, "A tithe of everything from the land, whether grain from the soil or fruit from the trees, belongs to the LORD; it is holy to the LORD" (Leviticus 27:30). Truly, the earth is the Lord's and everything in it. But God, in His grace and love, allows us to keep and enjoy 90 percent of His blessings and provisions. We return only 10 percent to Him as an act of Thanksgiving and gratitude. Take time to read Leviticus. You may have avoided this book many times; but it contains nuggets of wisdom, guidance, and practical teachings about how to love, serve, and approach God today.

DAY 11

In Leviticus 16, we read God's instructions to Moses concerning atonement for the sins of the people of Israel. In these instructions, we find a reference to "the scapegoat." This expression has found its way into modern parlance and conversation. We often refer to the act of assigning blame to someone or something as "scapegoating." We may make someone out to be the scapegoat for our mistakes or something that has not worked as planned. Usually, we misrepresent and misuse the idea of a scapegoat when it takes place in modern conversations and exchanges. But there was a real purpose and a real message behind the biblical concept of the scapegoat.

We read in Leviticus, "When Aaron has finished making atonement for the Most Holy Place, the tent of meeting and the altar, he shall bring forward the live goat. He is to lay both hands on the head of the live goat and confess over it all the wickedness and rebellion of the Israelites—all their sins—and put them on the goat's head. He shall send the goat away into the wilderness in the care of someone appointed for the task. The goat will carry on itself all their sins to a remote place; and the man shall release it in the wilderness" (Leviticus 16:20–22). The scapegoat symbolized that through the act of atonement, all of Israel's sins could be forgiven, never to return. The sins were sent away from the people and the nation, having been placed or laid symbolically on the goat.

The scapegoat was the "sin bearer" for ancient Israel. In this image of the scapegoat, we have a glimpse or symbol of the role that Jesus would fulfill at the cross in dying for the sins of the world and making atonement for our sins before the Father. Isaiah 53:6 says, "We all, like sheep, have gone astray, each of us has turned to our own way; and the

LORD has laid on him the iniquity of us all." Our sins were placed on Jesus, and His righteousness was given to us. Romans 5:8 says, "While we were yet sinners, Christ died for us." Jesus did for us what we could never do for ourselves—remove sin and satisfy our debts before the Father. Psalm 103:12 teaches us, "As far as the east is from the west, so far has He removed our transgressions from us." Sins that we confess, acknowledge, and repent of are placed at the cross where the death and blood of Jesus cover them and we are justified or declared not guilty.

Hebrews 9:28 says, "So Christ was sacrificed once to take away the sins of many; and he will appear a second time, not to bear sin, but to bring salvation to those who are waiting for him." And in 1 Peter 2:24, we read, "'He himself bore our sins' in his body on the cross, so that we might die to sins and live for righteousness; 'by his wounds you have been healed.'" Consistently through scripture, we discover that Jesus is the final and ultimate sin bearer. He removes our sins by His death for them. He makes us free, at peace, and restored with the Father through His passion at the cross. Give thanks today so that your sins can be forgiven and you can be made whole once again. The sins that once divided us from the Father have been covered and paid for by the only sinless One ever to live.

DAY 12

We all have ways of introducing ourselves. You might share your name or your vocation (or what you once did). You might share your address or hometown. You might share some details about your family. In Leviticus, God had a six-word way of introducing Himself. He said, "I am the LORD your God" (Leviticus 26:1b). And He said this more than once in Leviticus (and certainly more than once in scripture as a whole). The way that God chose to introduce Himself is significant and important. And there are some truths that we need to see. These truths carry meaning for us today.

First, God said, "I am." He simply is. God is the same yesterday, today, and forever. There has never been a second of existence without God. And there will never be a single second where God does not exist. The Bible makes no attempt to explain God's origin because He has no origin. He has always existed. He has no ending on the horizon. He does not give out, wear out, break down, or burn out. In Genesis 1:1, we read, "In the beginning, God ..." Again, God is. In Revelation, we read, "I am the Alpha and the Omega," says the Lord God, "who is, and who was, and who is to come, the Almighty" (Revelation 1:8). God has changelessly existed in the past, present, and future.

Second, God said, "I am the LORD." He is the great I AM. He is without an equal and cannot be captured in any idolatrous representation or efforts. God is the One who causes all things to be. To be the LORD means He is sovereign. He reigns—always and at all times. He does not share His throne or crown with any other entity. Satan learned this reality the hard way by being booted out of the presence of God. He is inextricably anchored to the throne of authority, control, and power. God spoke the creation into existence. God created time and the seasons. God made the laws of science and physics that govern how we live even at this moment as we write or read these words.

Third, God said, "I am the LORD your God." He introduced Himself as the God of Israel. He was also described as the God of Abraham, Isaac, and Jacob. God connected Himself to the affairs of history and today. The Bible says, "He is before all things, and in him all things hold together" (Colossians 1:18). Just as Israel could enjoy the favor of God, so can we. Many of the nations that surrounded Israel had their own particular gods, goddesses, or deities that they sacrificed and to whom they offered allegiances. But Israel was to be different. Israel belonged to the one true God of the universe. Their relationship was often likened to that of a marriage where Israel was to be betrothed wholly and completely to the Lord. Today, we are not to divide our faith and loyalty between God and lesser things. We are to be His people—to know Him, to walk with Him, to worship Him, and to trust Him.

We give thanks that God is real and that we can know Him and always lean on Him. He is infinitely more than we could ever imagine or begin to describe with human words and ways. Perhaps we are best suited to settle where Leviticus settled and simply recognize that the LORD is our God and to remember His words spoken long ago, "I am the LORD your God." David knew Him as a gracious and faithful shepherd. The disciples knew Him firsthand and face-to-face. Moses knew Him as the great liberator of Israel and as the One who parted the waters of the Red Sea. He is the LORD God.

DAY 13

When we read Leviticus, we learn about God's expectations for how we are to approach Him and how we are to live. We learn about His standards for holiness and righteousness. In Leviticus 11:45 specifically, we learn why God calls His people to be holy. The answer is simple. The Bible says, "I am the LORD, who brought you up out of Egypt to be your God; therefore, be holy, because I am holy." That verse deserves to be underlined in every person's Bible. There is some profound truth for us to see. First, we encounter the name and identity of God. He is the LORD. To see this word LORD in all caps reminds us of God's proper name. He is the great I AM. He is the One who causes all things to be. He is that He is. God is the great I AM. He is not an idol. He is not an artistically fashioned icon made from wood, stone, or precious metals. He is the LORD. There is no God but the LORD. He is without equal or comparison. Any effort to make a comparison of something to God fails and falls short.

Second, God tells us how to live. We are to "be holy." We are to live righteously and uprightly. We are to pursue purity in all ways and dealings. One way that holy living is practically expressed is found in Galatians 5:22–23 where we read about the fruit of the Spirit. Jesus tells us to love God, to love others, and to love as He has loved us. The Bible has the familiar refrain from Genesis to Revelation that we are to live in a holy way. We are to obey the Lord and to walk with the Lord. We are not to substitute our ways for His ways. Holy living is not something that we naturally do or pursue. We choose holiness with the help of the Holy Spirit living in us and guiding us into the things that are right, good, and true. Paul wrote in Romans 12:2 that we are to renew our minds rather than to just conform to the world in a default manner. When we renew our minds through scripture, prayer, and the indwelling of the Holy Spirit, we can seek God's good, pleasing, and perfect will.

Third, our motivation for being holy is God Himself. God tells us to "be holy because I am holy" (Leviticus 11:44). We are to be like God. That may seem daunting and overwhelming, but that is the unchanging standard that God has. We are not to do as we wish or settle for the lesser things. God called Israel to holiness and distinctiveness so that other nations might take note of Him because of how His people lived. Likewise, today, God calls us to live holy so that we reflect Him to those around us. We are to be salt in that we make people thirsty for the Lord we know and serve. We are to be light so we can direct others to the Lord by what they find in us and how we live.

Because God is God, He can make the rules and standards for how we are to live and the pathways we are to follow. Indeed, the Bible says, let God be true but every man a liar (Romans 3:4). That is to say, we are to trust God's standards above the standards of others or even our own. God's ways lead to light and life. The ways of the world lead to darkness and death. Even in the initial temptation in the Garden of Eden, Satan deceived Adam and Eve by casting doubt on God's standards and demands. When we turn from the standards of God, we are left with nothing else to trust or embrace as life-giving and life-changing. Israel needlessly and unnecessarily wandered in the wilderness for a long time because they disobeyed God and preferred their sour ways to His sweet ways. May we not follow that example. May holiness be the standard that we pursue, the carrot that we chase, and the manner by which we live. All other ways lead to death and despair.

DAY 14

Numbers is the fourth book of the Old Testament. In Hebrew, the name for Numbers means "in the wilderness" or "in the desert." This book is the fulfillment of the story of Israel's exodus from slavery and oppression in Egypt and their deliverance journey to gain or to lay hold of the land God promised to give them as far back as the patriarchs. But did you know that Numbers speaks of the coming of the Messiah? Already, even before Israel entered the land promised to them, God has laid the plans or groundwork for the coming of His Son Jesus to be the Messiah. We read in Numbers 24:17–19, "I see him, but not now; I behold him, but not near. A star will come out of Jacob; a scepter will rise out of Israel. He will crush the foreheads of Moab, the skulls of all the people of Sheth. Edom will be conquered; Seir, his enemy, will be conquered, but Israel will grow strong. A ruler will come out of Jacob and destroy the survivors of the city." These words were a prophecy spoken by Balaam. These words found their fulfillment in Jesus.

Many years before Bethlehem, there was a prophecy of Jesus's coming. The Father had put in place a plan to redeem the world through His Son. For generations, this promise would be held on to by faith and the confidence that in His way and in His time, God would bring forth the Messiah. He would crush the enemies of Israel but save all who received Him into His holy kingdom and family. His coming was "not near," but it was promised and certain to happen. These words from Balaam remind us to live by faith more than sight. We often cannot see where God is at work or what He might be doing. But we trust His Word and promises. We trust Him to keep watch over us and to grant us hope and a future.

A bit earlier in Numbers 6:24–27, we encounter the priestly blessing that the LORD gave to Aaron and his sons for how to bless Israel. We read, "'The Lord bless you and keep you; the Lord make his face shine on you and be gracious to you; the Lord turn his face toward you and give you peace.' So, they will put MY Name on the Israelites, and I will bless them." This ancient blessing reminded the people of Israel that indeed they belonged to the LORD. They were His people. Today, this blessing is often used at weddings to place the Name of the Lord over a man and a woman who become husband and wife. This blessing can be used at funerals and memorial services to remember that the one who has passed away has been raised to new life. It also encourages those who are still alive to remember that they rest and remain under the care of the LORD.

Numbers can often be a book that we rarely read and, even then, run through rather quickly. But we can easily miss the enduring messages, encouragements, and blessings that God has for us. One faith-building exercise you could do each day is to read and recite this Aaronic blessing in Numbers 6. Imagine the LORD speaking these words to you and over you. Receive this blessing in your life. Trust that God does make His face shine upon you and grant you peace. Remember, God is for you and loves you beyond anything you could humanly imagine. The prophecy and blessing we read are God's invitation to us to know Him, to seek Him, and to walk with Him. This invitation remains real and valid for us even today. There is no expiration or use-by date assigned to it. While God was fulfilling His purposes long, long ago in Israel, His eye was on the future as well and the day that His Son would come and people like us would turn to Him in the twenty-first century. Be grateful today for God's work and promises across the spectrum of time, nations, and boundaries. And welcome this God into your life today.

DAY 15

We know from reading the Old Testament that Israel roamed in the wilderness for a long time after leaving Egypt and before entering the land that God promised them. It was a forty-year-long time of wandering. That would be like starting something in 1983 and just now finishing it. But while they were in the wilderness, they were never alone. God had not forgotten about them or abandoned them. God had not chosen to play tricks with them or some sort of monumental game of hide-and-seek. Numbers 9:15–16 tells us that God gave guidance to the people. The Bible says, "On the day the tabernacle, the tent of the covenant law, was set up, the cloud covered it. From evening till morning, the cloud above the tabernacle looked like fire. That is how it continued to be; the cloud covered it, and at night it looked like fire." A cloud and fire. These simple natural objects represented enduring divine guidance to the people of Israel. Even today, God does not leave us without guidance and the promise of His presence with us in life. We have these blessings even when our situations or circumstances might suggest or persuade us to doubt Him and think otherwise.

God guides us today with His Word. It is a lamp for our feet and a light for our path. It does not change like the weather. God's Word is available to us—often much more available than we are inclined to open it and read it. Many Bibles sit idly on shelves and in closets gathering dust from an owner's lack of interest or willingness to read them. Those troubling or confusing moments we face in life can often be confronted by the promises, commands, and guidance we find in the Bible. God's Word speaks as clearly and as relevantly today as it ever has.

When we pray, we experience the guidance of God. He can speak to us, nudge us, and lead us in ways that are good and right. God will always lead us in concert with His Word. He is not the god of confusion. He is the God of clarity and correction. God can bring peace to anxious minds through prayer. God can comfort hurting hearts when we place ourselves humbly and wholly before Him. God can grant us the sweetness of forgiveness and the relief of His grace and pardon. Prayer is one way we can rest in Him.

Worship is yet another way that God guides His people. As we give glory to God in worship, we find that we are satisfied and filled with His presence and goodness. He brings fulfillment and grace to us in comforting ways. As we express our praise and thankfulness to God for battles that have been won, He gives us reassurance that He is with us always—even to the end of the age. Part of our worship, individually and collectively, is coming to the Lord for guidance. We recognize that He alone possesses perfect vision and wisdom into all things.

Occasionally, God can guide us through the words, wisdom, and witness of other believers. You may have Christian friends or family members you turn to often for counsel, help, and practical guidance. God can give us leadership and help through the lives of others. Near the end of Romans, in chapter 16, Paul gave a lengthy list of the names of fellow believers who had blessed and encouraged him. He certainly saw that God offered guidance through the names of these many brothers and sisters. Anyone you can trust for guidance will certainly only want your good and God's glory to prevail in any situation.

Israel came to see the cloud and fire as symbols of God's guidance to and for them. The people moved when the cloud moved and camped or stayed put when the cloud held in one place. God's guidance often leads us to move along or to stay in one place. And we can experience that guidance in some of the ways we have named today.

DAY 16

One of the best-known blessings in the Bible can be found in Numbers. Like Leviticus, Numbers is not a book that many people read often or at all. But like Leviticus, it is part of the biblical canon and deserves our attention and time. In Numbers 6, the LORD instructed Moses and Aaron about how to bless the Israelites. This teaching on how to bless the people would imply that God desires to bless His people and has designs for doing that. This ancient blessing reads like this: "The LORD bless you and keep you; the Lord make his face shine on you and be gracious to you; the Lord turn his face toward you and give you peace" (Numbers 6:24–26). You may have heard this blessing offered at a wedding or funeral. It is a comforting passage in the Bible. A few lessons stand out about God's blessings.

First, the LORD is the One who blesses us. Every good and perfect gift comes from above, from the Lord God (James 1:17). Blessings originate in the heart and mind of God. There is no reason to believe that God just randomly and winsomely drops blessings into lives much like you might toss a handful of sand at the beach. No. Rather, God blesses purposely and with forethought. And He blesses us so that the glory goes to Him. He blesses us so that we might be a blessing to others. God does not act in a random or scattered sort of way. Scripture plainly teaches that God always acts with purpose and precision in His deeds and ways.

Second, the LORD is gracious. He treats us much better than we have earned or deserved. He would be right to look away from us, but He chooses to see us and to make His face shine upon us. He would be right to cover His eyes with regret or embarrassment over who we are and what we have done. But He sees us with perfect understanding and knows the plans that He has for us. He remembers how we are made and that we come from dust (see Psalm 103). God's hand is open in the invitation for people to surrender their lives to Him through faith, trust, and new birth in Jesus Christ. Grace is the greatest blessing of all. It is by grace we are saved through faith. It was grace that drove God's plan for salvation in the first place.

Third, the LORD offers us peace. Peace is not the absence of pain or complete immunity from conflict or chaos. Rather, peace is a deep and abiding tranquility and stability in the face of such things as pain, conflict, injury, chaos, or things we cannot control. Peace is the confidence that God will protect us, provide for us, and propel us through such things while keeping us in serenity and contentment. God made a promise in Isaiah 26:3 that reads, "You will keep him in perfect peace, whose mind is stayed on You, because he trusts in You." Peace is a blessing. And peace is being content when all sorts of circumstances and challenges would suggest otherwise.

A bit later in the Old Testament, we find two blessings like the Aaronic blessing in Numbers 6. Psalm 31:6 says, "Let your face shine on your servant; save me in your unfailing love." Psalm 67:1 says, "May God be gracious to us and bless us and make His face shine on us." The next verse, Psalm 67:2, tells us why God chooses to bless us and what He hopes will happen through His blessings. We read, "So that your ways may be known on earth, your salvation among all nations." God blesses so He may be known and revered and exalted by the earth. He blesses us that we might be living, breathing, talking, and walking examples of His incomparable graciousness and goodness. We are advertisements and testimonials to Him and His salvation work. We declare the glory and praises that are due to Him.

DAY 17

We find a one-of-a-kind encounter in Numbers 22. I will bet you have never had a conversation with a donkey. You may have thought some people you have talked with acted like donkeys or maybe you have been guilty of acting like a donkey too. But we do not engage in conversations with donkeys or deer or goats or giraffes. Animals do not possess conversational English language skills as we do. We read about Balaam's exchange with his donkey in Numbers 22:28–31: "Then the Lord opened the donkey's mouth, and it said to Balaam, 'What have I done to you to make you beat me these three times?' Balaam answered the donkey, 'You have made a fool of me! If only I had a sword in my hand, I would kill you right now.' The donkey said to Balaam, 'Am I not your own donkey, which you have always ridden, to this day? Have I been in the habit of doing this to you?' 'No,' he said. Then the Lord opened Balaam's eyes, and he saw the angel of the Lord standing in the road with his sword drawn. So, he bowed low and fell facedown."

Perhaps the key phrase is "then the Lord opened Balaam's eyes." We have all had moments where God has opened our eyes to some particular truth or reality. There are times when we would not see what was plainly before us if God did not open our eyes to it. If you have not had such a moment, give it time. You likely will. God often has to open our eyes so we can see ourselves, His Word, His grace, or where we are in life. We may often be shocked by what we find or see when God opens our eyes. That shock could come from sins we have committed or those times when we have dismissed God from our lives. Repentance often begins by seeing ourselves as God sees us.

When it comes to opening our eyes, we are reminded of Jesus's healing of a blind man in John 9. Jesus is the light of the world so it makes sense that He possesses the power to restore sight to eyes that were once blind. When the man was asked about what Jesus had done, he replied, "I was blind but now I see" (John 9:25). Often it can be stated as simply as that. The Gospel opens blind eyes to salvation. The Holy Spirit often opens our eyes to the things that have blinded us—resentments, bitterness, anger, envy, jealousy, and pettiness. We have often been blinded to relationships that have been broken and to words we spoke that we should not have spoken. We have often been blind to situations where we should have asked for forgiveness or granted it to someone else. It is a powerful testimony today to say "I was blind, but now I see."

When the Lord opened Balaam's eyes, he bowed low to the ground and even fell facedown. Seeing truth for the first time has that kind of an impact. We can be stunned when God lifts the veil from eyes that have been blinded by indifference or sin. Acts 9:18 says that "something like scales fell from Saul's eyes (Paul) and he could see again." And Saul became Paul who proceeded to become Christianity's greatest preacher, theologian, and church planter. When God opens our eyes and we begin to see, good things inevitably come. Perhaps you would ask God to open your eyes today. Perhaps your eyes have been opened recently, but you need God's grace and strength to act on what you have seen or discovered. If God has opened your eyes, you can trust that He will help you to become and to do what He has for you.

DAY 18

The book of Deuteronomy comes from two different Greek words. *Deuteros* means second. *Nomos* means law. So putting those words together, we have the second law of Moses. One keyword that we find in Deuteronomy is the word *remember*. Israel was to remember God's character, deeds, and ways. Memory is a powerful resource for us as we live for the Lord and serve Him. We can remember His Word. We can remember what He has done for us. We can remember His grace and presence with us during difficult times.

Early in Deuteronomy, God tells the Israelites to get moving. It was time for them to move forward to take the land that the Almighty had chosen for them. They had stayed in one place for much too long, and the consequences were not good. The command came in this way, "The LORD our God said to us at Horeb, 'You have stayed long enough at this mountain. Break camp and advance into the hill country of the Amorites; go to all the neighboring peoples in the Arabah, in the mountains, in the western foothills, in the Negev and along the coast, to the land of the Canaanites and to Lebanon, as far as the great river, the Euphrates. See, I have given you this land. Go in and take possession of the land the Lord swore he would give to your fathers—to Abraham, Isaac and Jacob—and to their descendants after them'" (1:6–8).

There are occasions in life where God tells us to get moving. We have been in one place for too long. We can grow spiritually stale and stagnant at times. And that usually comes because we have sat down. So God rallies us up to get moving in a new direction. God may have blessings and wisdom for us if we dare to get moving and step onto the pathway that He has for us. Like Israel, we can get comfortable, too comfortable, in places that we have chosen. It is easy to linger in the weeds of the familiar, common, and everyday places of life. We can become so comfortable that we lose sight of what God may have for us to do. We might decide that worship is something we will confine to Sundays—maybe one or two a month. We might think we have read all there is to read in the Bible. We might leave prayer to those who are more eloquent of speech than we are. The enemy would love to move us to the margins of life where we are of little threat to Him or kingdom work.

God often has to break into those places to remind us to get moving again—to serve Him, to walk with Him, to live by faith, and to trust Him when the ways may not be 100 percent clear or easy. Another reason we may find ourselves stale or stagnant is we are tired—physically, emotionally, and spiritually. We may be teetering on the edge of burnout. We may feel like we are well past running on fumes. We are not running on anything. Burnout can be a dangerous place and a real place. If we fail to see it and name it, we could fall captive to it. Some extended time with God in Bible reading, prayer, journaling, and occasions for silence and solitude are good ways to arrest burnout if it has taken hold or to protect yourself against it.

Deuteronomy's opening message is a good checkup for us spiritually. We are called to see where we stand and how we got to that place. Complacency can rob us of vitality or could signal that we are running out of gas. But usually, staying where we are for long periods of time is not healthy. May we long for the Lord as David did in Psalm 63. When this future king was roaming in the desert of Judah, he wrote, "You, God, are my God, earnestly I seek you; I thirst for you, my whole being longs for you, in a dry and parched land where there is no water" (Psalm 63:1). When we thirst for the Lord, we will not remain where we are. When we drink from what He offers us, we find our thirst is quenched. If you are thirsty today, it might be time to drink from the Lord more than just hanging around where you are.

DAY 19

Deuteronomy is the fifth book of the Bible and the last of the five books that are traditionally ascribed to the collection called "the books of Moses." The name *Deuteronomy* means "second law," and the law that God had given to Moses was expounded and proclaimed before the people would enter the land God had promised to them. One of the keywords we discover in Deuteronomy is the word *remember*. The people were challenged to remember the LORD, His Word, and His ways. They were to remember what the LORD had done for them and how He had led them to the edge of the land that would be their lasting home. In Deuteronomy 8, we read, "Remember how the Lord your God led you all the way in the wilderness these forty years, to humble and test you in order to know what was in your heart, whether or not you would keep his commands" (8:2). A bit later, in the same chapter, we read, "But remember the Lord your God, for it is he who gives you the ability to produce wealth, and so confirms his covenant, which he swore to your ancestors, as it is today" (8:8).

These two verses call us to the word *remember*. As believers, memory should be important to us. Just as a family cherishes vacation or Christmas memories, we are to cherish our faith memories and stories too. We are to remember the LORD and His ways. We are to remember His blessings and provisions. We are to remember that God gives us abilities, blessings, creativity, and gifts with which we can serve Him and others around us. When we remember all that God has done and given, we are motivated to walk with Him and to stay with Him in faith and trust. As the word *remember* is used in Deuteronomy, the people are called to remember historic and significant acts that God performed on behalf of His people and to reveal His glory. The lesson for us is to remember that the LORD is the God of history. He works and acts in real ways, real situations, and real people.

One good exercise is to set aside time each day to recall where you have seen, heard, or experienced God at work. What has He done? When we are looking and listening for the LORD, we are much more likely to see and experience Him. Frankly, most of us have so many blessings that it is easy to lose sight of the Lord God and to think that we have won or gained these blessings by ourselves in our own strength. God made it clear to Israel that remembering Him and keeping His ways would be to their credit and benefit. We read, "See, I set before you today life and prosperity, death and destruction. For I command you today to love the Lord your God, to walk in obedience to him, and to keep his commands, decrees and laws; then you will live and increase, and the Lord your God will bless you in the land you are entering to possess" (Deuteronomy 30:15–16). We are not to take lightly the importance of knowing the LORD and walking in His ways. We are to live as different people and to live in distinct ways that bear witness to the Lord that we claim we know and serve.

Today, remember what the LORD has done for you and given to you. Remember where He has led and guided you. See His faithfulness and fingerprints in your life over the span of months, years, and even decades. The more that we see what God has done, the more that we wish to walk with Him and worship Him.

DAY 20

In Deuteronomy 1, we read about a rebellion against God. Amazing, isn't it? Amazing that people who were liberated from bondage, set free from slavery, and guided safely across the Red Sea would rise up in rebellion against the very God who did all these things for them freely, graciously, and faithfully! We read a bit of detail in Deuteronomy 1:41-42, "Then you replied, 'We have sinned against the Lord. We will go up and fight, as the Lord our God commanded us.' So, every one of you put on his weapons, thinking it easy to go up into the hill country. But the Lord said to me, 'Tell them, Do not go up and fight, because I will not be with you. You will be defeated by your enemies.'" We can easily be like these Israelites. We can take matters into our own hands and presume that we know better than God. We think that we can find a way forward that is at odds with what He has called us to be and to do. We always fail when we take matters into our own hands and act in ways that conflict with what God has said we are to do.

In Deuteronomy 1:43-45, we read the outcome of Israel's disobedience against God, "So I told you, but you would not listen. You rebelled against the Lord's command and in your arrogance, you marched up into the hill country. The Amorites who lived in those hills came out against you; they chased you like a swarm of bees and beat you down from Seir all the way to Hormah. You came back and wept before the Lord, but he paid no attention to your weeping and turned a deaf ear to you." God weighed in and judged the people. He judged their actions and their motivations. Their actions were rebellious and vain. Their motivations came from arrogance and the pursuit of self-glory. Even when they realized they had failed, God said their weeping and slow crawl back to Him were insincere and impious. It was more of a show than a true humble repentance and return to the Lord's side.

In life, we can choose our ways or God's ways, but we cannot have both. We can serve Him or serve something far lesser, but we cannot serve two masters. We can pursue the Lord's glory or we can chase after our own glory, but not both. As we read the early pages of Exodus, Leviticus, Numbers, and Deuteronomy, we see the people of Israel living stubbornly and defiantly. They needlessly pursued their ways and wishes in opposition to the Lord's will for them. There was no reason for them to wander that long in the desert except for their own pride and disobedience. They did it to themselves. To paraphrase an old saying, "They had met the enemy and the enemy was them." Their own arrogance and pride were their worst enemies, and they repeatedly stumbled over these things time after time. Remember, Lot ended up in Sodom because it looked good and right to him. At the end of Judges, the people did what was right in their own eyes. Pride can be a brutal and devastating sin. We see through sin-stained eyes at best.

Today, consider whether you have invoked your wisdom above God's. Have you chosen your ways above His? Have you acted in haste or delay when God has called you to do the opposite? Is there an ongoing rebellion in your life against God's plans and purposes? We occasionally have to ask very hard questions as we examine where we are and where God would have us to be. If you find the seeds of rebellion in your life, give them to the Lord. Put down that rebellion before it metastasizes and threatens to go and grow further. Surrender daily to Him and live in the serenity of His will and ways.

DAY 21

Near the end of his life and in the book of Deuteronomy, Moses sang to the people of Israel. He had led Israel out of Egypt, through the parted waters of the Red Sea and in the wilderness, but he would not enter the promised land. Because of his disobedience, God prohibited Moses from entering the new land. So Moses was entering the final stanzas of his life and leadership over Israel. As he sang, Moses declared these words, "Let my teaching fall like rain and my words descend like dew, like showers on new grass, like abundant rain on tender plants. I will proclaim the name of the Lord. Oh, praise the greatness of our God!" (Deuteronomy 32:2–3). Moses shared some truths that can still connect with us today.

First, we want our lives to be open to God's Word. May the truth and wisdom of God rain down on us like showers from the sky and like the morning dew on dry land. God's Word refreshes us and refills us. It is always available to us. We simply have to open it and embrace it. We are dry, parched, and even barren without His Word. Be intentional about pouring the Word of God into your life. Use the Bible primarily. In addition, you can look to some trusted Bible teachers and proclaimers who can help you understand God's Word.

Second, soak up scripture when you read it. What are these words saying to you here and now and the circumstances that you may be facing or battling? Read scripture with a pen or highlighter in hand so you can note the things that speak loudly to you and impact your walk with the Lord. Just as you might season or marinate food before cooking and eating, take time to let God's Word seep into your life and connect with you.

Third, proclaim the name of the Lord over the battles and trials that you may face. Keep the Lord's name in your mind. Speak His name prayerfully through the day when you feel tempted, threatened, thwarted, or tossed about. There is both power and strength in the name of the Lord. Keeping His name in mind allows us to realize that we do not live alone or walk alone. His presence is with us and goes before us. If we are followers of Christ, we wear His name. Our perspective in life is directly connected to our faith and belief in who the Lord is and that He will do what He has promised to do.

Fourth, praise the greatness of God. Look for reasons why you can praise Him. Look for reasons to be thankful and grateful. When we practice things like praise and gratitude, we discover that our heart grows. We become increasingly grateful and thankful. Name and acknowledge what He has done for you. We often find or fight our way through discouragement and battles by turning to gratitude and praise. When we see where God has been at work and how He has blessed us already, we find that some of our trials and battles begin to recede.

Moses sang another song in Exodus—shortly after reaching the other side of the Red Sea and escaping from the approaching Egyptian army. He sang, "The Lord is my strength and my defense; He has become my salvation. He is my God, and I will praise Him, my father's God, and I will exalt him" (Exodus 15:2). If you are a parent or grandparent, take time to teach your children or grandchildren the lessons of praise, giving thanks, and exalting the Lord. Invest in their faith and their walk with the Lord. Leave them a worthy legacy and heritage to trust and embrace. If you share your gratitude and praise with others, you even become a witness for the Lord and possibly open doors to share the Gospel—the greatest gift God has ever offered in His Son.

DAY 22

Joshua succeeded Moses as Israel's leader. After Moses died, God chose Joshua to lead the people in their conquest of Canaan. In some Bibles, the heading for Joshua 1 is "The LORD commands Joshua." The LORD assured Joshua that a blessing awaited both him and Israel if they remained true to the LORD's commands and instructions. God said, "I will give you every place where you set your foot, as I promised Moses" (Joshua 1:3). We learn that the Lord does honor our obedience to Him. This honor may not always be what we would expect or wish, but God does honor us. There are benefits and blessings to gain from walking with the Lord God. Moses and the generation that left Egypt in the great exodus could have enjoyed the promised land almost immediately if they had remained obedient and faithful to the standards that God had placed before them. But their disobedience would cost them dearly and leave them stranded unnecessarily in the wilderness where they would die. We often have to recognize that disobedience will never take us where we want to go. And defiance will never gain us the victories and blessings that God has for us.

Confidently, God promised Joshua protection and victory through this obedience. The Almighty promised, "No one will be able to stand against you all the days of your life. As I was with Moses, so I will be with you; I will never leave you nor forsake you" (Joshua 1:5). Likewise, we never have to worry about the Lord departing from us. He is faithful to His promises and faithful to His people. He is able to deliver us to salvation, eternal life, and victory over the enemy. We do not have to wake up each morning wondering whether the Lord is with us today or not. He is with us, and He does not forsake His people. We can draw strength from the Lord's message to Joshua in 1:9, "For the LORD your God will be with you wherever you go." This ancient promise remains relevant and valid today. We can claim it and cling to it for ourselves and the circumstances that we encounter today.

At the end of Joshua 1, we find the words "only be strong and courageous" (1:17). That command speaks to us. God calls us to be strong and courageous in our faith and service. We are to place our hopes and confidence in Him and serve wholeheartedly in the places where He may take or lead us. Someone once wrote that we should pray and trust like everything depends upon God and serve as everything depends upon us. There is truth in such a statement. When we trust in the Lord and seek Him, we do learn to serve with courage and boldness. And as we serve, we learn that God can be trusted to provide, bless, and enable us. You may remember Joshua's powerful words near the end of 24:15 when he declared to the people, "But as for me and my household, we will serve the LORD." We can stake a similar claim today to stand firm for the LORD no matter how situations, cultures, individuals, and adversity may challenge or accost us. We plant a flag of boldness, courageousness, faith, and service just as Joshua did. And may the Lord both bless and encourage Him as you follow and serve Him down the different roads where He may lead you on this day that He has made!

DAY 23

Judges is a fascinating book to read. We come across a variety of interesting people that God chooses or anoints to provide help and deliverance when Israel is in trouble. As we read Judges, we discover a familiar pattern of behavior. For a time, Israel is faithful to God. Then Israel falls into sin and departs from God. God punishes Israel by sending a neighboring country against them in battle. Israel struggles and cries for help. God then hears and raises up a judge. Israel is delivered and returns to the Lord for a season. And then Israel departs again. We call this Israel's "cycle of sin" or "cycle of apostasy." Judges 3:9 says, "But when they cried out to the Lord, He raised up for them a deliverer." The people often ignored the Lord until they realized they were in trouble and needed help. We can be guilty of the same practices—I know I can.

We can often identify with this pattern of behavior. We can easily fall into a cycle of sin, struggle, repentance, forgiveness, renewal, and sin again. And at the first indication of struggle or suffering, we call out to the Lord for help and deliverance. One of the more interesting judges is Gideon. There were two powerful assurances offered to Gideon as he worked to serve God and His people. An angel of the LORD promised the following to Gideon, "The LORD is with you, mighty warrior" (Judges 6:12b). Shortly later, the LORD Himself said to Gideon, "I will be with you, and you will strike down the Midianites as if they were but one man" (Judges 6:16). Twice, God assured Gideon that He was with him and would remain with him. Two assurances from God in the span of a chapter or an afternoon are powerful indeed.

We can take comfort in knowing that the Lord God is with us as well—in sorrow or celebration, certainty or confusion, day or night. God is with us in anxious times and in confident times. Psalm 56:3–4 says, "When I am afraid, I will trust in you. In God, whose word I praise, in God I trust; I will not be afraid. What can mortal man do to me?" God's presence with His people is a recurring theme in scripture. This reality is a faith-building certainty. Just as we use raw materials to build a house or an office, we also use raw materials to build our faith. The raw materials we use are the promises and assurances that God offers us in His Word. We can trust His promises and build with the certainties that He offers to us.

Whether we are walking with the Lord or simply struggling with where He is or even if we find ourselves in sin and rebellion, we know that we can call upon Him. He still forgives, encourages, helps, comforts, and convicts. We trust that God is able to do whatever needs to be done at the moment we call upon Him. A child looks to his parents to provide exactly what is needed and when it is needed. Likewise, we look to our Father to provide for us when we are in need. If you find yourself in a cycle of victory, struggle, and failure, seek the Lord today. Ask for His help to break that cycle and struggle once and for all. Victories are often won a day at a time or a step at a time. But as we walk with the Lord, we trust Him for victory just as Israel did in the days of the Judges.

DAY 24

Samuel is an interesting and large figure in the life of Israel. He was sort of a transitional figure away from the judges to the monarchy where Saul and later David assumed the throne over Israel. Some people suggest that Samuel might have even been the last judge. The circumstances of Samuel's birth were extraordinary. He was born to a childless couple named Elkanah and Hannah. His mother, Hannah, prayed fervently for a son. And God answered those prayers. After his birth, Hannah dedicated her son to the Lord's service. She said, "So now I will give him to the LORD. For his whole life he will be given over to the LORD" (1 Samuel 1:28).

Samuel served alongside Eli the priest. One evening, the LORD called out to Samuel. After some initial confusion thinking Eli was calling him, Samuel finally realized that the LORD was calling to Him. His response was, "Speak, for your servant is listening" (1 Samuel 3:10b). What a wonderful response for God's people! The Lord does speak today. The Lord continues to lead His people and shepherd them in ways that are both right and good. John Piper noted, "God is always doing 10,000 things in your life, and you may be aware of three of them." The point is God is at work. God is always at work. And God works in and through people. We want to hear Him when He speaks to us. There are some steps we can take to sharpen our listening and discerning skills so we can hear and understand the Lord.

First, God speaks through His Word. We possess the Bible today. God's Word is *not* outdated, old-fashioned, stale, and irrelevant. It is as relevant and urgent today as it has ever been. A commitment to reading scripture opens us to what God might have to say to us or to teach us. There is no magical amount to read. Some days you might explore several chapters. Other days may find you camped out on one single compelling verse that has captured your attention. God's people need to read the Bible. Biblical literacy today is alarmingly low. We have no reason to believe we will hear God speak if we choose not to read or study what He has already said and inspired.

Second, God speaks as we pray. God can grant us answers, assurance, peace, and clarity when we seek Him in prayer. We pray because we believe God works in response to the prayers of His people. Prayer does not always involve us talking. Prayer can often be times of silence and solitude. We can pray as we journal or write. We can pray as we walk. We can pray as God brings matters to mind. The purpose of prayer is to create an ongoing dialogue with the Lord about our lives and where He is leading us. This idea is expressed in scripture as praying without ceasing.

Third, God can speak to us through the counsel and guidance of other believers. We can be blessed by the wisdom, truth, and perspective that other Christians offer to us. And fourth, God can speak as we worship Him. A song, a sermon, a passage from the Bible, a testimony, and a chance to give become occasions where God can speak to us and move within us. Worship does not confine itself to Sundays with other believers. We can (and should) worship the Lord on other occasions during the week. The Lord is worthy of all the worship we can bring to Him.

A final way that God speaks is through the legacy, testimony, and example of other faithful believers—either alive today or already with the Lord. Consider some believers whom you hold out as role models. God often blesses us with the lives of faithful men and women whose examples speak volumes. And often, these role models continue to speak to us long after they have passed away. God can speak through giants of the faith like John Wesley, C. S. Lewis, Jim Elliot, Fannie Crosby, and Billy Graham. But He could also speak through the faith and example of people like parents, siblings, coworkers, Sunday school teachers, and friends who simply help you grow in Christ each day. Be as ready to listen to the Lord as Samuel was. Begin your day by saying, "Speak, Lord, for your servant is listening."

DAY 25

In 1 Samuel 8, the people of Israel complain about their lack of a king. They voice their discontent and anger to Samuel. Many in Israel desired to be like other nations with a king to rule over them and lead them. The people said, "Now appoint a king to lead us such as all the other nations have" (1 Samuel 8:5b). Immediately, we can see a problem in the people's thinking. And it is the same problem we can suffer from on occasion. The problem is believing that happiness and contentment come from getting what other people have. We fall victim to "if only" think. "If I only had this or that, I would be happy and everything would be good." We begin to pursue contentment based on what we find in others. We fall prey to thinking that everything will automatically improve if we could only be more like this person or that situation.

If you would like to have more square footage in your house, buying new furniture will not fix that problem. Similarly, trying to be like everyone else will probably not bring contentment and peace to a life that is lacking both. Trying to be like someone else's life is a lot like putting a size 9 shoe on a foot that fits a size 14. Shaquille O'Neal cannot wear your shoes or mine. He is a much bigger man. Comparative happiness is short-lived at best. Drawing comparisons with others will usually leave us more frustrated because we cannot live someone else's life.

A little further in 1 Samuel 8, we read, "And the LORD told Samuel: 'Listen to all that the people are saying to you; it is not you they have rejected as their king but me" (1 Samuel 8:7). In their pursuit of a king and to be like other nations, the people had rejected God in the process. It is easy to lose sight of the Lord when we are in hot pursuit of something that we believe to be a difference-maker in life. We can pursue bigger and better things, more of something, and a newer version of this or that and lose sight of God. I have met many people who reflect upon years and even decades of wasted and lost time when God was not a factor or feature in their lives. They were consumed by jobs, vacations, pleasure, good times, money, and a hundred other things. But the common factor in each case was trading God for the elusive belief that something else would make all the difference and bring the happiness that they so desperately craved and desired.

Any pursuit that rules out God is a fruitless and empty activity. We can no more find contentment without the pursuit of God than an orchestra can perform a concert without instruments. Israel failed to realize that their desire for a king was a rejection of God. And when we attempt to replace God with anything else, then we have rejected Him too. Rejecting God rarely happens all at once. And those who reject God will likely fail to see their rejection as clearly as they should. The enemy has blinded them. Those who reject God in their lives rarely go so far as to declare that there is no God. They just simply live like there is no God. Functional atheism is one of the biggest challenges churches face today. Functional atheism is where we may profess faith in God, but He places practically no role in how we order our lives. We never read the Bible. We only pray when we are in trouble. We worship when convenient. We do not tithe. We may not give at all. We do little if anything to grow our faith. We pay lip service to the Lord and say the right things, but inside, we are hollow and empty because we have functionally and practically rejected Him and written him out of our lives.

Children and grandchildren will directly learn from this functional atheism and likely grow up to live just as badly or, more likely, even worse. Passive Christians and believers usually produce children and grandchildren that are wholly disconnected and cut off from God altogether. If God plays no role in our lives from day to day, then how can we expect to hear the Lord say anything less than "depart from me, I never knew you?" (Matthew 7:23). These words are hard to hear. But you and I can do something now to reverse course and change where we are. If we hear these words in eternity, it is far too late to do anything. Is there a rejection of God that you need to walk back to today?

The message from 1 Samuel is simple and clear. Do not reject the Lord. Do not trade the Lord for the pursuit of other things. Do not build a life apart from the Lord. Embrace Him, love Him, worship Him, serve Him, and walk with Him. The words we read from 1 Samuel come as a wake-up call—get your life in order and do not settle for the same old things you have been doing!

DAY 26

Maybe one of the most beloved stories in the Bible is the one that involves David and Goliath. We know the outcome of this story—David killed Goliath and won the praise and favor of the nation. It was this young son of Jesse's first major battlefield win or conquest that made him a legendary figure. But it might be important to think about David's motivation for fighting Goliath when no one else ever answered the call. We are told that for forty consecutive days, Goliath challenged and defied the Israelites every morning. Mockingly, he called for someone to step forward to fight him—teasing and tormenting the army of Israel and Saul on every occasion possible. At last, David answered the call. The Bible says, "David asked the men standing near him, 'What will be done for the man who kills this Philistine and removes this disgrace from Israel? Who is this uncircumcised Philistine that he should defy the armies of the living God?'" (1 Samuel 17:26).

David took a stand for his nation and the army of Israel. But if we read closely, we see that he also took a stand for "the living God." This shepherd boy had grown weary of hearing this Philistine giant impugn and malign the name and character of the LORD. We know that David was called a "man after God's own heart." He was tired of hearing this giant defy, demean, and dismiss the LORD. It was time to take a stand. We all have moments where we can take a stand for the Lord. We often sing, "Stand up, stand up for Jesus." But do we? Do you? Do you look for ways to stand for the LORD and His gospel of hope and salvation? Do you stand, or do you shrink down and finally sneak away?

We often take a stand by how we live. We want to live consistent, righteous, and holy lives where we turn from sin and wickedness. We want to fill our lives with God's Word and daily dependence upon Him. We take a stand when we witness the Lord and speak of what He has done for us and given to us. We take a stand when we declare our thanksgiving and gratitude for the blessings and bounty that God has provided for us. Simply speaking of how God has blessed you is a witness in its own right.

We take a stand when we make a commitment to worship on Sundays even when the temptation is great to be elsewhere. We take a stand when we tithe and give our first 10 percent to the Lord when the temptation is great to hold on to that money and spend it in a different way. We take a stand when we teach our children and grandchildren the truth of the Bible and help them to know the Lord at a young and impressionable age. You make no greater investment in life than teaching truth to the children who are part of your life and preparing them to be faithful to the Lord in their lives.

Look for ways to stand for the LORD. You do not have to do this in a grandiose way that calls attention to yourself. Simply be a consistent example for Christ in every avenue of life. Speak for Him. Live for Him. Walk with Him. God does not give us puzzles to solve or difficult riddles to figure out. He calls us to be surrendered to Him and yielded to Him throughout life. He calls us to be His own. As we read in Psalm 107:2, "Let the redeemed of the LORD tell their story." If we know Him and walk with Him, we surely have a story to tell and a stand we can take.

DAY 27

2 Samuel is a continuation of the early years of Israel's monarchy. We learn of Saul's death and David's ascent to the throne as Saul's successor—chosen and anointed by God to assume this role. In 2 Samuel 7:16, we read, "Your house and your kingdom will endure forever before me; your throne will be established forever." These words were a promise that the Lord God made to David—an everlasting throne that would endure forever. We believe that this promise found its fulfillment in the coming of Jesus who would come from the line of David and be granted all authority in heaven and on earth. But there is another takeaway for us from this one passage. God works in the present with the future always in mind. Many of the actions that God undertakes today have ramifications in the decades to come or even well past our lifetimes. Consider for a moment the example of Revelation—the last book in the Bible. The Lord Jesus revealed to John the apostle the events of the last days and what would come to usher in the end of human history. John did not live to see that day, but he died with the assurance that God was in charge of history and would faithfully execute His plans and purposes to bring history to an end.

We have to remind ourselves that God works in us today with tomorrow in mind. God might bring a passage from the Bible to life today as you read and study scripture. And it could be that six months or a year from now you will remember that scripture and the power and promise it brought to you. And you will remember that God prepared you for today with that verse from months ago. God saw the future and gave you a passage to trust from His Word. God often teaches us life lessons today as a prelude for tomorrow. When we engage in spiritual journaling, we can look back at where God was at work teaching, shaping, and forming us for a moment that we had not yet seen or recognized.

In 2 Samuel, God was laying the groundwork for the coming of His Son Jesus from the line of David. No one in David's day or court would see Jesus or experience His miracles or teachings. But they could remember with confidence that the Davidic line would never perish from the earth. We often pray for months or years before we see or hear an answer to those prayers. And occasionally, we never see an answer. But God could be at work in and through us to bring an answer at a different time and at a time beyond our lives. Someone has said that the Gospel is concealed in the Old Testament and revealed in the New Testament. Or to put that another way, the Gospel is contained in the Old Testament and explained in the New Testament. God often works in our time with the future in mind. God prepares parents for the children He brings to them. God prepares a teenager or youth in a church retreat for a career that he or she launches a decade later.

Just because we may not see immediate evidence of God at work or God responding to our prayers does not mean He has forgotten us, ignored us, or abandoned us. Remember, His time is not always our time. And His ways are not always our ways. David placed his faith and confidence in God's promise to him and lived with the trust that God would bring the promise to fruition. David was a player or a part of God's larger plans and work. Sometimes we must recognize that we are players or parts too. We may not see the end or reap the harvest. But our mission is to trust unfailingly in God, to hold on unrelentingly to His promises, and to remain totally faithful to the things we can do and control as we await God's fulfillment of His plans.

DAY 28

1 Kings is a book of history in the Old Testament. In the beginning, David is nearing his death and preparing to hand off the throne to Solomon. One of Solomon's crowning achievements (and likely his biggest) was the building of the temple of the LORD in Jerusalem. While David had wanted to build this temple, it was Solomon whom God chose to complete the project. In 1 Kings 8, Solomon offered a prayer of dedication. We read, "Lord, the God of Israel, there is no God like you in heaven above or on earth below—you who keep your covenant of love with your servants who continue wholeheartedly in your way. You have kept your promise to your servant David my father; with your mouth you have promised and with your hand you have fulfilled it—as it is today" (1 Kings 8:23–24). In this portion of Solomon's prayer, the young king identified two powerful lessons about the Lord that we need to see.

First, God is incomparable and without equal. There is no comparison to the Lord God. There is no one like Him. Satan is not God's equal. He's not in any way comparable to God. Satan is a created being and cannot be held in comparison with the Creator God any more than we can. When we worship the Lord, we realize that we are giving our worship to the only One who is worthy of such things. Isaiah saw the Lord as high and lifted up. The Psalms testify to the majesty and greatness of the Almighty. God has no equal and no one who is even close to His standing or footing. In 1 Chronicles 17:20, in a prayer from David, we read, "There is none like you, O LORD, and there is no God but you, as we have heard with our ears."

Second, Solomon's prayer teaches us that God is trustworthy and reliable. He is a promise-keeper and a waymaker. We can build our faith upon His promises and Word. Whatever God promises, His hand delivers and honors. Solomon could observe the faithfulness that God showed to his father David. And Solomon knew this faithfulness firsthand as God honored and blessed him with wisdom and the great privilege of building this amazing temple. Psalm 37:3 says, "Trust the LORD and do good; dwell in the land and enjoy safe pasture." Perhaps today you have experienced family or friends or employers who have broken promises to you or even deceived you. Perhaps you find it hard to know what or whom to trust. Solomon teaches us that God is always faithful and true to His promises and His people.

When the temple was completed, the people had a place where they could gather before the LORD to offer gifts, sacrifices, offerings, and worship. But they also had a place where they could ponder the greatness of God and the faithfulness of His Word. These two realities help to strengthen us today. No matter what kind of day you may be having, you can remember that God is both great and good. You can remember that God is faithful and will continue to walk with you. Remember the words of Paul in Philippians 1:6, "Being confident of this, that he who began a good work in you will be faithful to carry it on to completion until the day of Christ Jesus."

DAY 29

1 Kings opens with the statement that when King David was old, he could not stay warm. No matter how many covers were put on him, he could not stay warm (1 Kings 1:1). We can easily imagine him buried beneath a pile of blankets. Maybe you're in that same state at times! The solution was bringing a woman named Abishag to lie beside him and help him stay warm. The Bible makes it clear that this arrangement was not an intimate or immoral one (1 King 1:2–4). Rather, this plan was a way to help an aging king stay warm. Maybe you can identify with his struggle to stay warm in these winter months.

Though David battled a problem with physical warmth, there are challenges we face to stay spiritually warm. We want our faith in Christ to be alive, growing, and warm. Spiritual coldness or apathy can often be a huge problem that some people battle. And others may not even realize how cold or apathetic they have become. To stay spiritually warm, we have to consider several important matters. First, we cannot stay spiritually warm if we have never had a born-again conversion experience where Christ became our Savior and Lord. We have to be able to identify a moment in life where we gave up on ourselves and everything else to place our full trust and all hope in Christ and Him alone. To answer the question "Do I know the Lord?" we have to look at the fruit we produce. Galatians 5:22–23 provides a list of the fruit of the Spirit. Do you see yourself growing in these ways? Would others say that you are growing? A fruitless life should be a sober reason for alarm and concern. No one will ever stay warm if he or she does not have a life-changing encounter with Jesus Christ. We cannot kindle a fire that does not exist in the first place.

But to stay warm, stay in the Word. Read your Bible consistently and reflectively. What is God revealing to you? Where is God correcting or counseling you? Have a plan in place to read your Bible consistently and thoughtfully rather than just occasionally reading whatever it falls open to and whenever you feel like it. We can hide the Word of God in our hearts (Psalm 119:11). The Word keeps hearts warm, clean and surrendered to the Lord Jesus. Next, develop some friendships with other believers who can help to disciple you and support you in your walk with Christ. Most of the time, this happens with one or two other believers with whom you can share your life, prayers, struggles, and victories. Proverbs 12:15 says that a wise man listens to advice. Proverbs 17:17 says that "a friend loves at all times, and a brother is born for adversity." The insulation of godly friendship can keep us spiritually warm.

Pray throughout the day. A dedicated prayer time is good to have. But we are not to limit ourselves just to an appointed prayer time each day. We can pray throughout the day (Paul counseled this practice in 2 Thessalonians 5:17). We can pray anytime and anywhere. Prayer is one more spiritual layer that God wraps around us. Commit time to worship on Sundays and during the other six days. Do not neglect coming together with other believers to give worship and glory to God (Hebrews 10:25). Use your life to serve the Lord. Find a way to share the Gospel each day. Find a way to offer your time and talents to the Lord in service and surrender. May you stay warm physically and spiritually. There is nothing we can do to control the weather or daily temperatures. But we can surely control the spiritual thermometer and the steps we take to stay warm spiritually each day.

DAY 30

In 1 Kings 2, David is nearing death. He's enjoyed a prominent place in Israel as a musician, writer, defeater of Goliath, and Israel's second king. He was not perfect, but he was called a man after God's own heart. His place in Israel's history remains secure even to this day. As we read 1 Kings 2:1–12, we discover some parting words and charges that David gave to Solomon—his son and successor to the throne of Israel. When we read these words, we find a mixture of things. David began with good counsel. "'I am about to go the way of all the earth,' he said. 'So be strong, act like a man, and observe what the Lord your God requires: Walk in obedience to him, and keep his decrees and commands, his laws and regulations, as written in the Law of Moses. Do this so that you may prosper in all you do and wherever you go and that the Lord may keep his promise to me: If your descendants watch how they live, and if they walk faithfully before me with all their heart and soul, you will never fail to have a successor on the throne of Israel'" (1 Kings 2:2–4). Walk with the Lord and obey Him was the central message. And those are commendable words to and for each of us.

But what follows is where we find the mixture. For example, David urged Solomon to show kindness to Barzillai but to bring judgment and execution upon Joab and Shimei. There were some long-stewing resentments that David carried to his grave. He even tried to perpetuate that resentment by charging his son Solomon to take care of these men not long after he had died. Looking at this scene of both kindness and resentment, we see some lessons that might help us as we live today. First, do not wait to show kindness. Do it now. You might choose to bless someone in your will or estate, but you might want to bring a blessing to someone here and now while you are alive. There is never a wrong time to show kindness to others—and especially if they have nothing to offer you in return. Blessing someone after you depart is fine and good. But seek to be a blessing here and now.

Second, do not carry resentment in life. Do not wake up each day with a burning bitterness or dislike inside you. If you do this, you only harm yourself and no one else. Pettiness, jealousy, getting even, and harboring bad feelings toward someone are no way to live. And you surely do not want to approach death with these kinds of feelings rattling around in your mind and heart. Make peace with those you dislike. Ask for forgiveness, or be quick to grant it to those who ask it of you. Pray for your enemies. Be kind to those who have hurt you or intended to harm you. We are all sinful, fallen people who have possibly been on both sides of resentment and bitterness—the perpetrator and the recipient. Relieve yourself of any bitterness, and lighten the load that you carry in life.

Third, keep short accounts with others. Do not put off to the end of life what you could easily and credibly do today. We often daydream about "one day" or "someday," but those times often never come and in the midst of daydreaming we lose today. Take action today if you have some unsettled accounts where you need forgiveness or have the kindness to show to someone else. Seize this day or moment as a time to do that.

Fourth, and this is a hard lesson to learn, there will be many people who simply never measure up to what you want them to be or the standards you have. They will not. They will disappoint you and frustrate you. They will provoke and aggravate you. But you are likely the same way yourself in someone else's eyes. No, people do not always act as we would like or measure up to what we would like to see. But you and I do not always measure up either. We come up short. We fail. We fall short of the glory of God and the standards or expectations that other people may have for us. There is no perfect Christian, no perfect preacher, no perfect church, no perfect teacher, and no perfect doctor.

And finally, at times, all we can do is shake hands and love the other person but still perhaps disagree or deal with some disappointment. We cannot control or reprogram others as we want them to be. Leave that to God who can change hearts, minds, and lives. Keep on loving those who disappoint you. Seek good for them. Do good to them. And live graciously with them. You will never be disappointed that you offered someone a spirit of graciousness and goodness. May we live humbly today and seek to complicate the lives of others far less. May we not live painful lives or hold on to the pain that others have inflicted on us. You and I, as followers of Christ, remain "works in progress" because God, thankfully, is not finished with us yet.

DAY 31

2 Kings continues with the history of ancient Israel and Judah. It continues to record the events of the various kings all the way up to Judah's exile in Babylon. In 2 Kings 5, we find the healing story of Naaman who had been afflicted with leprosy. The Bible says he was a "great man in the sight of his master and highly regarded, because through him the LORD had given victory to Aram. He was a valiant soldier, but he had leprosy" (2 Kings 5:1). Like anyone suffering from leprosy or another disease, he wanted to be healed and whole again.

Naaman went to visit Elisha in the hope of receiving the healing he so desired and needed. We read the following: "Elisha sent a messenger to say to him, 'Go, wash yourself seven times in the Jordan, and your flesh will be restored and you will be cleansed.' But Naaman went away angry and said, 'I thought that he would surely come out to me and stand and call on the name of the Lord his God, wave his hand over the spot and cure me of my leprosy. Are not Abana and Pharpar, the rivers of Damascus, better than all the waters of Israel? Couldn't I wash in them and be cleansed?' So, he turned and went off in a rage" (2 Kings 5:10–12). Naaman was angry, enraged even, because the Lord was not going to heal him as he had planned or expected. "Why not this or that," he muttered to anyone who would listen. Imagine being on the cusp of healing but just too proud or ornery to receive this miracle!

He suffered from what we might call the "what-about-this syndrome." At times, we can suffer from this syndrome as well. It is worse than leprosy. This syndrome is where we want God to work according to our expectations more than His. We want God to do what we want Him to do rather than submit ourselves to His plans and purposes. This syndrome is an on-demand approach to life where we expect God to snap things in order according to our wishes and ways. Naaman wondered, "What about this river? Why don't you just wave your hand and say some words and heal me here and now?" What about, what about, what about? This kind of babbling can sound like us too. God gives us a message to hear or a pathway to follow, and we don't like it so we begin to toss the alternatives that we believe are better. This battle is essentially the same one we see played out in the Garden of Eden for the first time with the serpent, Adam, and Eve challenging and doubting what God had planned.

Naaman was given something rather simple to do in order to experience healing. But this instruction from Elisha moved Naaman out of his comfort zone or the small world where he felt most secure and most in control. The "what-about syndrome" is where we are reluctant to let go and trust God, to give up our control to see where He might lead and take us. This battle of wills between God and us can be intense. There are occasions in life when all we can do is let go and trust God's ways and for God to provide for us. This letting go could be a change in jobs, a physical move, a career change, a decision about where to attend college, trusting God for healing, and looking to the Lord to answer your prayers and questions in His time and by His means.

Faith and trust are hard. They are shaped and formed in the furnaces and trials of life. As Peter taught us, we often must set Christ apart as Lord over situations and battles that we cannot control or win by human power alone (1 Peter 3:15). The good news for Naaman is found in 2 Kings 5:14, "So he went down and dipped himself in the Jordan seven times, as the man of God had told him, and his flesh was restored and became clean like that of a young boy." And when Naaman complied with God's instructions, he was healed, made whole, and restored just like the skin of a young child and not a diseased man. From Naaman's life, we learn the lessons of trust, faith, and obedience. We must trust God if we call upon Him. We have to have faith in God's answers. And we have to obey Him and go wherever He takes us. Maybe today, we're due for some lessons in trust, faith, and obedience. If we will learn these lessons, the rewards are ours to enjoy.

DAY 32

1 Chronicles is another history book in the Old Testament. It is considered by many to be a historical supplement to 1 and 2 Samuel and 1 and 2 Kings. 1 and 2 Chronicles tend to focus much more heavily on the history of the southern kingdom of Judah. One of the prevailing themes or thoughts that we find in 1 Chronicles is the sovereignty of God. He is clearly God and Lord over the affairs of both Judah and the earth. A little more than midway through 1 Chronicles, David paused to offer a psalm of thanks to the Lord in I Chronicles 16:8-36. Two important thoughts stand out in David's Psalm. He said, "Give thanks to the LORD, call on His name; make known among the nations what He has done" (16:8). And he said, "he remembers his covenant forever, the word he commanded for a thousand generations" (16:15). We acknowledge God's sovereignty by our gratitude and by our trust in His faithfulness to a "thousand generations."

Let us consider those thoughts that stand out for us to see. First, we learn to be thankful people. We learn to express our thanks to the Lord God who is the Giver of every good and perfect gift or blessing. And in our gratitude, we make the Lord known to others. We reveal Him through our sense and expression of gratefulness. You may know people who are exceedingly grateful and thankful for all the blessings that they possess and enjoy. Second, we learn that God remembers His people and His promises. God's memory extends beyond today or this generation. His memory extends out to generations to come far beyond our days and times. David knew, and we can know, that God is always at work with the future in mind. The events of today play a role in His unfolding plans and purposes. God is not caught off guard by tomorrow or next week. He is already at work with the future in mind as He writes out His purposes in history.

A bit later in this psalm of thanks, David wrote about the singular nature of the Lord God. We read, "For great is the LORD and most worthy of praise; he is to be feared above all gods. For all the gods of the nations are idols, but the LORD made the heavens" (1 Chronicles 16:25–26). David played a word game with his readers. He is saying that GOD is the GOD of all gods. We might turn things or people into gods or place our allegiance with things or people. But God is the GOD of anything else we might be tempted to chase or pursue. David wrote of God's awesome and incomparable nature by declaring that the LORD made the heavens and all the things of creation from which we might make or fashion idols. In human ignorance and defiance, we fail to realize that the LORD GOD made the very things that we are often tempted to turn into idols and worship with our lives and talents. What we might elevate to the status of an idol by our attention, affection, and adoration was made by the GOD of all gods.

David ended his psalm of thanks by challenging his readers to praise God in an unrelenting way—or to praise the LORD God forever. "Praise be to the LORD, the God of Israel, from everlasting to everlasting" (1 Chronicles 16:36). David's message to us is to never stop giving praise or thanks to God. Let praise and thanks be in your heart and on your mind constantly and continuously. The Maker of all things deserves all the praise and thanks that we can make and offer for His glory. We likely have little trouble asking God for help or petitioning God to be at work in our lives. But we often have to grow in our sense of praise and gratitude. And may today mark a starting line or trend where we do just that.

DAY 33

2 Chronicles is a continuation of Old Testament history. Most of Judah's kings were idolatrous and wicked and led the nation on a course of spiritual ruin and depravity. One exception was King Uzziah. We read this about Uzziah, "He did what was right in the eyes of the Lord, just as his father Amaziah had done. He sought God during the days of Zechariah, who instructed him in the fear of God. As long as he sought the LORD, God gave him success" (2 Chronicles 26:4–5). This simple assessment teaches us some valuable lessons. First, anyone should seek the Lord. God calls both kings and commoners to come to Him and to seek Him. We never reach a status in life where we can retire from seeking or serving the Lord. The Lord graciously invites us to know Him, love Him, and serve Him. King Uzziah wisely knew that He could not lead his people without guidance from the Lord God.

Second, success can be defined in a different way. Culture and the world have ways of defining success, standing, or wealth. Scripture has a different way. A successful life makes a way and a place for the Lord. We do not live by our standards, and we do not do things our way. We take a knee before the Lord and begin to define success and faithfulness as He defines them. King Uzziah was blessed by God because of this monarch's humility and for his choice to yield himself before God. We would do well to remember the warning of 1 Peter 5:5b, "God opposes the proud but gives grace to the humble." We can humble ourselves willingly or we can leave it to God to bring humility to us. There were kings who faced humility at the hands of the Lord because of their persistent, willful stubbornness and rebellion. May we never reach the point where God must humble us because of our pride or sinfulness.

Third, we learn that Uzziah was instructed in the fear of the Lord. We are to fear the Lord—not in the sense of a scary movie, ghost stories, or like we might fear a crime taking place. Rather, we fear the Lord from the perspective of reverence and honor. We give to Him what rightfully belongs to Him—our worship, adoration, respect, and reverence. We love Him because He first loved us. We want to be careful not to develop a casual, careless, haphazard relationship with the Lord whereby we only call upon Him when we need or want something. To fear the Lord means we walk with Him and cling to Him at all times, in all ways, and on every occasion.

Near the end of 2 Chronicles, another king named Josiah led a period of revival and renewal in Judah after a copy of God's law had been found. Amazing, isn't it, that the people had become so detached from God's Word and ways that it was news when a copy of the law was found! We live with Bibles so close by that we find it hard to imagine life without the Word close to us. It was said about Josiah, "He did what was right in the eyes of the LORD and walked in the ways of his father David, not turning aside to the right or to the left" (2 Chronicles 34:2). Shortly after the finding of the copy of God's law, Josiah led the people in a reading of it and a recommitment to keep and honor this Word. The lesson for us is to know God's Word and ways and to live in them and with dedication to them. May we also live in a way that others see evidence of that commitment and devotion in us. Folks should know we are devoted to the Lord and His Word and ways before we ever have to open our mouths to say one single thing. There should be evident indications of the depth to which the Word and ways of God have penetrated our heart, mind, soul, and being. The lesson from 2 Chronicles is clear for all to see. Ignorance of God, His Word, and His ways will uniformly lead to ruin and decay. But the opposite is equally true. Walking with God, understanding His Word, and seeking to follow His Ways will lead to life, joy, and success in His eyes.

DAY 34

Ezra offered leadership to Judah near the end of the Babylonian exile and in the days that followed. The book that carries his name is ten chapters long and details the rebuilding of the temple and the return of Ezra and others to Jerusalem. The work that God gave him to do was not easy, but it was crucial to the reestablishment of the Jewish people in the land God had originally promised them. In Ezra 7, he wrote, "Because the hand of the LORD my God was on me, I took courage and gathered leading men from Israel to go up with me" (Ezra 7:28b). Ezra knew he needed God's help to complete the mission that was entrusted to him. He was wise enough and humble enough to seek courage from the Lord God. There certainly may be missions and occasions where we feel inadequate to do what God has for us. In such times, Ezra is an example. We seek the courage we need from the Lord. Note also that Ezra did not work alone. He gathered others to go with him. God can graciously give us the company and blessings of others to help bear the weight of the work He has for us to do. Often, all we have to do is ask God for a trusted brother or sister to go with us and to stand beside us. Remember, Moses had Aaron, Paul had Barnabas and Timothy. Even Jesus leaned upon Peter, James, and John.

Ezra's ten chapters have some important works about repentance, confession, and forgiveness. He led the people to acknowledge their sinfulness and the role that the disobedience of their ancestors had played in the punishing exile in Babylon. Ezra led the people to pray these words, "What has happened to us is a result of our evil deeds and our great guilt, and yet, our God, you have punished us less than our sins have deserved and have given us a remnant like this. Lord, the God of Israel, you are righteous! We are left this day as a remnant. Here we are before you in our guilt, though because of it not one of us can stand in your presence" (Ezra 9:13, 15). Confession is important for us today. We have to acknowledge our sinfulness and failure before the Lord. When we confess our sins, God is faithful and just and offers grace and forgiveness for those sins (see 1 John 1:9). We are not to treat sin and disobedience lightly. Some folks often like to dismiss sin and minimize it by saying everyone sins or we all do it or there is always grace and God will always forgive us. But the Bible is clear that we are not to be casual about sin, whimsical about it, or even de-emphasizing it as we might minimize a paper cut.

Paul said this about sin, "What shall we say, then? Shall we go on sinning so that grace may increase? By no means! We are those who have died to sin; how can we live in it any longer?" (Romans 6:1–2). Jesus Himself told a woman whom he had forgiven to go and sin no more (John 8:11). John wrote, "You know that he appeared in order to take away sins, and in him there is no sin. No one who abides in him keeps on sinning; no one who keeps on sinning has either seen him or known him" (1 John 3:5–6). We are to see sin as God sees it. We are to treat it as seriously as God does. Ezra's confession and treatment of sin help us to see that we are to deal ruthlessly with any sin or disobedience that we find in our lives. Unaddressed or ignored sin can grow and metastasize just like cancer in the body. We are to give no room or occasion for sin to grow. Isaiah offered us this warning, "Woe to those who call evil good and good evil, who put darkness for light and light for darkness, who put bitter for sweet and sweet for bitter!" (Isaiah 5:20). Perhaps today, Ezra inspires you to seek courage from the Lord and to live courageously for Him. Maybe this ancient man convicts you of sin and disobedience or even a cavalier attitude about such things that need correction. Scripture can comfort the afflicted and afflict the comfortable.

DAY 35

Nehemiah was a builder—or more properly, a rebuilder. He was commissioned by God to rebuild the tattered and broken walls of Jerusalem. He gave up a position of prestige and comfort in the Persian king's court to take this position of service. When he heard that his beloved Jerusalem was lying in trouble and disgrace, he cried (Nehemiah 1:3–4). As we read Nehemiah, we immediately recognize that he faced opposition and encountered resistance as he tried to rebuild the walls. He replied to his opponents in a clear and determined way. "I sent him this reply: 'Nothing like what you are saying is happening; you are just making it up out of your head.' They were all trying to frighten us, thinking, 'Their hands will get too weak for the work, and it will not be completed.' But I prayed, 'Now strengthen my hands'" (Nehemiah 6:8–9).

This response from Nehemiah to his opponents gives us some help in dealing with naysayers and opponents today. We can encounter resistance as we seek to serve the Lord and do the work He has for us. But these verses give us at least four strategies that we can use. First, keep any opposition or trouble in perspective. Do not make it out to be bigger than it is. There is an old saying about making mountains out of molehills. Do not elevate inconveniences into life-and-death matters. Keep your head straight and your emotions under control when you encounter trials and headwinds in life. Satan would love to distract you from what God has given you to do. Some of his strategies involve making as much noise as possible to divert and distract us from where the Lord is leading. He throws up a lot of mud with the hope that some of it will stick and throw us off guard or off stride. Second, keep fears in perspective. Much of what we fear in life never really comes to pass. A lot of fears can be exaggerated and inflated beyond normal. God is always greater than our fears so we have little to worry about. John said, "Greater is He who is in you than he who is in the world" (1 John 4:4). Entrust your fears to the Lord. Be honest about them. Be transparent. Acknowledge them before the Father who loves you, and take comfort in His protective grace. Your fears may not completely go away, but you can navigate through them with the Father's help.

Third, trust God to supply the strength and resources necessary to do anything that He has directed you to do. When God calls, He equips. When God confirms us to His service, He qualifies us for it. God's strength is made known in our weakness and even perfected in our weakness. Remember what the Lord said to Paul, "My grace is sufficient for you, for My strength is made perfect in weakness" (2 Corinthians 12:9). And fourth, you can believe that God will supply what you need exactly when you need it. God may not bring His grace or blessings in advance, but He will certainly not be late in delivering them to you. And He will not forget you or leave you to fend for yourself. Nehemiah noted His reliance upon the Lord God. "Our enemies lost their self-confidence because they realized that this work had been done with the help of our God" (Nehemiah 6:16b). God brought these ancient enemies to shame and ruin.

Near the end of Nehemiah, in chapter 13, he wrote the word *remember* several times. He knew that God had remembered him and would remember him. He knew the Lord's memory was and is flawless and perfect. He never doubted that God would act in the right ways and at the right time. Such a foundational value is critical for us today. We can bank on these certainties as we make our way through life each day. Nehemiah teaches us to remember the Lord because He surely remembers us.

DAY 36

Esther has a rather surprising claim to fame as a book of the Bible. It never mentions the name of God. Not even once. It is the only book in the Bible that contains no mention or reference to the name of God. While this book named Esther does not directly mention God, it most certainly and clearly reveals God at work on behalf of His people to bring His purposes to completion and fulfillment. Though His name is not captured or written in the book, we can easily see evidence of His fingerprints and His hand at work.

God worked through Esther to save and deliver the Jewish people. Perhaps the key verse is Esther 4:14, "For if you remain silent at this time, relief and deliverance for the Jews will arise from another place, but you and your father's family will perish. And who knows but that you have come to your royal position for such a time as this?" The phrase "for such a time as this" is the one we often remember in connection with Esther and her work. The principle that this phrase illuminates remains true even today. God often calls us to work, to serve, and to go for "such a time as this." God gives us the opportunity to serve Him and His purposes. We may not always know why God makes such a choice. And a full explanation is not usually necessary for us to serve the Lord. Often, we may not have any explanation at all—just a gnawing, restless sense that God has something for us to do.

When God presents us with an occasion to serve, we usually have two choices. Obedience or disobedience are the choices. We can disobey and decline the occasion to serve like Jonah first did when God called him to preach in Nineveh. Or, we can obey like Peter, James, and John did when Jesus offered to make these fishermen fishers of men. We can respond affirmatively and positively as Esther did and bring God's ways and purposes to high places or even unfriendly places. If you are looking for some way to serve the Lord or to become a difference-maker, there is usually no shortage of ways, places, and occasions where you can serve the Lord and reveal Him to others. Start where you work or live. Perhaps God has you there for such a time as this. There is work that God would like to fulfill through you where you already are.

When I was in Poland in May of this year, God had clearly raised Polish believers to serve Ukrainian refugees. This service involved listening, encouraging, feeding, comforting, and meeting these refugees where they were at that moment in life. Service does not always look like a Billy Graham crusade or a month spent in some of the direst and most distressed places on the planet. God often uses us right where we are, and He has put us there for a reason. Generally, that reason is to make Him known to others and to share His Gospel and grace with others. Look around your location. Pray about the place where God has you living or working. What could God be doing? Where is God already at work so you can join in with Him and what He is doing? We know with confidence that God is at work in the world. We simply need to decide whether we join Him in that work or refuse to do so.

We can get bogged down by guilt over all the times when we did not see or hear God when He called us to join Him. The enemy can trick us into thinking that our time has passed and the opportunity is gone. We can also get distracted and sidetracked if we look too far into future opportunities or ways to serve the Lord. The enemy can trick us into inactivity and passivity as we just sit idly by waiting for tomorrow. May we focus our eyes on our times and places so we can serve God at such a time as this and in such a place as this. It is a privilege to be used by the Lord and to join in whatever He may be doing. May we be as attuned to the movements and work of God as Esther was and be available for a time and place of His choosing.

DAY 37

Job is a fascinating book to read. It tells the story of a man who had almost anything, lost practically everything, and then regained even more after his time of testing came to an end. Along the way through the book and life of Job, we encounter and discover some powerful lessons about God. For example, we read, "Dominion and awe belong to God; He establishes order in the heights of heaven" (Job 25:2). God is majestic and in control. His throne in heaven is firmly anchored in His governance of the creation. God is in control—forever, fully and faithfully. When our lives may be spinning and swirling, we can take comfort in knowing that God reigns.

In Job 28:28, we read that "the fear of the Lord is wisdom." This message reflects what we read repeatedly in Proverbs. To know God, to reverence God, to walk with God, and to humble ourselves before God is where wisdom begins. If we wish to enjoy lives of wisdom and discernment, we have to make room for the Lord in our lives. We do not add God to all the other busyness and clutter we might have gathered in our lives. Rather, we clear space for the Lord and make Him the center of our existence and who we are.

The eternal nature of God is revealed in Job 36:26. We read, "How great is God—beyond our understanding! The number of His years is past finding out." God is. He simply is. The Bible makes no attempt to defend or to define the existence of God in the opening pages of scripture. Genesis simply states, "In the beginning God." Job encountered the LORD God as one who is. The human mind can neither completely define nor completely comprehend God. We accept His existence by faith and trust. Any "god" that we can completely understand or describe or define is not God. Such a god is the creation of human minds and human hands. Job draws us to the reality of the God who is. Remember the way God revealed His Name and character to Moses—the great I AM. Not "could be" but "I AM."

In Job 38, God speaks and responds to the affairs of Job and his friends in the previous chapters. The Lord answered Job in this way, "Where were you when I laid the earth's foundation? Tell me, if you understand" (Job 38:4). We are reminded of just how small we are and how glorious and great God surely is. The Lord's words to Job can humble us every bit as much as they likely humbled Job and his friends. We can often find the Lord's majesty and power on display in the creation itself. Consider these words from God, "Have you entered the storehouses of the snow or seen the storehouses of the hail, which I reserve for times of trouble, for days of war and battle? What is the way to the place where the lightning is dispersed, or the place where the east winds are scattered over the earth?" (Job 38:22–24). There is enough evidence of God in the creation for us to conclude that He is real and alive today.

Near the end of Job, he learns a crucial lesson that carries weight and purpose for us even today. "I know that you can do all things; no plan of yours can be thwarted" (Job 42:2). God wins. God always wins. His purposes and plans prevail. We can be confident that God will do what He says and carry out His sovereign will. If we think the world is going out of control or that nothing makes sense, we come back to the reality that God cannot be thwarted, stopped, or halted. He will prevail. He will endure. His plans will reach their fruition and conclusion. We can trust God and place our highest hopes in Him. Job's life was an adventurous one, but in the end, he came to know God in some deeper and more enduring ways. His faith was unshakeable. Take time to read Job's forty-two chapters and prepare to meet God in possibly some new ways but certainly in ways that build and edify your faith.

DAY 38

Psalms is the longest book in the Bible as it spans one hundred fifty chapters. In these chapters, you find a host of themes, emotions, reactions, convictions, and worship. Some of the more beloved passages of scripture can be found here—Psalm 23, Psalm 46, Psalm 121, Psalm 91, Psalm 8, and Psalm 51, to name just a few. Psalm 46, for example, was one of Martin Luther's favorite psalms and an inspiration for his hymn "A Mighty Fortress Is Our God." Psalms opens with a statement about a blessed man. "Blessed is the one who does not walk in step with the wicked or stand in the way that sinners take or sit in the company of mockers" (Psalm 1:1). And Psalms ends with a praise offered to the Lord. "Let everything that has breath praise the LORD. Praise the LORD" (Psalm 150:6). It certainly makes sense to say that a blessed life is going to result in praises and worship offered to the Lord God.

Psalm 119, the longest chapter in the Bible, drives home the importance of God's Word and the life that it brings to those who read it, ponder it, meditate upon it, and study it. We are told, "Your word is a lamp to my feet and a light for my path" (Psalm 119:105). Just a bit earlier, we read, "Your word, O LORD, is eternal; it stands firm in the heavens" (Psalm 119:89). God's Word is inspiring and life-giving when we engage it and reflect upon it. When we engage God's Word, the result is always good. Time with scripture helps us to recognize sin and helps us to navigate a course away from wrongdoing. "I have hidden your word in my heart that I might not sin against you" (Psalm 119:11). A psalm read every day would be an inspirational boost to your life.

Psalm 23 is where we turn when we are seeking the familiar and comforting presence of God's promises and protection. We are assured that we do not walk or journey through life alone—whether we are roaming mountain peaks or struggling through a deep and even dark valley. For many people, Psalm 23 is a "go-to" passage when they are facing a trial or battle. It is a comfort when we have lost loved ones. When we read the story of David's life, we can see how God used the situations and circumstances that he faced to inspire him to write a passage like Psalm 23. David's life was riddled with ups and downs.

Psalm 113:3 gives us a lesson in praising God. We read, "From the rising of the sun to the place where it sets, the name of the LORD is to be praised" (Psalm 113:3). We learn to create a lifetime of praise—from the beginning of each day to the end. We can consistently bring praise to the Lord with our lives. Every day brings a reason to praise the Lord. And we praise the Lord simply because He is God and worthy of the praise that we bring to Him. Psalm 111:2 teaches us to look deeply into the deeds of the Lord God. "Great are the works of the LORD; they are pondered by all who delight in them" (Psalm 111:2). Psalm 8 begins and ends in the same way: "O LORD, our Lord, how majestic is your name in all the earth" (Psalm 8:1 and 9).

Reading through the Psalms could take a little time. It is a long book, and some chapters are long. But investing in Psalms is a way to enhance your praise, thankfulness, and understanding of God's character and ways. We learn to rely upon the truth of Psalm 46:1, "God is our refuge and strength, an ever-present help in times of trouble." Have a great Tuesday! Praise the Lord today in some way, and let Psalms be a guide for how you can do that.

DAY 39

Psalm 32 speaks to the important matters of confession and forgiveness. Just think for a moment about how wonderful forgiveness feels. If you have asked for forgiveness from someone and received it or granted forgiveness to someone who asked you for it, you likely felt a sense of peace and contentment wash over your mind and spirit. I heard someone describe forgiveness as an overwhelming sense of joy. And it is. David knew this feeling. He wrote, "Blessed is the one whose transgressions are forgiven, whose sins are covered. Blessed is the one whose sin the Lord does not count against them and in whose spirit is no deceit" (Psalm 31:1–2). We are blessed when we experience God's forgiveness. What an amazing relief to know for certain that we are forgiven and that God does not count our sins against us! Blame gives way to release. Remorse yields revival and renewal.

We can know the joy of God's forgiveness at any time. We can approach His throne of grace with humility and confession and know that we are heard. His ears do not fail to hear our feeble cries. God does not "count" or "reckon" our sins against us. Our sins are buried in the sea of God's grace—forgotten and scattered as far as the east is from the west. The word *count* implies recordkeeping or bookkeeping. When sins are forgiven, God no longer keeps those records. The records are destroyed and forever forgotten. They are as shredded as receipts you might run through your shredder at home. The debts, ledgers, or books of sin were settled decisively and once and for all at the cross when Jesus gave His life as the full and required payment for sin. Psalm 130:3 says, "If you, Lord, kept a record of sins, Lord, who could stand?" Paul said in Romans 8:1, "There is now no condemnation for those who are in Christ Jesus."

David contrasted the joys of forgiveness with the miseries of harboring sin and persisting in it. He wrote, "When I kept silent, my bones wasted away through my groaning all day long" (Psalm 32:3). The sting of shame and guilt seeped all the way into David's bones. Even now, we often feel the weight of guilt and shame when we know that we have sinned against God and when we have done the very things we should not have done. The enemy often likes to manipulate or exploit that guilt or shame. The enemy will often try to persuade us that we are hopelessly and unforgivably wrecked or ruined. Yet we have to remember that no sin is beyond God's grace to forgive. No sin was too great for the cross of Christ to make payment for. The only sin that is too severe or too late is to die without Christ and His promise of life and salvation to all who believe in Him as the way, the truth, and the life (John 14:6).

David said that the burden of unconfessed and unforgiven sin was heavy and sapped his strength just like exertion and fatigue can wear us down in the heat of a summer day (Psalm 32:4). If we allow Satan to burden us with shame and guilt, then we have allowed ourselves to be marginalized or sidelined in the game of faith. A believer who is unnecessarily burdened by guilt has been effectively neutralized by the enemy. We can easily lose our passion to serve the Lord and worship Him. Keep short accounts with God. Confess your sins when you recognize them. Ask God to make you sensitive to the enemy's snares, thickets, and fiery darts of temptation. Remember the promise of 1 John 1:9—if we confess our sins, God is faithful and just to forgive those sins and to cleanse us from all acts of unrighteousness and rebellion.

At the end of Psalm 32, David calls us to sing to the Lord. Our shame has been replaced by a song. Our guilt has been replaced with His righteousness. We can rejoice in the Lord because our sins have been given to Him and deposited on the cross. David wrote, "Rejoice in the Lord and be glad, you righteous; sing, all you who are upright in heart!" (Psalm 32:11).

DAY 40

Psalm 51 is a passage of confession and contrition. David wrote this psalm after his ordeal with Bathsheba and conspiring to arrange the murder of her husband, Uriah. Nathan confronted then King David about his sinful conduct, and Psalm 51 was the king's response. When we read this chapter in the Bible, we discover the depth of David's confession and sorrow before God. We have a standard for what contrition and repentance look like still today.

Psalm 51:17 says, "My sacrifice, O God, is a broken spirit; a broken and contrite heart you, God, will not despise." Sorrow over sinful behavior looks and feels like a broken spirit. This kind of sorrow brings a certain heaviness and weightiness to the soul. It is almost like an elephant sitting on your chest. We are not to be indifferent toward our sins or oblivious to them. We are not to minimize them. We are not to compare our behavior to someone else and try to persuade ourselves (or even God) to believe we really have not done anything terribly wrong—at least when compared to this person or that person. We may persuade ourselves to believe that we are not as bad as we could be. Comparative righteousness or guilt has no value.

Psalm 51 shows us how to feel about sin and how to acknowledge sin. First, we are to feel a sense of brokenness. We have broken fellowship with God and chosen our ways above His and a love for something else above a love for Him. If we find that we are persisting in sin and pursuing an ongoing sinful lifestyle, habit, or behavior, then we have to ask if we have ever come to know the Lord in the first place (Romans 6:1–2, 11–14). We are not to be blind to sin and to convince ourselves that we can continue to sin because grace will bail us out. Such a notion is unconverted thinking and a desire to have it both ways (or even, as Jesus said, to attempt to serve two masters).

Second, we are to approach God in humble contrition and sorrow. David wrote, "Have mercy on me, O God, according to your unfailing love; according to your great compassion blot out my transgressions" (Psalm 51:2). David was asking God to blot out his sinfulness—to erase it, to remove it, and to cancel it. What David had once found to be so enticing and alluring had, at last, become disgusting and repulsive to him. When we see our sinfulness against the backdrop of God's holiness and righteousness, it does become repulsive to us as well. We see the disobedience for what it is. The satisfaction and energy we might once have felt have turned to emptiness, impotence, and shame.

Third, we approach God with humility. We set aside our pride to recognize that we have sinned against our Maker. We have not just done the wrong thing. We have sinned against the One who made us, loves us, and gave His Son's life for us. Though we might sin against an institution, an organization, or another person, all sin is really against the Lord. David knew this. "Against you, you only, have I sinned and done what is evil in your sight; so you are right in your verdict and justified when you judge" (Psalm 51:4). We have to see, with humility, that sin is not just a silly mistake at the moment or an inconvenient lapse in thought. No, it is an act of trespass against the One who is the embodiment of love, purity, and righteousness.

Take time to explore the depth of David's words in Psalm 51. His approach to confession is worth considering and practicing. Confession can enrich our walk with the Lord and anchor us in a desire to live uprightly, blamelessly, and righteously. Verse 17 reminds us once again that God does not despise a broken and contrite heart. Rather, He welcomes the humble, the broken, and those who seek Him and His healing grace. As we make our way through the Lenten season, may we recognize the depth of our sins and the power of the cross to heal and forgive. And may our love for the Lord triumph over any affection we may have for the things and ways of sin.

DAY 41

Sometimes we hear the expression "pay it forward." And we often speak of "paying it back." When we are overcome with gratitude, it can be easy to wonder how we can express what we feel. Could we "pay it back"? Should we "pay it forward instead"? You may be surprised to know that the writer of Psalm 116 struggled with how to be grateful for what the Lord has done. In Psalm 116:12, we read, "What shall I return to the LORD for all his goodness to me?" Have you ever asked that question? Have you ever found yourself in utter amazement over what the Lord has done for you or given to you? I suspect many of us have wrestled with these questions. There is no way we could pay God back for what He gives us—grace, love, forgiveness, healing, second chances, and daily provisions. By asking this question, the writer of the Psalms makes us think. He invites us to explore how we might answer that simple question in a difference-making way. There could be a few answers to the question that the psalmist raised.

First, we can tell God we are grateful. We can make time to express our gratitude and thanksgiving for what the Lord has done. We can tell God that we are grateful just as we might offer thanks to a friend or family member who has blessed us in some sort of special way. God does not need us to pay Him back; the earth is His and everything in it. But like any good father, He delights in hearing the gratitude of His children when they have received His rich blessings.

Second, we can use what God has given to us to bless others. We are not to hoard blessings or simply collect them for selfish reasons. God blesses us so we can bless others. God gives to us so we have resources with which to serve and honor Him by serving those around us. We have all been given far, far more than we have any right to deserve or expect. So we can use this abundance of blessings to serve those around us.

Third, we can recognize what we have been given. We may need to widen our eyes and ears so we can more clearly see and hear what God has done for us. We want to pay attention to what God sends to us. His blessings can often come through other people. He often even chooses to bless us directly without the intervention or assistance of others. It might be helpful to develop the habit of acknowledging three blessings every day that you can cherish and name. Keep a list of things that you can review.

Fourth, speak about what God has done. Tell others about the blessings and grace that God has given to you. Peter wrote, "Always be prepared to give an answer to everyone who asks you to give the reason for the hope that you have" (1 Peter 3:15b). One way we can witness for the Lord is by speaking about what He has done for us and given to us. We should not only count blessings; we should also declare them and talk about them too. Your testimony may encourage someone else in ways you could not have envisioned.

Fifth, we can draw near to the Lord and deepen our relationship with Him. Indeed, the psalmist tells us how we can be grateful to the Lord in the next verse of Psalm 116. We read, "I will lift up the cup of salvation and call on the name of the Lord" (Psalm 116:13). We return to the Lord a love for Him and an eagerness to spend time with Him. We often desire time with those we love. And if we love the Lord and rejoice in what He has done, we will want to draw near to Him and walk with Him in greater ways. When we recognize His goodness, we will surrender to Him in love and loyalty, dependence, and devotion.

DAY 42

Psalm 130 is often called a Psalm or a song of ascent. This grouping of special psalms spans the chapters between Psalm 120 and Psalm 134. These verses were often sung on the way up to Jerusalem by worshippers as they approached the city and the temple. These psalms were seen as ways to extol the Lord and to praise the Lord for His greatness and glory. These psalms centered the minds of worshippers upon the Lord and His ways. Psalm 130 speaks to waiting for the Lord and hoping in the Lord. Waiting often involves hoping and hoping involves waiting. And God can be found both in our waiting and our hoping. The Bible says, "I wait for the LORD, my whole being waits, and in his Word, I put my hope. I wait for the Lord more than watchmen wait for the morning, more than watchmen wait for the morning. Israel, put your hope in the LORD, for with the LORD is unfailing love and with him is full redemption" (Psalm 130:5–7). There are some truths in these verses that stand out for us to see.

First, we often have to wait for the Lord. We can be impatient, but He is not. We can be sluggish and slow, but He is not. Our schedules are not His schedule, just as His ways are not our ways. The Lord, at times, may slow us down. He may graciously ask us to wait or to slow down. Haste can lead to impulsiveness. Impulsive actions or decisions can often leave us in desperate places. Waiting may be one way that God saves us from ourselves. When we wait on the Lord, we can linger in His Word, approach Him in prayer, and confidently know that He will open the right doors at the right time. Waiting is not God's judgment or cruelty. In fact, waiting could be a wonderful expression of His grace at just the right time.

Second, we can always put our hopes in His Word and in Him. As we have said, we can trust God's Word and the God of the Word. When we wait in the Word, we are growing in the wisdom and truth of God. We may even discover that much of our haste and impulsiveness is selfish or even sinful in nature. We might have cloaked our plan in some self-appointed righteousness, but scripture has revealed it to be sinful and selfish. As we wait on the Lord, we continue to do the last thing or mission that He has entrusted to us. We continue on in devotion and dedication to whatever He has given us to do. We must not lose sight of what God has entrusted us to do while looking for something else or something different.

Third, as we wait on the Lord, we want to ensure that our hopes are in line with His. Our hopes and dreams in life should give us occasions to serve Him, honor Him, bless Him, and glorify Him. We can easily treat God like a gift card or a vending machine and see Him as simply existing to bring us happiness and satisfaction. But waiting on the Lord allows us to see our hopes for what they are. To be a follower of Christ means we trust Him with our present and our future. We never want to stray from Him, and we never want any future hopes to lead us away from Him.

God is the waymaker. He makes a way for us to be healed, forgiven, strengthened, and blessed. He removes confusion and replaces it with clarity. He rolls back the darkness and replaces it with His light. Remember the words of John 1:5, "The light shines in the darkness, and the darkness has not overcome it." Waiting may not be easy, but it can be rewarding. As you wait for God to work, you may well look back and see that the time spent waiting was more rewarding to you than what you were waiting for God to do. If you are in a season of waiting, do not waste the time. Grab the Word and hunker down to see what God has to show you and to teach you. And when the waiting ends, you will be even more ready to embrace what God has for you.

DAY 43

Proverbs is known as a book of wisdom. It was written by Solomon—a man blessed by God with wisdom and understanding. And incidentally, Solomon gained his wisdom simply by asking God for it. His wisdom reached legendary status. "King Solomon was greater in riches and wisdom than all the other kings of the earth. The whole world sought audience with Solomon to hear the wisdom God had put in his heart" (1 Kings 10:23–24). In Proverbs, Solomon endeavored to bring the wisdom of God into the realm of ordinary, normal human activity—finances, relationships, work, parenting, conflict management, conversations, and worship.

Proverbs began with an important lesson. "The fear of the Lord is the beginning of knowledge" (1:7a). To know fear and reverence God is a continuing theme in this book. A bit later, we discover two of the most beloved and quoted verses anywhere in the Bible. "Trust in the Lord with all your heart and lean not on your own understanding; in all your ways submit to him, and he will make your paths straight" (Proverbs 3:5–6). We learn that we can lean into God at any time and for any reason. He can straighten our crooked paths and crooked people. It is important to seek and follow the Lord's wisdom because, as Solomon wrote, "There is a way that seems right to a man, but in the end, it leads to death" (Proverbs 14:12).

Proverbs can help us to strengthen our worship and prayer life. We read that "the Lord is far from the wicked but He hears the prayer of the righteous" (Proverbs 15:29). We want to ensure that sin and wickedness do not get in the way of our prayers and walk with the Lord. Evil cannot take us anywhere that is good. Solomon wrote, "if a man pays back evil for good, evil will never leave his house" (Proverbs 17:13). By contrast, the Lord God is always a safe place to turn. We will never regret a decision to turn toward Him in faith and trust. God is our refuge and our strength. "The name of the LORD is a strong tower; the righteous run to it and are safe" (Proverbs 18:10). God's protection is an undefeatable castle or fortress where His people remain safe in His care.

Proverbs 31:10–31 features the beautiful passage of scripture often referred to as the virtuous woman or the woman of noble character. People will often request that this passage be read at the funeral of a saintly woman who has gone to be with the Lord. In Proverbs 27, we learn that godly men can bless and benefit each other. Solomon wrote, "As iron sharpens iron, so one man sharpens another" (Proverbs 27:17). Since Proverbs spans thirty-one chapters, a person could gain a graduate-level education in wisdom by committing to read a chapter a day over the span of a month with thirty-one days. Proverbs is a book that beckons us to read it again and again. The wisdom we discover cannot be exhausted with one reading. Two cardinal values that we encounter consistently in Proverbs are humility and the fear of the LORD. "Humility and the fear of the LORD bring wealth and honor and life" (Proverbs 22:4). We discover the kind of life that God blesses and honors when we commit to reading the wisdom that Solomon described.

Much of what we read may strike us as profoundly common sense. Yet often today, common sense can be in short supply. Proverbs speaks a word to many of the ordinary, everyday things that we encounter as we go about the work that God has assigned to us. One final example of godly common sense is found in Proverbs 20:19 where we read, "A gossip betrays a confidence; so, avoid a man who talks too much." Be careful with what you say and those to whom you say it. We know that words can be destructive and harmful so we must measure and choose them carefully. Choose a month where you go deeply into Proverbs to discover the wisdom that awaits.

DAY 44

Ecclesiastes is often attributed to Solomon. The opening verse simply says that what follows are "the words of the Teacher, son of David, king Jerusalem." While Solomon is not specifically named, assuming him to be the teacher is a reasonable conclusion. This book is part of the Bible's collection of "wisdom literature." It opens with a rather frustrating or discouraging message. "Meaningless! Meaningless! says the Teacher. Utterly meaningless! Everything is meaningless" (Ecclesiastes 1:2). While this book opens on a down note, it ends on a high one. We read, "Now all has been heard; here is the conclusion of the matter: Fear God and keep his commandments, for this is the duty of all humankind. For God will bring every deed into judgment, including every hidden thing, whether it is good or evil" (Ecclesiastes 12:13–14). We might conclude that a meaningless life or situation can find purpose and meaning when it is turned over to the Lord for His wisdom and guidance. Solomon's own life was marked by moments of great faith and discernment and moments of great disappointment and disobedience. If you find yourself struggling in a meaningless place or time, turn to the Lord and walk with Him. We do not have to wallow in a meaningless place or state.

Twice in Ecclesiastes 12, we are told to "remember" the Lord. We are not to lose sight of Him in the days of youth or even when we reach a mature age. We are to know Him, see Him, walk with Him, and lean upon Him. Often, when we lose sight of God, life can be reduced to a state of meaninglessness. Nothing seems to be right or to work out the right way. Human efforts and ways alone can usually end in frustration. Solomon wrote in 2:11, "Yet when I surveyed all that my hands had done and what I had toiled to achieve, everything was meaningless, a chasing after the wind; nothing was gained under the sun." These words remind us of Jesus's admonition to lay up treasures in heaven and not to make the things of this earth and this life the be-all and end-all of our existence. Jesus said, "Do not store up for yourselves treasures on earth, where moths and vermin destroy, and where thieves break in and steal. But store up for yourselves treasures in heaven, where moths and vermin do not destroy, and where thieves do not break in and steal. For where your treasure is, there your heart will be also" (Matthew 6:19–21). Jesus is reminding us to live always in view of eternity. We are to know that there is much more to life than what we can see, hear, feel, or experience.

Ecclesiastes 3:1–8 is a brief lesson on time. Most of us recall the familiar refrain of "a time to." The message is life moves rapidly—almost like a swift-moving river that can transport a raft or canoe speedily through the waterways. Life changes quickly—almost like the scenery outside your windshield on a long interstate drive. We are to navigate life's rapidity and quickness with the Lord as our guide and master. In Ecclesiastes 5, we discover this amazing statement: "Therefore stand in awe of God" (5:7b). And we are to live in awe of God and to stand in amazement and wonder of who He is and what He can do. How much of your day is spent in awe of God? Are you in the wonder of His blessings and provisions in life? Scripture calls us to give both awe and adoration to the Lord God.

You could read Ecclesiastes rather easily and briefly. The words of the Teacher challenge our thinking and how we have chosen to live. As you read this book, take the words of 7:13 to heart and "consider what God has done." Consider indeed, and even count the ways God has blessed you or provided for you. The Teacher came to learn, recognize, and realize that God is sufficient for us. "This only have I found: God made humankind upright, but men have gone in search of many schemes" (7:29). True wisdom lies in looking less at the schemes of the world and more at the Lord and His ways.

DAY 45

The Song of Solomon is often called the Song of Songs as well. Both names work for the same book. It is part of the literature section of the Old Testament (along with Psalms, Proverbs, and others). When we read this book, we immediately think that we are reading love poetry or perhaps eavesdropping on some love letters exchanged between a couple separated by great distance but, nonetheless, wanting to reconnect with each other. Indeed, the book has been criticized by some for its sensuous language. What are we to make of this book today? Well, it is included in scripture because scholars and faithful interpreters came to believe that it was a collection of love poetry describing the relationship that God enjoyed with His people Israel. It has been seen as a spiritual allegory symbolizing the love and affection between God and Israel and perhaps even, later, Christ and the Church for which He died.

In Song of Solomon 2:16a, we read, "My lover is mine and I am His." We are reminded of the certainty of God's love and the permanence of that love. His love does not waver or change. It remains constantly in the life of the believer. It is this profound love that calls us back to the Lord if we wander away from Him or choose our ways above His ways. In 1:4b, we read, "We rejoice and delight in you; we will praise your love more than wine." God's love is incomparable and without an equal. We give thanks for His love more than we would be thankful for the finest earthly treasures that we might gain or acquire. Solomon presented the idea that no matter how much earthly treasures or experiences may bless us and enliven us, the love of God is far greater and far more precious to us.

As we approach the end of Solomon's poetry, we read in chapter 8, "You who dwell in the gardens with friends in attendance, let me hear your voice" (8:13). God longs to hear His people. He desires to hear us worship Him with words of praise, trust, and thankfulness. He desires to hear us call upon His name in trust and faith. He desires to hear us call out to Him in prayer. He desires to hear us raise His name above all names and declare our unfailing trust in Him. We may not audibly hear the voice of God today, but we can sense His voice in scripture as we pore over His Word and discern His will for our lives. We can hear His voice in prayer and in the guidance of His Holy Spirit.

In Song of Solomon 8:14a, the Lord calls us to "come away." We are to leave our sins and idols behind to trust Him fully, totally, and completely. We are to walk with Him and no one else. We are to place our full trust in Him and not the things of earth. When we come away, we are reminded of the first disciples who dropped their nets and urgently left behind everything to follow Christ and Christ alone. When some disciples were turning away from Jesus, Peter stepped up and asked, "Where would we go?" When we come to the Lord, we do so fully and completely. As the hymn sings, "No turning back, no turning back." Perhaps today, the Lord is calling you to come away to Him and with Him—leaving behind all others and all else for His sake and His glory.

DAY 46

In Song of Songs 7:4, we find these words: "Your nose is like the tower of Lebanon looking toward Damascus." What does this mean? At first read, we might think it is not very kind or neighborly to say that about someone. But the comparison matters. In Solomon's day, this statement would have been complimentary and flattering. The tower was in a lofty and invincible position. It would have commanded both respect and awe. So this verse is a way of saying that someone's nose was distinct, prominent, and even enviable.

Another rather surprising verse is Song of Songs 4:2. We read, "Your teeth are like a flock of sheep just shorn, coming up from the washing." This comparison was a way of saying that someone's teeth were beautiful and almost perfect. A freshly shaved and washed sheep would have glistened brightly in the midday sun. Likewise, perfect teeth command attention and capture our vision. One person said this verse meant that not a single tooth was missing—perhaps a rarity in biblical days when modern dental care and dentists were not available. To speak these words meant that someone had been blessed with lovely teeth—and such a blessing was a rare sight in the days of King Solomon.

The lesson is we may never know what captures someone's attention. Even the smallest details or actions we might have minimized or long forgotten can be used by God for the good of others. God can use us in many ways to be witnesses for the Gospel and to draw others to Him. The way you handle a crisis could be a witness for someone to see. The words you speak might land at just the right time upon the ears of someone who needs to hear them. A note you write or a text you send could bless someone at the right time and with the right message.

Consider someone whose faith you might admire or respect. Perhaps there is something admirable in that person's faith that you could bring and incorporate into your own faith. There could be someone who looks to you as an example or even a role model for faith. Polish your faith like you might brush your teeth. Point others to Christ like a nose might point to Damascus (okay, a bit of a stretch, but the idea is to live prominently and noticeably for Christ). Another perspective might be to take as much time to care for your spiritual life and your faith as you do for your physical health or appearance. Invest deeply in prayer time, worship, Bible reading, sharing your faith, tithing, and inviting others to participate in our church. Share the Gospel. Practice sharing your testimony and how God has blessed you. Do not neglect your faith or leave it unattended any more than you would neglect to take a shower, wash your clothes, or comb your hair.

God's Word gives us many different lessons and examples to drive home the important message that we are to be devoted to the Lord and diligent about our faith every day—not just the holidays or the convenient days. Every day matters because every day is a day that the Lord has made. Even something ordinary like teeth and noses can remind us to polish our faith and to point others to Christ with the way we live. Make the most of every opportunity the Bible teaches us. And God can work through practically anything that we dedicate and offer to Him.

DAY 47

Isaiah is the first of the Bible's major prophets. It is a long book that spans sixty-six chapters. He was generally regarded as the greatest among the Old Testament prophets. He gave a compelling call to repentance that still resonates today: "Come now, let us settle the matter," says the LORD. "Though your sins are like scarlet, they shall be as white as snow; though they are red as crimson, they shall be like wool" (Isaiah 1:18). God promises to transform us and to forgive our guilt when we return to Him. A bit later, we learn that God will transform nations as well. We read this good news: "He will judge between the nations and will settle disputes for many peoples. They will beat their swords into plowshares and their spears into pruning hooks. Nation will not take up sword against nation, nor will they train for war anymore" (Isaiah 2:4). Isaiah takes us into the throne room of God where he saw that God was thrice holy. "Holy, holy, holy is the Lord Almighty; the whole earth is full of His glory" (Isaiah 6:3).

Also in Isaiah 6, we find a stirring call to service that has led many Christians into missions and ministry. "Then I heard the voice of the Lord saying, 'Whom shall I send? And who will go for us?' And I said, 'Here am I. Send me!'" (Isaiah 6:8). Today, may we aspire to be just as willing and eager to serve the Lord and to answer the different calls that He may make to us—whether full-time or part-time, whether local or far away. The prophet is also a herald of Christmas—proclaiming and declaring the coming of Jesus about 760 years before that first Christmas night in Bethlehem. Consider the magnitude of that prophecy. It would be like a prophecy first spoken in 1263 that finds fulfillment today in 2023. Isaiah 7:14 is the often-quoted scripture at Christmas that tells us a virgin will conceive a child. And Isaiah 9:1–7 tells us that a child is born to us.

We often sing and read these words during the Advent season of waiting and anticipation: "For to us a child is born, to us a son is given, and the government will be on his shoulders. And he will be called Wonderful Counselor, Mighty God, Everlasting Father, Prince of Peace."

Isaiah touched all the important bases. Isaiah 53 is often called the "Calvary of the Old Testament" as it speaks to the suffering and death of Jesus for the sins of the world. We find unmistakable evidence of the cross in these words: "But he was pierced for our transgressions, he was crushed for our iniquities; the punishment that brought us peace was on him, and by his wounds we are healed. We all, like sheep, have gone astray, each of us has turned to our own way; and the LORD has laid on him the iniquity of us all" (Isaiah 53:5–6). On Maundy Thursday or Good Friday, we often turn to Isaiah 53 to see the depth of our Lord's suffering and the severity of the price that was paid for our salvation. Isaiah 43:2 is a great encouragement to us as we go through life's battles and trials. "When you pass through the waters, I will be with you; and when you pass through the rivers, they will not sweep over you. When you walk through the fire, you will not be burned; the flames will not set you ablaze." We know the Lord walks with His people—just as He led Israel out of Egypt in the Exodus and just as He abided with His servants in the fiery furnace we read about in Daniel.

Isaiah gives us many foundational promises we can claim and hold on to during the challenges of life. We are neither forgotten nor forsaken. He even spoke briefly about the coming new heaven and earth in Isaiah 65. We take comfort in knowing that God has the future well under control. "Behold I will create new heavens and a new earth. The former things will not be remembered, nor will they come to mind" (Isaiah 65:17). Taking two chapters a day, you could easily read Isaiah in just over a month and enjoy his many amazing promises for yourself and to use as you encourage others.

DAY 48

The prophet Isaiah had much to say about both the first and second coming of Christ. In chapter 42, he depicted Christ as "the Servant of the LORD." He said that the Father "delighted" in His Servant (Isaiah 42:1). The prophet spelled out some of the work that was expected of the LORD's Servant (or Christ) when He came into the world. We read, "I, the Lord, have called you in righteousness; I will take hold of your hand. I will keep you and will make you to be a covenant for the people and a light for the Gentiles, to open eyes that are blind, to free captives from prison and to release from the dungeon those who sit in darkness. 'I am the Lord; that is my name! I will not yield my glory to another or my praise to idols'" (Isaiah 42:6–8). A few lessons stand out for us to see in this prophecy.

First, Christ is our righteousness. He lived the perfect life that God expects of everyone. We have not lived perfect lives, but Christ did. Through faith, His righteousness is credited to us. We are given the life He lived in exchange for our sins that He carried to the cross. As we make our way through life, it is important to remember that Christ not only lived the life we could not live but also died the death that we should have died. He gave up His righteousness to us only to take our sinfulness in exchange. The righteousness that we receive from Him becomes safely and securely credited to us. It is more secure than your bank account.

Second, Christ promises to hold and keep His people. He does not lose anyone. Consider His words in John 10:28, "I give them eternal life, and they shall never perish; no one will snatch them out of my hand." In His first coming, Christ has saved and secured us so that we will be ready to join Him in His second coming or His return to gather His people to be with Him. We can be confident that He will not lose us. We may struggle to keep track of possessions and personal items, but the Lord does not lose sight of us. His watchful eye is ever aware of where we are.

Third, the Lord opens blind eyes and frees captives from prisons. In short, He changes our lives and circumstances. We can now see the truth of God and understand the Gospel message. We can be freed from sinful ways, dangerous habits, and destructive lifestyles. He has come to open the prison cells that once held us captive. We begin to recognize how awful sin and disobedience are and just how far such things have pushed us away from the Father. Jesus declared that He is the light of the world. It is the light that He brings to us that allows us to see clearly and to see the truth He brings to us.

Isaiah wrote, "I am the LORD; that is my name!" (Isaiah 42:8a). Whenever LORD is all capitalized in scripture, we must remember that it is the Name that God revealed to Moses at the burning bush. LORD is the great I AM God. LORD means the One who causes all things to be. When Jesus used the expression "I am" seven different times in John's gospel (such as "light of the world," "good shepherd," etc.), He was taking the divine name upon Himself. Jesus clearly identified with the great I AM name for God or LORD. Jesus can save us because He is the LORD and He is mighty to save. And when He comes again for His people, He will come in rapturous glory and conquest.

Our response to all that the LORD has done is to sing a new song unto Him (Isaiah 42:10). Sing "His praise from the ends of the earth." As we live, we look back at the cross not only in remembrance, but also look forward to the Lord's coming once again. He has not finished His work with this earth or history. To know Christ, to walk with Christ, and to live for Christ secures our place with Him. May we submit and surrender to Him each day so we can join Him in His coming.

DAY 49

Jeremiah was the second of the major prophets in the Old Testament. He was called the "weeping prophet." He spoke God's Word during some dark days in Judah—the final days of Judah's existence before the Babylonian exile and then for several more years into the time of exile and captivity. He called the people out for their sins but also gave them the promise of renewal and restoration. God was not finished, and the last word had not yet been written. In chapter 1, this prophet taught us a lesson about the intimate way that the Lord knows us. We read, "The word of the Lord came to me, saying, 'Before I formed you in the womb I knew you, before you were born, I set you apart; I appointed you as a prophet to the nations'" (Jeremiah 1:4–5). The Lord knows His people and has plans for them. As Jeremiah would later say in one of his most often quoted passages, "'For I know the plans I have for you,' declares the Lord, 'plans to prosper you and not to harm you, plans to give you hope and a future'" (Jeremiah 29:11). We can take consolation today in knowing that our lives and existence are not futile or frustrating. God does have a purpose and meaning that He can bring to any life.

Seeking the Lord is an important mission in life. Jeremiah gives us a primer on how to seek the Lord each day. We read, "Then you will call on me and come and pray to me, and I will listen to you. You will seek me and find me when you seek me with all your heart" (Jeremiah 29:12–13). Seeking and knowing the Lord are not mere hobbies or pastimes. To know the Lord is the most pressing or urgent calling in our lives. And Jeremiah challenges us to seek Him with heart, mind, soul, life, and everything. We learn from Jeremiah that faith in God is rewarded and honored. Such an investment of faith and trust does not return to us void. "But blessed is the one who trusts in the Lord, whose confidence is in him. They will be like a tree planted by the water that sends out its roots by the stream. It does not fear when heat comes; its leaves are always green.

It has no worries in a year of drought and never fails to bear fruit" (Jeremiah 17:7–8). In a turbulent and often changing world, we find our footing and stability in the Lord and the trust we place in Him. We seek to hear Him and to believe Him above the noise of the world around us.

Chapter 18 of Jeremiah is the powerful story of the prophet's trip to the Potter's House where the Lord taught him that Israel was like clay in His hands. God could build and shape the people and the nation if they would only trust Him. The same can be said about us today. God can work in those who place their trust and hopes in Him. We might not always see the evidence of His work and hand as immediately as we might like. But our trust, prayers, and seeking are not done in vain. God is at work in all who call upon His Name and place their hopes in His hands. What could God do in your life today as you look to Him?

Jeremiah delivered a stark warning about forgetting the Lord. "My people have committed two sins: They have forsaken me, the spring of living water, and have dug their own cisterns, broken cisterns that cannot hold water" (Jeremiah 29:13). When we turn from the Lord to *any* other thing, we find that we have made a bad and tragic choice. We have turned to wells and cisterns that are empty and have no life-giving power to offer us. If Jeremiah spoke to us for a minute today, he might likely tell us to lift our eyes beyond the things around us, to see God and walk with Him, and to abandon the ways we have chosen in favor of His ways. Seeking the vain and empty things is like running until your feet are bare and your throat is dry, said Jeremiah (2:25a). "Your sins have deprived you of good" (Jeremiah 5:25). But the Lord awaits, like the loving Father He is, for His people to return to Him while the window is open and there is still time. Consider whatever business you might have before the Lord and quickly attend to it today.

DAY 50

In addition to his prophecy, Jeremiah is also credited with writing Lamentations. One reason he is often called "the weeping prophet" is his writing of Lamentations. As the name would suggest to any casual reader, it is about lamenting and mourning. He wrote about the ruin of Jerusalem and his country and the misery of the people who were suffering affliction at the hand of God through the Babylonians. He grieved over the situation his people endured and experienced. But there was also the promise of renewal and restoration. We read a familiar passage in Lamentations 3:22–23, "Because of the LORD's great love we are not consumed, for His compassions never fail. They are new every morning; great is your faithfulness." These words helped to give rise to the great hymn of faith "Great Is Thy Faithfulness." But we can also build our faith on a passage like this. At least four valuable truths stand out for us.

First, the Lord is never absent. He is never missing in action. He is always present and present with us. We can often say what Jeremiah said, "Because of the Lord." No situation is ever too dire or too stressful for the Lord. No matter is ever a lost cause when the Lord is present and near to us. When a battle arrives in your life, think of God before you think about the battle. Think about God's presence with you. He is much more real than any battle we may encounter. We can speak the name of the Lord over any crisis or battle that may come our way. As Peter would remind us, set Christ apart as Lord!

Second, because of the Lord and His love for us, "we are not consumed." The word for *consumed* means "completed" or "finished." No trial can destroy us. No trial can rob us of the most essential matters of life and faith. We are not "finished" whenever a trial comes our way. Noah was not "finished" by the flood. God provided an ark. Joseph was not "finished" when his brothers hated him and conspired to do away with him. God granted him favor and safety even while he was in an Egyptian prison. Battles do not have to beat us or whip us.

Third, God's love or "compassions" never fail. We never have to wonder whether God loves us or not or whether that love has changed or weakened. God's love remains constant and consistent throughout life. We can take confidence and rest in His love. The word used for *fail* can mean spent or empty. There is no bottom to the well of God's grace and love. Indeed, His compassion is new every morning. Just like sunrise is new each day, so is God's love renewed and expressed every day. It comes to us in new and dynamic ways with each new morning. It is always sufficient for us. His love is not exhausted by our trials or battles. He puts no limits or boundaries on His compassion. We have not earned it or deserved it. Yet God freely shows His love to us.

And fourth, God's faithfulness to us is great and awesome. He does not betray us or turn His back on us. He is not cowered or intimidated by the battles we encounter in life. The word used for "great" can also mean many. So God's faithfulness can be expressed and demonstrated in many different ways. The word that Jeremiah used for "faithfulness" can mean firm, stable, and steadfast. God's faithfulness does not waver or change. It is not subject to the whims and winds of the world. God will always remain faithful even when we are not or life is not.

Though Lamentations does imply sorrow or sadness, we should not discount the hope that we can find in Jeremiah's message. Hope does not come from a change in one's circumstances or the mere absence of battles. Hope comes from the Lord. Hope is what we have amid any trial we face. Often, in scripture, we see that suffering and hope are welded together. Suffering brings hope. And hope endures despite suffering. Remember, Good Friday led to Easter. We live in a fallen world today with the hope that one day we will be with the Lord forever and safely in His keep. Great is His faithfulness indeed!

DAY 51

Ezekiel is the third major prophet found in the Old Testament. His name means "God strengthens," which is a good name for a prophet to have. One of this prophet's key phrases is "I am the LORD." This statement reminds us of two realities. First, there is a Lord God. And second, we are not Him. Perhaps today, you need to be reminded that God is real and He is the great I AM. He is as alive and real today as He was at the moment of creation when He called for light. Knowing this truth *can* make a difference in your life as you rely on His power and strength. In Ezekiel 11:19, the prophet wrote about the return of the people from judgment and exile. We read, "I will give them an undivided heart and put a new spirit in them; I will remove from them their heart of stone and give them a heart of flesh." In short, Ezekiel described the new birth that we enjoy as followers of Christ. The heart is changed. The mind is changed. And we live a new life given to us by the work of Christ at the cross and the empty tomb.

One of Ezekiel's most celebrated passages involves the vision of the dry bones in chapter 37. He recognized the futility of man's ability to come back to life on his own. Only God can bring life and vitality to dry and once-dead places. "Therefore, prophesy and say to them: 'This is what the Sovereign Lord says: My people, I am going to open your graves and bring you up from them; I will bring you back to the land of Israel. Then you, my people, will know that I am the Lord, when I open your graves and bring you up from them'" (Ezekiel 37:12–13). If you find your faith in a dry season, do not despair. Trust the Lord. Look to the Lord. Lean upon the Lord. He can bring new life, new hope, and new encouragement to you. The dryness can be removed with a return to scripture reading, prayer, journaling, worship, and keeping an ongoing dialogue with the Lord God.

In Ezekiel 28, Ezekiel directed a prophecy against the King of Tyre. Some believe this prophecy was directed more against Satan who was portrayed as the earthly king of Tyre. In the prophecy, we find a warning against pride and its many dangers. We read, "Your heart became proud on account of your beauty, and you corrupted your wisdom because of your splendor. So, I threw you to the earth; I made a spectacle of you before kings" (Ezekiel 28:17). Pride led to Satan's downfall and casting down from heaven and the presence of God. Pride was part of the original fall in the Garden of Eden where Adam and Eve became convinced that they could pick their ways above God's ways and not suffer any consequences from such a choice. Pride is dangerous today. And when we find ourselves acting pridefully, we need to remove such things from our lives—casting them to the cross for healing and forgiveness.

Ezekiel ended with a declaration that we need to hear clearly today. It is the kind of statement that we could post on our refrigerator or a sticky note on a desk or table. The prophet concluded his prophecy with these four words, "The LORD is there" (Ezekiel 48:35). And indeed, He is. God is there. God is with us. The whole message of Christmas is the presence of God with us. The Holy Spirit indwells His people today. He lives in us and with us and becomes our counselor and companion through the turns and demands of life.

DAY 52

Daniel is the fourth and final major prophet of the Old Testament. He prophesied as a captive in Babylon during the Babylonian exile suffered and endured by Judah. Some of his prophecies are biographical in nature, some intended for his immediate audience of exiles in Babylon, and some were future in outlook and remain unfulfilled to date. One of his main themes is the sovereignty or reign of God over the affairs of people of all ages and times. God's kingdom and reign are eternal in nature—never ending and never passing away. In Daniel 2:20–21, he praised the Lord with these words, "Praise be to the name of God for ever and ever; wisdom and power are His. He changes times and seasons; He deposes kings and raises up others. He gives wisdom to the wise and knowledge to the discerning." We learn to celebrate the wisdom and majesty of God and to humble ourselves before such wisdom and power.

Daniel was known as a dream interpreter and for doing a bit of time in a lion's den for refusing to worship as the king demanded. He was a man who chose not to eat at the Babylonian royal table and defile himself with the king's food—preferring instead the healthy food of his people and culture. One lesson Daniel teaches us is his unwavering walk with the Lord and not succumbing to the temptations and mores of the times and conditions that surrounded him. Be wary of what you indulge in—and not just food, but the things you invite into your mind, heart, or life. He was not easily deceived into Babylonian ways and misled from the ways of God and the hand of God. Often today, we can be overwhelmed by whoever has the loudest voice, makes the grandest promises, or seems to be the strongest or most powerful. But Daniel just faithfully walked with the Lord and always leaned upon the Lord while turning down much of the noise that surrounded him.

One of the key verses in Daniel is 1:8, which says, "But Daniel resolved." He was not going to mix His faith in the Kingdom of God with the ways of the empire. We have to be cautious today and discerning. We have to be careful not to confuse the kingdom of God with the empires of this world. You may remember when Jesus was tempted by Satan, that one of the temptations involved Satan delivering the kingdoms of the world to Jesus if Jesus would only bow to Satan's ways. But our Lord refused—preferring the ways of the Father to the ways of the enemy. Loud, boastful, and outrageous ways and empires do not deserve to be mixed or conflated with the ways of the Lord. Hold fast to all that is right, true, and good. The New Testament prioritizes the fruit of the Spirit to the weapons and ways of the world. If you cultivate the fruit of the Spirit, you will find that the need to live or act combatively might start to diminish and disappear.

In Daniel 9, we read a great prayer of confession that the prophet offered on behalf of himself and his people who had sinned against God. He shows us how to confess our sins and acknowledge our waywardness before the Lord. "Lord, the great and awesome God who keeps his covenant of love with those who love him and keep his commandments, we have sinned and done wrong. We have been wicked and have rebelled; we have turned away from your commands and laws. We have not listened to your servants the prophets who spoke in your name to our kings, our princes and our ancestors and to all the people of the land" (Daniel 9:4b–6). Daniel acknowledged the character and righteousness of God, the sins of Judah, and the reason he and Judah were in the exile predicament they were in. That is a powerful way to pray. As you pray, follow Daniel's lead. Praise and declare the majesty and glory of God. Humbly and honestly confess your sins and failures. Declare your emptiness and powerlessness apart from God and His grace and help. Be a Daniel today—a figure of character, faith, and devotion who walked with the Lord.

DAY 53

Hosea was an Old Testament prophet who preached and prophesied about the same time as two other biblical prophets—Isaiah and Micah. He spoke primarily to the northern kingdom also known as Israel. God called Hosea to act out a prophecy in real life and in real time. It was a matter of not just declaring God's Word to people but actually modeling the message itself. God's command came to Hosea in this way: "When the Lord began to speak through Hosea, the Lord said to him, 'Go, marry a promiscuous woman and have children with her, for like an adulterous wife this land is guilty of unfaithfulness to the Lord.' So, he married Gomer daughter of Diblaim, and she conceived and bore him a son" (Hosea 1:2–3). This marriage was to symbolize Israel's betrayal of the Lord and turning away from the Lord to pursue idols and false gods. The betrayal that Hosea experienced at the hands of his wife Gomer would symbolize the betrayal that God had experienced at the hands of His people Israel.

We often do not think much about idolatry today, but it is real and remains a temptation or sin for us today. We can easily transfer the love and loyalty that belong to the Lord to something else. We can allow something else to claim our minds and hearts. Possessions, money, jobs, hobbies, and life goals can all become idolatrous and take the place of God in our thinking, devotion, and worship. God is the giver of every good gift and blessing. But it can be easy, often too easy, to love the gifts and blessings more than we love the Giver of such things. Satan often works in subtle ways—even ways that are hard to sense or detect. He can often turn our heads and hearts away from the Giver to the gifts and blessings that we enjoy.

Hosea gave a stern warning near the end of his prophecy. We read, "Return, Israel, to the LORD your God. Your sins have been your downfall" (Hosea 14:1). Two things stand out for us to see. First, there are times when we simply must return to the Lord. We have wandered and roamed away. We have chosen courses and pathways that lead us away from the Lord and toward a thousand other things. These things may not be inherently bad, but they become sinful because they draw us away from the Lord. The enemy does not particularly care about whatever pathway may lead you away from the Lord so long as you choose one of them. He will gladly give you a thousand options. Second, sin is a downfall. Sin is always wrong. Adam and Eve lost their place in the world's first and only perfect garden because of their disobedience to the Lord. We deserve death and judgment based on how we have lived. When we return to the Lord, Hosea told us what happens. "I will heal their waywardness and love them freely, for my anger has turned away from them. I will be like the dew to Israel; they will blossom like a lily" (Hosea 14:4–5a). Restoration comes to those who repent. God does offer a second or third chance for those who come back to Him and leave their love for sin behind so they can embrace Him again.

As a preemptive warning against sin, Hosea ended his prophecy with this message for us to consider: "Who is wise? Let them realize these things. Who is discerning? Let them understand. The ways of the Lord are right; the righteous walk in them, but the rebellious stumble in them" (Hosea 14:9). Each day, we have to decide that the ways of the Lord are right and good. God's ways lead to life and well-being both here and in the world to come. Perhaps today you would hear the words of Hosea in a new way. The prophet bids us, "Come, let us return to the Lord" (Hosea 6:1a).

DAY 54

Joel was a minor prophet who delivered a message from God to the southern kingdom also known as Judah. His message was one of great earnestness—judgment was imminent upon the nation because of their sins. If we looked for a key passage in Joel to consider, we might choose Joel 2:12–13. In these verses, we learn some timely lessons about God's way of dealing with us. We read, "'Even now,' declares the Lord, 'Return to me with all your heart, with fasting and weeping and mourning. Rend your heart and not your garments.' Return to the Lord your God, for he is gracious and compassionate, slow to anger and abounding in love, and he relents from sending calamity" (Joel 2:12–13). Joel teaches us four relevant lessons from these two verses.

First, we learn that we can return to the Lord. We can come to the Lord for the first time or we can return to Him after a season of roaming or wandering away from Him. Like the father in Jesus's parable of the prodigal son, our Father's arms are always open and ready to receive us back into the fold. We live in a day of grace and invitation. We enjoy the unearned and undeserved favor of God. And we live with His invitation to come to Him. Perhaps you have departed from the Lord in some way. Maybe today you return to Him and leave behind the diversions and distractions that have pulled you away from Him.

Second, we learn about the urgency of returning to the Lord. Joel used the expression "even now." There is not a better time to come to the Lord than now—here, now, and at this time. Why delay until later the unfinished business that you have with the Lord now? We have no guarantees of tomorrow or next week or next year. But we do have the gift of "even now." We are invited to return to the Lord at this moment. No time is better to seek the Lord than now and the moment at hand. This could be a life-changing moment for you.

Third, when we return to the Lord, we make a change of heart. People in Joel's day often made an outward demonstration out of rending their garments to show that they were serious about repentance and contrition. But at times, their outward display did not lead to an inward change. The rending was more show than substance. God calls us to change our hearts. It is the heart that is wicked and in need of repentance and change. Jeremiah 17:9 says, "The heart is deceitful above all things and beyond cure. Who can understand it?" The heart is where we begin to plot sinfulness and wickedness. We might understand the heart today as the mind, the will, or the human way of doing things. God says that when we return to Him, a change of character is in order.

Fourth, we learn that God is patient, slow to anger, and abundantly compassionate. He desires to see His people return to Him. It is not His wish to see anyone languish in sin and rebellion and the consequences of such things. Today, God's Spirit continues to call people to forgiveness and reconciliation. Maybe you are one of those people the Lord is calling today. He can and will relent from sending judgment if we return to Him. Joel gave his readers a vision of the coming day where God's Spirit would be poured out upon His people. We know this as the Day of Pentecost where the Spirit descended upon believers. We read, "And afterward, I will pour out my Spirit on all people. Your sons and daughters will prophesy, your old men will dream dreams, your young men will see visions" (Joel 2:28). The Spirit of God is still at work today. He convicts, calls, comforts, and counsels us. Perhaps today, He convicts you of your need to return to the Lord. Maybe He calls you to serve in a new way. Possibly He comes to comfort you in a time of uncertainty and worry. Maybe He counsels you to understand what God is doing in your life. Prophets almost always call us to see and know the Lord in new ways. What does the Lord have waiting for you today?

DAY 55

Amos was another minor prophet in the Old Testament. His name means "burden" or "burden-bearer." Perhaps you have felt like that was your name too. Some people bear the burden of long-term health problems that never seem to go away or even get better. Some carry the weight of grief that has lingered for decades. Some seem to carry financial burdens that never really change or go away. Amos's burden was to pronounce judgment on the people of Judah. This righteous judgment from God was pronounced on a people who had become decidedly unrighteous in words, behavior, and actions. The Lord had concluded, "They do not know how to do right" (Amos 3:10a).

Ironically, the people of Judah were pushing away and resisting their only hope—the Lord God Himself. Their unrighteousness could be addressed only by the righteousness of God. Poor Amos carried the burden of declaring God's Word to people who would neither hear him nor change their ways in response to his message. Ultimately, their stubborn sinfulness would result in their judgment by God and exile at the hands of the Babylonians. At one point, God clarified the role for Amos to play. We read, "Amos answered Amaziah, 'I was neither a prophet nor the son of a prophet, but I was a shepherd, and I also took care of sycamore-fig trees. But the Lord took me from tending the flock and said to me, Go, prophesy to my people Israel. Now then, hear the word of the Lord.' You say, 'Do not prophesy against Israel, and stop preaching against the descendants of Isaac'" (Amos 7:14–16). The key message for Amos was not to stop preaching and prophesying. He was to continue to do what God had given Him to do.

Occasionally, we have to carry burdens and possibly for a protracted period of time. The manner in which we carry those burdens can often bear witness to the Lord in the presence of others. Our willingness to carry burdens can often be an example or encouragement to others. Elisabeth Elliot often spoke of burdens as being the portion that God had chosen for her or others. The way we carry that burden is a faith story or testimony. As people of faith, we have to recognize that we do not live or carry burdens in our strength alone. God's grace is sufficient for us and will see us through the dark times and life's valleys. God often does some of His finest work in the face of burdens and struggles.

Amos gave Judah a great measure of hope near the end of his prophecy: "The days are coming," declares the Lord, "when the reaper will be overtaken by the plowman and the planter by the one treading grapes. New wine will drip from the mountains and flow from all the hills, and I will bring my people Israel back from exile. They will rebuild the ruined cities and live in them. They will plant vineyards and drink their wine; they will make gardens and eat their fruit. I will plant Israel in their own land, never again to be uprooted from the land I have given them," says the Lord your God (Amos 9:13–15). Even in the direst of times, God has plans and possibilities for us. We can see His light dawning and His grace breaking through the burdens.

If you find yourself carrying burdens today, be encouraged. God's grace is sufficient in the presence of burdens. God is at work in the midst of burdens. And God has seen the purposes that He wishes to accomplish through the burdens. Hold on to the Lord God as Amos did. Continue to do what God has given you to do. And trust that God will bring forth something good and glorious in the end. Just as Judah was restored following the exile, God is a restorer today as well. Burdens are never the last word for those who hold on to the Lord.

DAY 56

Obadiah is probably not a place in the Bible where you have routinely, or even recently, read and studied. It is only one chapter or twenty-one verses long. We know virtually nothing about this prophet or his background. He focused his prophecy on God's coming judgment of Edom for that nation's cruelty toward Judah. God would extend His care and protection over His people and shield them from the wickedness of another nation. That much was certain. The prophet did make it clear that the "Sovereign LORD" had given him this message to deliver. In fact, twice in verse 1, Obadiah made it clear that God had spoken to him. We read, "The vision of Obadiah. This is what the Sovereign Lord says about Edom—We have heard a message from the Lord" (Obadiah 1). Though we may not visit Obadiah very often for Bible study or guidance, it is part of God's Word and worthy of our reflection and consideration.

We do find a relevant warning in Obadiah 15 that can speak or connect with us today. The prophet wrote, "The day of the Lord is near for all nations. As you have done, it will be done to you; your deeds will return upon your own head." Like Hosea, Obadiah seems to be saying that if we sow the wind, we will reap the whirlwind. We tend to reap what we sow. If we sow seeds of division or discontent, we will experience the same thing in our lives. If we live maliciously or callously, we can expect that such experiences will visit our lives as well. The contrast is also true. Living graciously, generously, or kindly will likely mean that we enjoy the same as well. There is an old saying that reminds us that once we have made our beds, we will have to lie in them. There is truth to this statement. We often have to deal with circumstances of our own making. We have to handle situations that we have helped to create—whether good or bad. We rarely live in a vacuum or in isolation.

Jesus once said, "No one can serve two masters. Either you will hate the one and love the other, or you will be devoted to the one and despise the other. You cannot serve both God and money" (Matthew 6:24). Obadiah's message seems to say that we must be careful about the master we choose to serve. We need to be certain that we have sought the Lord and chosen the Lord above the host of things we might find on earth. Things, people, possessions, and objects will often leave us disappointed and empty. But no one ever regrets coming to the Lord. The Lord God is never the wrong choice or bad choice. The Lord will never leave us feeling empty inside.

Obadiah warned in verse 3 that "the pride of your heart has deceived you." The things we might desire or pursue may look good or pleasing to us, but we soon discover that they have no staying power or permanence. The pride of the heart persuades us to believe that we can go our own way and not suffer for it. This pride leaves us convinced that we know best and that what we wish to pursue is best for us. We see this pride on display in the Garden of Eden where Adam and Eve trusted their own eyes and a serpent more than the clear commands and teachings of the Lord who had told them what to do and what not to do.

This small prophet is worth your time and reading. God can use this prophet to encourage us to go deeper into His Word. A few moments in Obadiah might lead you to another prophet, the Gospels, the Psalms, or one of Paul's letters. The words of Obadiah can spark recognition and remembrance of other scriptures where you might wish to camp as well.

DAY 57

Jonah may be the best known of the minor prophets. His four chapters are presented as a short story and easily read that way—a leading character, plot, twist, turn, and resolution. His story can be read rather quickly. We meet Jonah as a man who would rather do anything than the one thing God had called him to do—preach to the city of Nineveh. So rather than preach, he chose to run away. Running turned into sailing, and then sailing gave way to swimming when a violent storm arrived that landed Jonah in the water after having been thrown overboard by the crew (Jonah 1:12).

After spending three days and three nights in the belly of a big fish, Jonah offered a moving prayer: "From inside the fish Jonah prayed to the Lord his God. He said: 'In my distress I called to the Lord, and he answered me. From deep in the realm of the dead I called for help, and you listened to my cry'" (Jonah 2:1–2). Isn't it good to know that we can pour our hearts out to the Lord—even in moments of deep despair and distress? We can approach God without pretense and without masking our feelings and fears. We can unburden ourselves before Him knowing that He hears us and welcomes us. Jonah cried out to God at a time when there was little else to do and nowhere else to turn. Desperation can often become a fitting altar where we do serious business with God through our prayers.

Jonah spoke these words near the end of his prayer: "I will say salvation comes from the Lord" (Jonah 2:9b). And salvation does come from the Lord God. The One who made us and gave His life for us is powerful and mighty to save. Soon, Jonah would be delivered from the fish and head off to Nineveh. This encounter with the Lord through prayer gave Jonah the courage and motivation that he needed to do what God had first called him to do—preach to a city that was lost and suffering mightily in their sins and waywardness. Perhaps you have a sense that God is calling you to a season of change in your life—to take a step of faith and trust and do something that He has for you to do. Maybe, like Jonah, you too have wandered and roamed away. You have resisted and even disobeyed what He has called you to do. Maybe the restlessness that you feel is an indication that a change is in order for you.

You might find comfort in the rest of Jonah's story. He did go to Nineveh and preach—and successfully so. The city repented and turned to the Lord. The response was so overwhelming that God relented and refrained from the judgment that He had intended for Nineveh (Jonah 3:10). We might expect Jonah to be deliriously happy about this outcome. But he was not happy—indeed his reaction was the opposite. He was angry at the Lord's compassion and started to sulk and pout. It is very easy to miss what God is doing or what He has done. We can easily get caught up in ourselves and not see the good that God may be doing all around us. Today might be the occasion when you begin to see what God is doing in your life and in the lives of those around you. Perhaps today you begin to celebrate God's power and presence and compassion when you see it displayed and revealed. Many times, we can be like Jonah—running, pouting, sulking, and even blind to the good happening around us. Perhaps we pray for God to grant us greater vision and greater faith—vision to see Him and faith to trust Him.

DAY 58

Micah was a prophet to Judah and Israel whose time paralleled that of Isaiah. The name Micah means "who is like Jehovah." His name alone tells us that his highest allegiance was to God alone in declaring a word or message that the people of Judah and Israel needed to hear. Perhaps the best-known verse is Micah 6:8, which says, "He has shown you, O mortal, what is good. And what does the Lord require of you? To act justly and to love mercy and to walk humbly with your God." We learn from this verse that justice, mercy, and humility are never wrong. We always serve the purposes of God whenever we endeavor to live out those virtues.

Though Micah made it clear that God's judgment and punishment were looming, he also offered hope to the people. Near the end of his prophecy, Micah said, "Who is a God like you, who pardons sin and forgives the transgression of the remnant of his inheritance? You do not stay angry forever but delight to show mercy. You will again have compassion on us; you will tread our sins underfoot and hurl all our iniquities into the depths of the sea" (Micah 7:18–19). Some very important truths stand out for us to see in these two verses. First, God is incomparable and without an equal. There is nothing to which we can compare God. There is no person worthy of such comparison. The ways of God and the character of God stand without equal. Any understanding or ideas we might have about God are not complete and imperfect. And what we know about God, as revealed in scripture, is only because God has chosen to make that known to us. We would not discover that by ourselves.

Second, God is the only One who can forgive. We are sinners—probably no one would debate this reality. While we may sin against others, all sin is ultimately committed against God because God is the One who determines right and wrong. Remember what David said when he was confronted by Nathan about his sins. David made his confession in this way: "Against you, you only, have I sinned and done what is evil in your sight; so, you are right in your verdict and justified when you judge" (Psalm 51:4). Recognizing that God alone can forgive underscores the importance of regular examination and confession. We want to be rigorous in dealing with sin. We want to acknowledge it and ask for God to deliver us from it. We are not to allow sin to linger in our lives. Rather, we want to feel and think the same way about sin that God does.

Third, God is merciful. He delights in showing mercy, Micah said. The Lord is willing to offer grace and mercy to those who seek it and call upon His name for it. We should be just as merciful toward others—offering forgiveness when others seek it and ask for it. When sins are confessed and owned, we can then move toward mercy and reconciliation. Remember how seriously God takes sin—He offered up His Son to die for sin because sin had to be judged and punished and could not be excused or dismissed.

And fourth, God remains compassionate at all times. We never have to doubt the depth and sincerity of God's love. It is real, and it is enduring. God's love is not conditional or contingent as we sometimes are about our love and how we express it. We can count on the presence of His love. He does not always love our behavior or the things we do, but He does love us and is at work to redeem and reconcile us. Micah is a short prophecy—only seven chapters long that could be easily read in one sitting. Spend some time with Micah and let his prophecy speak to you with the same freshness and relevance that it did for Judah and Israel many years ago.

DAY 59

Nahum is an unusual name and a short book found near the end of the Old Testament. His name means "compassionate" or "one who is full of comfort." He directed his prophecy primarily against Nineveh and declared the judgment and destruction of Nineveh at the hands of God's designed punishment. Some people suggest the key verses of Nahum are 1:7–9. We read, "The Lord is good, a refuge in times of trouble. He cares for those who trust in him, but with an overwhelming flood

He will make an end of Nineveh; He will pursue his foes into the realm of darkness. Whatever they plot against the Lord he will bring to an end; trouble will not come a second time." There are several truths that stand out in these three verses.

First, Nahum declared the goodness of God. About this, there should never be any debate. God is good, uniformly good always. There is never a time or situation where the character of God should be in question. God exists. God is. And God is good. He reveals His goodness in His blessings, grace, kindness, and mercy. God does discipline, and He does deal with sin. But these actions from God are expressions of His goodness as well. He sees and knows full well what unchecked sin and rebellion lead to whenever they are pursued. God is the standard for all goodness because He is inherently good.

Second, God remains a refuge for His people and particularly so during times of trouble and hardship. If life has dealt you a bad hand, you can look to the Lord. If life has dealt you an uncertain hand, you can look to the Lord. If life has dealt you an unfair hand, you can look to the Lord. The Lord is our refuge. We can lean into Him and lean upon Him. He does not turn away those who seek Him earnestly and sincerely.

Remember the powerful language of Psalm 46:1–2, "God is our refuge and strength, a very present help in trouble. Therefore, we will not fear, though the earth be removed, and though the mountains be carried into the midst of the sea." As our refuge, God is a permanent and everlasting place of contentment and security for His people.

Third, we can entrust our foes and enemies to the Lord. We can trust that God will deal with those who mean us harm and pain. We can pray for our enemies and treat them justly and fairly. We do not have to take matters into our own hands. Just as God is our refuge, He is also our justice. He will deal with those we entrust to Him. We do not have to live with revenge or vengeance in mind.

Fourth, God knows the end of His plans. God always acts with purpose. Sometimes He acts to discipline. At other times, He acts to deliver us. Occasionally, discipline and deliverance work together for our good in the present and the future. We are not living random lives that are at the mercy of mere chance. We are serving a God who has purposes and plans that He is writing out in and through the lives of His people. Whether the present time is good for you or bad, rewarding or challenging, there is the hope of God bringing the good work He has started in you to faithful completion. Nahum knew this and placed His hopes in the Lord. He knew that Israel would be delivered and that the enemies of Israel would be dealt with by God's perfect judgments. Take comfort today in knowing that you can lean into the Lord and He is strong enough to receive you.

DAY 60

Habakkuk is a prophet with a strange name and a short book. He was one of the minor prophets in Israel's history. He prophesied primarily to Judah but has a message for anyone who may be asking some difficult and hard questions in the face of life situations and circumstances. He opened with a complaint that many of us have likely voiced at one time: "How long, LORD?" (1:2a). At times, we are inclined to ask that question. How long must something go on? How long must something last? How long till we have an answer from the Lord? We can often find ourselves with more questions than answers. Usually, we are asking this kind of question when we are facing some trials and unsettled times that tax us emotionally or physically and take a spiritual toll on us. And occasionally, the answers we do have may not be all that satisfying or encouraging to us. But even as we ask such questions, we trust the outcomes and results of the Lord and hold on to Him.

Near the end of his second chapter, Habakkuk offered us a glimpse of the Lord that was similar to what Isaiah 6 revealed. We read, "The LORD is in His holy temple; let all the earth be silent before Him" (2:20). What an encouragement! Even amid questions and complaints, the prophet reminded us that God remains on the throne (or in His temple). We look to the Lord in awe and wonder. Sometimes the answer to our complaints and questions is simply reminding ourselves that the Lord is on the throne and that He remains in charge of this world and us. When things around us may look absurd or even unbelievable, we take comfort in knowing that God has not changed and He has not moved off the throne. He is the bedrock to which we anchor ourselves.

One of the signature passages of the Bible is found in Habakkuk. He wrote, "Though the fig tree does not bud and there are no grapes on the vines, though the olive crop fails and the fields produce no food, though there are no sheep in the pen and no cattle in the stalls, yet I will rejoice in the Lord, I will be joyful in God my Savior.

The Sovereign Lord is my strength; He makes my feet like the feet of a deer; He enables me to tread on the heights" (Habakkuk 3:17–19). In a word, Habakkuk said that when nothing is going right, we can still look to the Lord and find our contentment and security in Him. God's power is never contingent upon our prosperity or success. When it seems that all is lost, our faith can endure because we place our faith in the One who is eternal and everlasting. He neither changes nor weakens.

Habakkuk teaches us to find joy and contentment in the Lord and our walk with Him—not in circumstances or the successes or failures we may experience in life. We rise to new heights and new places through our faith in the Lord and not the things we might have achieved by human power or capabilities. Habakkuk is well worth our time to read. He gives us a vision of God who is majestic, everlasting, and all-powerful. His prophecy can help us reset our faith if we have taken our eyes off the Lord and what He is able to offer us and do for us. Even at the end of struggles and battle-filled days, we can easily say, "Yet will I rejoice in the Lord."

DAY 61

Zephaniah was another one of the Old Testament's minor prophets. Like many other prophets, he had a message of judgment that he received from the Lord God. In his three chapters, he prophesied primarily to Judah and some surrounding nations. Apparently, according to verse 1, Zephaniah was a descendant of King Hezekiah of Judah. Some who read this Old Testament prophet see chapter 1 with some end-time, final judgment imagery. We read, "'I will sweep away everything from the face of the earth,' declares the Lord" (1:2). The earth as a whole has not yet met the full or final judgment of God. That time is looming at some moment in the future. But the prophet does promise that God will set right anything that is wrong. He will not allow unrighteousness and wickedness to prevail.

If we carefully read Zephaniah 1:7, we find that he emphasized a spiritual discipline that has value for us to this day. We read, "Be silent before the Sovereign LORD, for the day of the LORD is near." Keeping still and silent before the Lord is one way to worship Him and one way that we grow in our faith. Silence, solitude, and solemnity are ways of turning down the volume of the world and turning up our awareness of God's presence with us. Entering into and maintaining silence can be difficult. But when we embrace silence before the Lord, we find just how fulfilling it is to step away from the noise and clutter of the world around us. The demands of life can easily encroach upon us to the point that we lose time with the Lord and even sight of the Lord. Silence brings us back to the first and best things—knowing and walking with the Lord God.

While Zephaniah proclaimed judgment from God upon Judah, he also held out the prospect of renewal and restoration. This judgment would not endure or last forever. God would give Judah a new day and a new life.

Zephaniah made this promise on God's behalf: "Then I will purify the lips of the peoples, that all of them may call on the name of the LORD and serve him shoulder to shoulder" (Zephaniah 3:9). Lips that once cried out to idols and offered worship to the same would be made right and righteous once again. The lips of Judah would sing of God's greatness and offer worship in His Name. The lips that once called on empty gods and equally empty promises would turn to call on the Lord and profess allegiance to His promises.

Zephaniah challenges us today to think about how and what we profess. Do we chase after and hold on to the empty promises of this world, or do we trust God? Do we offer worship to the tangible things that we own (or that own us), or do we bring our worship to the Lord who has made us and saved us? Do we give away our loyalty and allegiance without much thought to who receives it from us? Prophets often challenge us with unpopular and inconvenient truths that we cannot dismiss lightly or easily. But God can set right any heart that is divided or broken. God can redeem worship that has been offered in the wrong ways and the wrong sources. God can make us well again and heal us just as He healed Judah and restored the people. If we ever want to consider what has first place in our lives, we need only to look at our calendar and our money. Where do we spend our time and our blessings? Today, as you consider Zephaniah, read his brief prophecy for yourself. See what He might say to you about your worship and the ways you live before the Lord.

DAY 62

Have you ever had a gnawing sense that God had something important and special for you to do? The prophet Haggai certainly did. He is regarded as "the prophet of the temple." His mission was to motivate people to finish rebuilding the temple and to return to the worship that God expected of His people. A dedicated temple and holy worship were critical to Judah's restoration after the exile. Indeed, God judged Judah through exile, at least in part, because their manner of worship had become sinful and idolatrous to Him. The nation's worship had become much more human centered and human advantaged than it ever should have been. We are to take worship seriously because God surely does. He sets the standards by which we approach Him and worship Him. Haggai said as much in 1:5 and 7 when he wrote, "This is what the LORD Almighty says: 'Give careful thought to your ways.'" Remember, our ways are not His ways. Our thoughts are not His thoughts. So we are to evaluate our ways and thoughts by His. One of Haggai's themes is for God's people to give sober and careful thought to their ways—in any season or circumstance.

Haggai made it clear that the time had come for the people to rebuild the temple. They were to cease their delays and procrastinations. They were to put an end to the excuses. God was demanding a change in tone and behavior. The time was at hand to do the work He had plainly commanded them to do. Haggai wrote, "This is what the Lord Almighty says: 'These people say, "The time has not yet come to rebuild the Lord's house."'" "Then the word of the Lord came through the prophet Haggai: 'Is it a time for you yourselves to be living in your paneled houses, while this house remains a ruin?'" (Haggai 1:2–4). God was tired of the people's slowness and even laziness. He spoke through Haggai and demanded a change.

If we delay our obedience to God, then we have only further entrenched our disobedience to Him. Delayed obedience is really immediate disobedience. Deferred obedience is really unending disobedience. We might make ourselves feel better by promising to get around to something one day, a soon-to-come day or some other time. But all the while, we are persisting in doing things our way rather than being useful servants of the kingdom. Imagine standing before the Lord one day and giving an account of your life when all you can say is what you intended to do or planned to do or put off doing. My guess is you will be profoundly grieved by the Lord's reaction to your excuses and explanations. The right time for obedience is now. The season for obedience is always at hand.

Some of the most essential ways we can grow in our faith are often the very things we neglect or postpone doing. Those ways include Bible reading, prayer, tithing, worship, serving, church attendance, and sharing our faith with others. Perhaps today, you would adopt an excuse-free life and begin to do the things you know God has for you to do and to live in the ways that He has for you. Just imagine the kind of influence you would have in your home, workplace, school, and church if you made a decision to do these essential things that God has for you to do. Frankly, God may not give us big things to do until we are faithful in the small and essential ways that He has for us. When you begin to do what God has for you to do, you develop a life of "saying yes to Him" and living for Him. So as we began, do you have a sense that God has something for you to do? Your answer should be a resounding yes because He surely does. Stay on task with the basic spiritual steps and disciplines that God has placed before you. And then look for new things and new ways that God may bring to you.

DAY 63

Zechariah's name means "God remembered." And in the days of his prophecy, the people needed to know that God had remembered them. He prophesied about the same time as the prophet Haggai. His message was aimed primarily at the Remnant of Jews that had returned from the Babylonian exile to resettle in the land that God had originally given His people. He delivered a message of hope to the people who heard him. He also had some words to speak about the coming end of history where God draws everything to a close according to His purposes and for His glory. One of the earliest verses we read in this prophecy is a recipe for spiritual revival and renewal that works to this day. We read, "Therefore tell the people: This is what the LORD Almighty says: 'Return to me,' declares the Lord Almighty, 'and I will return to you,' says the Lord Almighty" (Zechariah 1:3). We see three truths in this verse that can speak to us today.

First, revival and renewal are possible. Our faith can be strengthened, and our walk with the Lord can be deepened. If we are frustrated or stagnant in our faith, we certainly do not have to stay that way. We can live again. We can experience renewal and a fresh encounter with the Lord. Second, if we return to the Lord, He will return to us. He will bring new life and new hope to those who trust Him and seek Him. The Lord takes great delight in renewing His people. He is overjoyed when His people turn to Him and walk with Him in new ways of trust and worship. And third, this promise is backed up by the assurance and character of God: "This is what the LORD Almighty says." We are not looking at a human promise or a mere statistical chance or probability. God assures us that He will do this for us. We have a 100 percent guarantee.

As a supplement to this promise in Zechariah 1:3, we can turn to Zechariah 4:6 where we read, "This is the word of the Lord to Zerubbabel: 'Not by might nor by power, but by my Spirit,' says the Lord Almighty." The renewal comes from the Lord. And God brings renewal by His Spirit and not by power or might. The renewal comes when our spirit is touched by His and when our faith walk through life reaches out to walk with Him. God does not promise renewal with the loudest sounds and brightest lights. He brings renewal when sincere hearts return to Him in sincere ways. He is often most experienced in subtle and simple ways.

A bit later in Zechariah, we read a prophecy concerning Christ. "Rejoice greatly, Daughter Zion! Shout, Daughter Jerusalem! See, your king comes to you, righteous and victorious, lowly and riding on a donkey, on a colt, the foal of a donkey" (Zechariah 9:9). This verse is often shared on Palm Sunday. We can also see in this prophecy an image of Christ coming into human hearts and lives that turn to Him. He is righteous and victorious and comes into those who humble themselves before Him and seek Him. The proud generally believe they need nothing. The conceited rarely look beyond themselves. But to those who seek the Lord in humility, they find Him ready to enter their lives with victory, righteousness, and goodness. In this same measure, Zechariah spoke of God's work among His people in 12:10. We read, "And I will pour out on the house of David and the inhabitants of Jerusalem a spirit of grace and supplication. They will look on me, the one they have pierced." We encounter God's grace in full measure through the cross and the death of His Son. Through His piercing, stripes, and blood, we are healed and made whole again. Our wickedness is replaced with His righteousness, and the debts that separated us from the Father are forever settled and paid for. Renewal and revival are possible even for those whose faith is most weary and frayed. Salvation and renewal both come from the same source—from the One who was pierced for us. May God encourage you and renew you as you begin a new week.

DAY 64

Malachi is the last of the minor prophets and the final book of the Old Testament. He was the last prophetic voice until the emergence of John the Baptist who heralded the coming of Jesus as Israel's long-awaited and long-anticipated Messiah. As the last prophet for a long time, we would reasonably expect that his message should be heard and applied. One of Malachi's keywords is "return," as in God's people returning to Him in all the ways they have departed from Him. We read this promise in Malachi 3:7, "Return to me and I will return to you," says the Lord Almighty. This recipe for revival works anytime and anywhere for anyone who wishes to walk with the Lord. Sliding away from the Lord can often be a gradual, glacial thing. The pace away from the Lord is often not fast or sudden. It can be a slow compromising slide where we begin to think more highly of our ways than we do His ways. In perhaps a distinctly Baptist way, we often call this "backsliding." The expression makes sense because we could be thinking more with our backsides than the brain God gave us. We become less vigilant and less diligent in our walk. We begin to put some distance between ourselves and spiritual disciplines that we know to work whenever they are tried—worship, Bible reading, prayer, tithing, serving, testifying, and faith sharing. Slowly, other things begin to take over and take priority.

Return. That word can come to us as both a command and an invitation. God says to return because nothing else is right when we are separate and disconnected from Him. If we have departed from Him, then nothing else really matters until that breach is repaired and we have come back to Him. But God also loves us and enjoys fellowship with us. Return is an invitation to come back to the One who loves us more than anyone else and desires to enjoy us more than anyone else. Return could be an inviting command and a commanding invitation. It is a declaration that God's hand is both open to us and extended to us. He is like the father in the parable of the prodigal son who is looking for the wayward and wandering boy long before the boy sets his sights on his loving father. Like an old advertisement for a motel chain, God has left the light on for us, anticipating and calling us to return to Him.

Malachi 3:17 says, "'On the day when I act,' says the Lord Almighty, 'they will be my treasured possession. I will spare them, just as a father has compassion and spares his son who serves him.'" God treasure us! That statement might seem overwhelming and even too incredible to believe, but He does. We have it on the authority of His Word. God lavishes His compassion on His people just as an earthly father enjoys and lavishes love on his son. Those who return to the Lord are spared and saved from the pitfalls and missteps that come from wandering away and rejecting the Lord's entreaties and invitations. As the days of summer begin to run out, perhaps you would ponder if there are ways where you can return to the Lord. Perhaps you are looking at a season of separation and disconnection where the Lord has been little more than an afterthought or an often overlooked distant relative. The good news is you can return. As the Old Testament prepared to transition into the New Testament and the new covenant that God was making in Christ, the people were called to return. God's last word before Christ was *return*. And as Malachi pointed out in his last verse, a return to the Lord pays dividends in the family as well, as parents return to their children and children return to their parents. Bring a blessing to your life and home today. Return to the Lord. Walk with and enjoy Him again.

DAY 65

Can you imagine someone growing tired of God? Can you imagine someone wondering what good comes from a relationship with the Lord? How would one grow tired or bored by the amazing ways and power of God? Malachi suggested that Israel had grown tired of God or even pushed God away. We read the prophet's mournful words: "You have said, 'It is futile to serve God. What do we gain by carrying out his requirements and going about like mourners before the Lord Almighty?'" (Malachi 3:14). Hard to fathom that Israel would have grown frustrated with God! He had built them into a nation, given them land, led them out of Egypt, and freed them from slavery. But Malachi said the people believed it was "futile to serve God." It is dangerous and reckless to push God to the margins of life. To ensure the same conclusion cannot be drawn about us, we can take several important steps or actions.

First, remember what the Lord has done for you. Remember how He has blessed you. Remember what He has given to you. Never forget about the Lord and never live a day without talking and walking with Him. We can easily find ourselves at a distance from God if we neglect opportunities to connect with Him each day. Be intentional about seeking the Lord and seeing the Lord. The more you seek the Lord, the more you will find yourself seeking Him and wanting time with Him.

Second, lose the ego. Only God is God. We are not God. Life is not about what makes us happy or what fulfills us. Life is about bringing glory to God. Life is about serving Him and elevating Him above ourselves or anything else. We are not to make life about ourselves and what we can gain from it. A lot of the things that we enjoy or make a big deal out of will perish. They are not suitable for eternity. Money, material things, and much of what we may accumulate will not travel into eternity with us. We lose the ego when we make life about serving the Lord and laying up treasures in heaven.

Third, God's ways are right and good. We never have to worry about God's ways or Word leading us astray. Culture can be a bad influence. Some people can be bad influences. Even friends can pull us away from the Lord and water down our zeal for Him. But when obeying the Lord and following Him are our top priorities, then we are on a pathway that is good. Do not be ashamed of the Lord and His ways. Leave behind anything that comes into conflict with your faith and your walk with Christ. Eagerly walk with, obey, and love the Lord!

And fourth, refresh your faith. If life seems futile and your faith seems that way, take time to freshen it up. Pray for God to revive or renew you. Ask God to reveal any sinful ways or behavior in your life. Spend some extra time in prayer and Bible reading. Psalms is a great place to start for refreshing your faith. You find a range of emotions and situations where the writer is calling out for God to make His grace and refreshing power known to His people. Do not let the enemy convince you that serving the Lord is futile or empty. He would love to persuade you to give up and sit down. He may not persuade you to walk away from God, but the enemy will be happy just to nudge you to the margins or sidelines of faith a little more each day. Satan often patiently sows seeds of discontent in hearts and homes. Be aware of His schemes and strategies. He is skilled in subtlety.

Malachi brought his prophecy to an end with a powerful word—*remember* (4:4). Remember the Lord. Remember to serve Him. Remember Him throughout your days. If we are thinking of the Lord and walking with Him, we reduce the likelihood that we will grow frustrated or think that our faith is futile. Remember where the Lord has been at work. Remember what the Lord has entrusted to you. And walk boldly with Him.

DAY 66

Consider the number of words you might speak in an average day. The number is likely well into the thousands when all conversations and occasions, big and small, are taken into account. How often do your conversations involve the Lord—either speaking to Him directly or about Him in the company of others? The prophet Malachi had a wise word for us about the many words we speak. He wrote, "You have wearied the Lord with your words. 'How have we wearied him?' you ask. By saying, 'All who do evil are good in the eyes of the Lord, and he is pleased with them' or 'Where is the God of justice?'" (Malachi 2:17). He seems to suggest our words can be disturbing or disquieting to the Lord. Perhaps we even offend God with what we say. There could be several ways this is true.

First, we could make promises we never keep and pledges that we never honor. We can make grand promises to serve God in some way yet fall short in keeping those commitments. We can promise to pray more, read the Bible from beginning to end, to tithe, and yet fail to do those very important things. We are usually disappointed when others break promises they make to us. Likewise, we can "weary" God with promises that we make yet fail to honor. We can even weary God by distorting reality with our words by calling evil good or good evil. We can redefine sin in a way more suitable or soothing to us.

Second, we can honor God with the tone and tenor of our language. James pointed this out for us to see. He wrote, "With the tongue we praise our Lord and Father, and with it we curse human beings, who have been made in God's likeness. Out of the same mouth come praise and cursing. My brothers and sisters, this should not be. Can both fresh water and salt water flow from the same spring? My brothers and sisters, can a fig tree bear olives, or a grapevine bear figs? Neither can a salt spring produce fresh water" (James 3:9–12). The same mouth that praises God can often curse others. The same mouths that praise God can often provoke others. Lies, cursing, idle talk, gossip, and malicious whispers can wreck lives, families, marriages, and even the church. Yet we often think little about the inconsistency between the words we use in worship and the words we use in daily life. God sees the inconsistency and calls us out for what we have done.

Third, the Bible teaches us to be people who can get by on a few words. Jesus said, "All you need to say is simply 'Yes' or 'No' anything beyond this comes from the evil one" (Matthew 5:37). We should be honest enough that we do not need to reinforce a simple answer with words that give us a little wiggle room or latitude if we are playing loose with the truth. A convoluted answer to a simple question may be someone's way of not speaking honestly or truthfully in response. Our Lord is teaching us to be people of integrity and character so a simple answer like yes or no can be accepted and trusted by others as right and true.

Fourth, we might bring weariness to the Lord when there is a long time of silence between our occasions for worship and prayer. We have chosen and used words in many other ways and for many other reasons, but it may have been a long time since we prayed or worshipped with our words. God may be wearied by your silence and distance because you have not drawn close to Him for quite a long time. You could change that reality today. You could confess your silence and absence and seek His forgiveness. The Bible warns against long prayers that seek attention and flattery from others. But a stark lack of prayer is no better. If you have not spoken to the Lord lately, how can you call Him your Savior? Worship God with your words, and do not leave Him weary. Welcome Him and do not leave Him waiting. Seek Him and do not snub Him.

DAY 67

As you likely know, there are four Gospels in the Bible. Matthew is the first one. He was also known as Levi and was one of the first twelve disciples called by Jesus. Like the other disciples, he had a checkered past, but the Lord called him and changed him dramatically by making him a fisher of men. When the Lord called to him, he left everything behind and followed in an instant. His particular Gospel had Jewish readers as his primary audience as he wrote to persuade them to believe that Jesus perfectly fulfilled their messianic expectations and was the kingly Messiah the nation had long anticipated. In Matthew's Gospel, we find the Sermon on the Mount where Jesus took the law to a higher level and raised the bar for holiness.

In Matthew 13, we read Jesus's parable of the sower. As a certain farmer scattered seeds, the seeds landed on different types of ground—a hard pathway, rocky terrain, thorny land, and finally good soil. The seeds took root in the good soil and flourished. Jesus explained the good soil in this way: "But the seed falling on good soil refers to someone who hears the word and understands it. This is the one who produces a crop, yielding a hundred, sixty or thirty times what was sown" (Matthew 13:23).

A few lessons stand out for us. First, we need to recognize that seed is always being sown. Some people will sow good seeds into our lives while others will sow seeds that are harmful or even destructive. I recently noticed a "seed-cleaning" operation this summer that endeavors to ensure that farmers are planting good, pure, and productive seeds that have not been mixed with undesirable or even harmful seeds that could ruin crops or pasture land. Be discerning about the influences that you allow into your life. Not every teacher brings what is good, wholesome, and true.

Not every teacher desires to draw you closer to the truth of the Gospel. Deception reigns in our world today.

Second, be ready for the truth that God brings to you as you read His Word, pray, worship, and trust Him. God often opens our eyes to things that are wrong that we once held to be right. Likewise, God often sows into our lives seeds and lessons that convict us and call us to give up things we once treasured or pursued. One of the Spirit's roles is to convict us of the important things that God would have us know. We are never to close our eyes or lives to the truth of scripture. The Spirit is sowing into us as we trust Him and lean into Him each day.

Third, prepare the soil of your life for God's truth and ways to be sown in you. We prepare this soil by making a commitment to read the Bible and pray. We must carefully prioritize worship and fellowship with other believers. Surround yourself with trusted and faithful believers who can help open your eyes to where God is at work and what He is doing. Choose a day every few months and enjoy a spiritual retreat. Get alone for half of a day to read the Bible, pray, praise God, and listen to His voice. Practice some times of silence and solitude. Being alone with the Lord is a time-honored spiritual discipline that has encouraged and blessed believers for generations.

Matthew concluded his Gospel with a promise that we can cling to every moment of every day—whether we are in sorrow or celebration. Jesus said, "And surely I am with you always, to the very end of the age" (Matthew 28:20b). Christ is with us! Christ is for us! Christ walks alongside us! What a promise, and what a way to end the first Gospel!

DAY 68

Mark is likely the earliest of the four Gospels. This Gospel was also a source for both Matthew and Luke. Together, the first three Gospels are often called the synoptic Gospels because of the similarities they share with each other. Mark's Gospel is the shortest of the four. In his Gospel, Mark wrote with a sense of urgency or immediacy. Indeed, a keyword to describe this book might be *immediately*. For example, Jesus was pursued by a large crowd in Mark 6:31–34 when he sought rest and time to reflect. Earlier, in Mark 3:20, such a large gathering of people crowded into the house where Jesus and His disciples were that there was no time to eat a meal. Urgency and immediacy. Indeed, as followers of Christ, there are things that demand our time, attention, and focus. We are to tend to these priorities with urgency and immediacy. Knowing the Lord and walking with the Lord are the greatest missions we have in life.

Mark's Gospel immediately jumped into telling the story of Jesus's life, deeds, and ministry. Barely a quarter of the way into chapter 1, Jesus announced the good news of the Gospel. We read, "'The time has come,' he said. 'The kingdom of God has come near. Repent and believe the good news!'" (Mark 1:15). Two verses later, Jesus called His first disciples, "'Come, follow me,' Jesus said, 'and I will send you out to fish for people.' At once they left their nets and followed him" (Mark 1:17–18). This theme of urgency and immediacy is reflected in the verses we just read. First, Jesus announced that God's timing had arrived. The Gospel was ready to be revealed in fullness and completion. Jesus's time had come—the hopes and expectations of the prophets were at last fulfilled in Jesus's appearance. And second, Jesus made it clear that the Kingdom of God had taken a bold step forward. It had entered into the world and the realm of human existence.

The Kingdom had come not to rival or topple Rome but to live within the hearts and lives of all who welcomed and received the Lord Jesus. There was no stopping the kingdom when it came to Christ. Crucifixion did not stop it. Rome failed as well. Satan came up short. And history has not halted the kingdom's march and progress. We are still seeing the kingdom break into places that are dark, lost, and hurting even today.

Third, we see that repentance cannot wait. We are to deal with sin swiftly and sincerely. We are not to allow it to accumulate in our lives. When we repent, we leave sin behind and replace it with the good news that Jesus came to offer us. And this good news translates into a good and new life. Never sign a peace treaty with sin. Resist it. Repent of it. Refrain from it.

Fourth, this new life leads to a new mission—becoming a fisher of men and women. We seek to draw others to Christ like a fisherman enjoys reeling in the daily catch. We live to bring glory to Him and to make His Gospel known far and wide. Jesus commanded His first disciples to "come" and to "follow" Him. The same command stands today—we are beckoned to come to Christ and Christ alone, leaving behind all other things. And we are beckoned to follow Him—no turning back and even if no one chooses to go with us. We follow Him—unwaveringly and unreservedly. Now that is urgency and immediacy!

DAY 69

In Mark 5, Jesus was busy. He healed a man possessed by demons. He raised a dead girl to life. He healed a sick woman. Near the end of this remarkable chapter, Jesus said to a man named Jairus, the father of the dead girl, "Don't be afraid; just believe" (Mark 5:36). No better words could have been spoken to that grieving heavyhearted father. Those five simple words form the foundation for a life-changing faith. On many occasions, we have a choice between fear and faith. We can pull back or step forward. We can run away or walk ahead. Fear can rob us of faith, but faith can conquer fear. Jesus's message to that broken and bewildered father can challenge us in several ways.

First, faith is always in a person. Faith is grounded in Jesus Christ. We do not place ultimate faith in other people, objects, or an ever-changing world. To do so is a recipe for disappointment and discouragement. We place our faith in Jesus who is the same yesterday, today, and tomorrow (Hebrews 13:8). He is everlasting and worthy of our faith and trust. People will disillusion us. Circumstances can change. Possessions can be lost. But Jesus remains. No one ever regrets coming to faith in Jesus. He is the way, the truth, and the life (John 14:6).

Second, we always face our fears with faith. We might even say that we "faith our fears." Such a statement is not necessarily good grammar or sound syntax, but it makes great sense and great theology. You may recall the time in Mark 4 when the disciples were terrified by a sudden storm that popped up while they were with Jesus in a boat. The disciples had already resigned themselves to a certain stormy death. They went so far as to ask Jesus, "Teacher, don't you care if we drown?" (Mark 4:38b). After Jesus woke up and calmed the storm, He said to His disciples, "Why are you so afraid? Do you still have no faith?" (Mark 4:40). The disciples were more worried about that storm they saw with their eyes than they were comforted by the One who was sleeping in the boat with them. But we have been there too. When we live by sight, we can find ourselves frightened and even overwhelmed on occasion. But when we live by faith, the things that confront us do not seem to be nearly as scary as we have made them out to be.

Third, faith is believing that God always has the last word. Defeat does not define us. Situations do not have to take us hostage. We can trust the momentary troubles we experience and encounter with the Lord. Ultimately, we know that one day God will make right all that is wrong. Until that day comes, we trust God to provide for us here and now. He is our shield and defender. He is our provider and protector. He is gentle, good, and gracious.

Fourth, faith is believing that God can handle anything we give to Him. His arms are not too frail or weak to take what we entrust to Him. We can go boldly and confidently before His throne of grace knowing that we will be received, welcomed, heard, and loved. Daily prayer time is that golden moment when we can release to the Father all that has troubled us and trapped us. The enemy would love to convince us that we are simply stuck with certain things and that God has forgotten us. In those moments, we remind ourselves of Jesus's words of triumph: "Don't be afraid; just believe" (Mark 5:36b).

DAY 70

The Gospels are full of miracles Jesus performed. And each is astounding to consider. Frankly, is there such a thing as a "minor" miracle? A miracle is a miracle. It is the inbreaking of God's power into a situation that seems lost, hopeless, unfixable, or even dead. In Mark 6, Jesus walked on water. Just before this astounding feat, He had been praying alone on a mountainside, having dismissed His disciples by sending them to a boat and telling them to go on ahead of Him to Bethsaida. Mark 6:49–50 tells us that the disciples had two distinct reactions to the sight of Jesus walking on water. First, they mistook Him for a ghost. And second, they were terrified by what they saw. Their reactions are understandable even today. We are not confronted by such a sight in our day-to-day lives. Walking on water seems extraordinary and unthinkable—unless, of course, it is Jesus doing the walking.

Jesus spoke to His anxious disciples and said, "Take courage! It is I. Don't be afraid" (Mark 6:50b). Jesus's words were the first-century equivalent of "Chill out. I'm good and you are good too." There are a few lessons that stand out in words to His disciples. First, the Lord said, "It is I." By saying these words, Jesus invoked the divine name "I AM." In the Greek language, the wording is "ego eimi" or "I AM." Jesus used this same expression in seven bold declarations in John's Gospel. By using this expression, Jesus signaled that the One walking on the water was the same One who spoke to Moses at the burning bush. Jesus comforted His disciples by saying, "The One you see is the great I AM and I AM is the One you see." Hopefully, this explanation is not confusing to you. Just know that Jesus was saying more than "it is me." He is using the Holy Name of God often translated as LORD in the Old Testament.

Second, Jesus reminded the disciples that He was with them. Indeed, He was walking directly toward them. He had not sent them on a fool's errand. He had not forgotten them. And when Christ is with us, there is no reason to fear. Indeed, our fears can take leave. There is no greater comfort than knowing the Lord is with us and watching over us. We claim this promise even in the valley of the shadow of death as Psalm 23 reminds us.

Third, Jesus called His disciples to look at Him and not the water or the boat. We often lose sight of the Lord today. We can lose sight of Him in the miseries of the moment or the challenges before us. Except for Joshua and Caleb, the Old Testament spies that Moses sent to scout out the promised land saw the giant size and stature of the people they would have to fight. They were ready to quit before the first battle. They lost sight of God when they looked at how big their enemies were. By contrast, David never saw Goliath's size. This shepherd boy with his slingshot saw the greatness and glory of the Lord. The lesson for us is simple and even obvious. See the Lord more than you see trials and battles or even those who would threaten you.

And fourth, Jesus "climbed into the boat with them" (Mark 6:51a). He joined them. He has joined us too. Jesus is our Immanuel or "God with us." We are not alone and never will be. He has come to be with us. And He remains with us through the presence and power of the Holy Spirit who lives within us. He is our consoler, counselor, comforter, and companion. You never make a journey, reach a decision, or face the dawn of a new day without the assurance that the Lord has climbed into your life with you. He is there—as much as ever. And He can calm the wind and the waves and set you on a course for safe harbor.

DAY 71

We occasionally find ourselves in embarrassing circumstances. Often, those situations can be funny. And it is probably good to laugh at ourselves at times and to laugh along with others about something we have done. There was an embarrassing situation that took place just before Jesus's crucifixion. Mark explains the situation in this way: "A young man, wearing nothing but a linen garment, was following Jesus. When they seized him, he fled naked, leaving his garment behind" (Mark 14:51–52). Who was that man? Imagine being stripped of your clothes and left with nothing to do but run away! Most Bible students believe this unnamed young man was actually Mark himself. This story is not included in Matthew or Luke. But Mark makes mention of it. Some people suggest that Mark was making a cameo appearance in the story of Jesus's arrest, trial, and crucifixion. But there are some lessons we can take from this story.

First, the Bible says that this man was "following Jesus." He was doing exactly what Jesus called others to do—"follow Me." To follow Jesus would suggest some sort of connection or association with our Lord. He was not a casual fan. He likely was not a curiosity seeker or some fringe character just trying to get a look at what was happening—not a rubbernecker at a traffic accident. Following Jesus remains the Lord's call today to all who would come to know and love Him in a saving relationship. When you follow someone or something, you devote your time and attention to that person or thing.

Second, this young man "fled" from Jesus. The disciples had fled too. Almost everyone had abandoned Jesus at that point. You may recall that Jesus even issued a warning or prophecy that those most loyal to Him would flee and fall away as the cross drew near (Mark 14:27). Peter and the disciples strongly denied that they would ever desert Jesus or abandon Him (Mark 14:31). But they did—and without putting up too much resistance at all. And honestly, we have deserted or abandoned the Lord too. We have walked away. We have chosen our ways above His ways. We have loved ourselves more than Him. We may not have lost our clothes in those times when we fled from the Lord, but we may have lost our character, our fellowship with Him, or our devotion to Him. To flee from the Lord would suggest that something else has captured our attention more than Him.

Third, this young man had a second chance. If this unnamed man was in fact Mark, then he went on to write the Gospel that bears his name. He would also participate in a mission trip with Barnabas and Paul. During that mission trip, Mark would flee again—abandoning Paul and the work of the Gospel. But once more, he would experience restoration and renewal (1 Timothy 4:11). There are occasions in life when we have to walk back to the Lord because we have turned away. We choose a different route or course than the One that He has chosen for us. You may be in a situation today where you are ready to walk back to the Lord—to experience His grace and renewal once again. Mark shows us that even the most embarrassing of circumstances cannot keep us from the healing and cleansing power of God's grace. We can walk back to Him. We can be reclothed and remade by His power.

And there is a fourth lesson—embarrassing and regrettable moments do not have to hold us captive. They do not have to define us. We can leave them behind and move beyond them. We can learn from them. Most of us would not want to be defined by or reduced to our worst moments in life. Experience can be a good teacher, and if an experience brings us closer to the Lord, then it just may have been a divine appointment all along with God's fingerprints on it. It just may be that Mark is using this story to say, "If I can bounce back from this unbelievable situation, then there is hope for you too."

DAY 72

We know Luke in two ways—as a physician and as a scripture writer. He was inspired by the Holy Spirit to write the Gospel known by his name and the book of Acts. Indeed, some people consider Luke and Acts to be a two-part work that complements each other almost like a two-volume book or a hit movie followed up by a sequel. Luke's Gospel contains the beautiful birth story of Jesus that we often ponder in amazement at Christmastime. Luke tells us the very purpose of his writing: "With this in mind, since I myself have carefully investigated everything from the beginning, I too decided to write an orderly account for you, most excellent Theophilus, so that you may know the certainty of the things you have been taught" (Luke 1:3–4).

Luke made it clear that he had looked carefully into the birth story of Jesus—much like a physician would examine a patient or look seriously into the reason for a patient's sickness. He then prepared an "orderly account" of the events of Jesus's birth, death, resurrection, teaching, miracles, and ministry much like a physician would have detailed records and information about a patient's medical history and prognosis. He then wrote to assure Theophilus of the certainty of what he had learned about Jesus as the Son of God and Savior of the world. Much like a physician today might seek to persuade you to see the benefits and value of certain medicines or healthy practices, Luke wrote to persuade his readers to know and trust Christ and Christ alone with their lives and faith.

In Luke 5:31–32, we read, "Jesus answered them, 'It is not the healthy who need a doctor, but the sick. I have not come to call the righteous, but sinners to repentance.'" Using the language of a physician, Jesus made it clear that He came for those who need forgiveness, healing, and a second chance. Jesus came to offer us forgiveness and a new life with Him. In Luke 8, Jesus calmed a storm and demonstrated His mastery of nature. This calming of a physical storm assured the first disciples (and us too) that Christ is able to calm the storms of life—whether they rage in nature or in the minds and hearts of humans who are desperate for recovery and relief. We can entrust our life battles and storms that rage in us to the One who can calm them down and set us on a new course in life.

Shortly later, in Luke 8, the Lord healed a demon-possessed man who had been oppressed "for a long time" (Luke 8:27). With this healing, our Lord demonstrated His power over the spirit realm and the battles that Satan launches against us. With the help of Christ, we put on the full armor of God to take our stand against the evil one and his ways of domination and oppression. Luke, ever the physician, points His readers to Jesus as the one and only cure to evil and spiritual oppression from the enemy. In Luke 9, Jesus fed a multitude of people that numbered at least five thousand men and likely many more women and children. Here, Luke portrayed Jesus as the One who cannot only provide physical food and literal bread but also as the One who feeds the heart and spirit of humankind as well. Jesus Himself is the bread of life and the only One who can sustain us for a lifetime and for eternity. Just as your doctor would encourage you to develop good eating habits, Luke points us to Christ alone to feed us and nourish us through our relationship with Him.

We can make our way through Luke's Gospel and find multiple examples of him presenting his case as a physician might do—examining evidence and possibilities before reaching a diagnosis or even prognosis. When you read Luke's Gospel, find yourself in the verses, stories, and encounters that He presents. In Luke 24, we read the story of Jesus walking and talking with two followers on the road to Emmaus as the Lord explained the scriptures to them and further explained everything that had happened through His death and resurrection. Luke plays a similar role to us today. He walks us through the Gospel message and meticulously, like a physician, shows us what Christ has done and why that should matter to us. Enjoy Luke's Gospel and walk slowly with him as he shows you the greatness and glory of our Lord.

DAY 73

As we know, fishermen were among Jesus's first disciples. Matthew 4, Mark 1, and Luke 5 all detail Jesus's call to these men. Each of the Gospels presents some detail and perspective on that call. In Luke's Gospel, we read this account: "When Jesus had finished speaking, he said to Simon, 'Put out into deep water, and let down the nets for a catch'" (Luke 5:4). When these men followed Jesus's instructions, the results were amazing. They caught so many fish that their nets began to break, and the boats were so full of fish that they began to sink (Luke 5:6-7). Lesson: taking Jesus at His word and trusting Him can produce profoundly amazing results—more than you can imagine!

Perhaps you have a sense that the Lord is calling you to "deeper waters." Maybe there is something that God is nudging you to do. Maybe there is an unfulfilled calling in your life that you know without a doubt has come from the Lord. You may have played life safe for a long, long time—preferring not to take a risk or even to act in faith. God often calls us to life's deeper waters. And in such places, we learn invaluable lessons about faith, trust, surrender, and what it means to be a disciple.

In order to learn to swim, you must at some point move to the deeper end of the pool. The safety of water where your feet touch the bottom and you can stand upright is not really swimming. That's just standing in a pool of water. We often limit our faith in God to what we can reasonably manage or accomplish. We do not expect much else. We often ask God to bless what we are already comfortably and feasibly doing rather than trusting Him to shape us and make us beyond what we may be. At first, Moses did not want to trust God in the deep waters of confronting

Pharaoh and leading Israel out of Egypt. He had all kinds of objections and excuses. But Moses finally took God at His word.

There was a rich young man (some Bibles say he was a ruler too) who came to Jesus asking some serious questions. But he did not like Jesus's answers. Our Lord called him to move into deeper waters and to take steps of unparalleled faith and trust. I suppose this young man preferred a simple answer or for Jesus just to affirm what he had already been doing. But Jesus pushed him to be and to do something far more. And this man walked away—choosing the shallow and comfortable waters where he had long been dwelling to the deeper waters and deeper life that Jesus offered him.

Faith cannot be described as getting our feet wet but as keeping our heads dry. Getting our feet wet is but a step to something better. We often must let go of the familiar and manageable to experience what the Lord may have for us. The Lord very well could call us to get wet from head to toe as we serve and follow Him. Remember, Jesus could have called legions of angels to fight to save Him from the cross. But Jesus took the cross instead. And He took the cross so we would not have to take it. Faith is often measured by the crosses we carry, the deep waters in which we swim, and our willingness to choose His ways over our ways. Stepping into the deep waters may open our eyes to see the Lord more clearly than ever before. And if the Lord leads us to deeper waters, we can trust He is with us and He knows the way before us. Remember, God never abandoned Israel in the Exodus. Though the people were often defiant and disobedient, God led them by a pillar of fire and cloud, through the Red Sea, and across the dangerous terrain of the wilderness. God continues to lead His people as they obediently follow Him into the deeper waters.

DAY 74

John's Gospel presents a portrait of Jesus that is different from the first three Gospel accounts. John opened with a recognition of the eternal nature of Jesus and the embodiment of God in the flesh. We read, "In the beginning was the Word, and the Word was with God, and the Word was God. He was with God in the beginning. Through him all things were made; without him nothing was made that has been made" (John 1:1–3). Jesus is God, and God came in the flesh and body of the One we call Jesus. He was and is the Word of God. John wrote, "The Word became flesh and made his dwelling among us. We have seen his glory, the glory of the one and only Son, who came from the Father, full of grace and truth" (John 1:14). In this one verse, John the apostle conveyed three powerful truths for us to consider.

First, John wrote about the incarnation of Jesus: "The Word became flesh." God took human form in the person of Jesus, His Son. The Son entered into the human and earthly realm to complete the salvation work of the Father. Second, the Son of God came to dwell among us. The language is literally "pitched His tent among us." Christ came to identify with humanity and was like us in every way with the exception being His innocent and sinless nature and life. He lived the life that God expects us to live. The Creator entered into the creation and walked among us. Third, Jesus was (and is) the embodiment of truth and grace. His life, death, and resurrection convey to us all that we need to know about the ways of God. He perfectly embodied the grace that we so desperately need. The coming of Christ opened the way for fallen people like us to know and access the Father.

When you read John's Gospel, you come across seven profound I AM statements made by Jesus. These I Am statements include "I AM the bread of life," "I AM the light of the world," "I AM the door of the sheep," "I AM the resurrection and the life," "I AM the good shepherd," "I AM the true vine," and "I AM the way, the truth, and the life." These statements where Jesus invoked the expression "I AM" remind us of the divine name of God disclosed at the burning bush to Moses. By clearly making these seven statements, Jesus made the bold declaration that He is God—He shares the divine name and nature of His Father. Other religions may have a founder, but Christ is God. In John 3, we read about Jesus's encounter with Nicodemus where our Lord teaches us about the importance of a new birth and a new life. Indeed, we find one of the Bible's most beloved verses. "For God so loved the world that he gave his one and only Son, that whoever believes in him shall not perish but have eternal life" (John 3:16).

Reading John's Gospel account is both a joy and an education. It is a joy to know that the Lord is available to us and loves us unfailingly each day. His great love led Him to a cross that held your name and mine, but He willingly took that place. This Gospel is education because we learn that Jesus was, is, and always will be God. He is the Almighty One and the Ancient of Days. The apostle John ended His Gospel with an amazing look back at his friend, teacher, and Lord. He wrote, "Jesus did many other things as well. If every one of them were written down, I suppose that even the whole world would not have room for the books that would be written" (John 21:25). If you wrote a gospel about Jesus, what would you choose to emphasize? What truths, miracles, or teachings would resonate most with you? While Matthew, Mark, and Luke all began their accounts of Jesus with genealogy, birth stories, forerunners, and earthly events, John started his account of Jesus with eternity, wanting us to know that His Lord is the LORD. May God bless your reading of John.

DAY 75

It was an innocent dinner party that we read about in John 12:1–11. And quite a party it was. It is not every day that you get to eat with someone who has been raised from the dead. And it is not every day that you have a chance to eat with someone who raises people from the dead. But there was Lazarus—happy, healthy, and home. And there was Jesus—Lord, Master, Savior. It is also not every day you get a chance to have dinner with Jesus. But there was Jesus—just a few days before most of Jerusalem would turn against Him and call for His cruel crucifixion. Lazarus and Jesus were likely talking when we pick up the story. Just imagine a man raised from the dead talking to another man who would soon die and rise from the grave as well. Lots to discuss!

John tells us Martha was serving and Mary was anointing Jesus's feet with a pint of nard and a bottle of perfume. John says the house was filled with the fragrance of perfume. It was one of those all-too-few moments that Jesus had where He could simply enjoy the company of friends and those who loved Him and held on to His every word. It was the kind of moment that Jesus is worthy to enjoy all the time—for eternity even. Jesus is worthy. And worthy is Jesus. He is worthy of the best we can bring to anoint and honor Him.

On another side of the story, we hear from Judas who complained that this anointing was a total waste of good money, good perfume, and good time. He concocted a cover story about selling the perfume to help the poor, but he really had visions of helping himself to the money since his reputation was that of a thief. Judas cared little about saving a few shekels here or there. He slowly watched his expectations and wishes fade from view as Jesus lived according to the plans of the Father and did not meet the whims and wishes of His soon-to-be betrayer. This protest from Judas was a portent of things to come on Thursday night stretching into Friday.

We really have two competing visions of Jesus. Will we enjoy Him and His company, or will we scrutinize His every move? Will we cherish the chance simply to call Him Savior or look for ways we do not think He will ever measure up? We really have four choices to make when it comes to Jesus. We can serve Him as Martha did. We can make our lives about making Him known and serving Him on every occasion. We can commune with Him as Lazarus did. It makes sense to want to be with the One who has saved us from every awful thing we have ever done. We can worship Him, as Mary did with her anointing. We can lavish our love, devotion, dedication, and trust upon Him. We can offer everything we have to Him—call Him Lord of all and Lord of us. The fourth choice is to turn from Him, as Judas did. We can turn away, walk away, even betray Him. We can come up with reasons for why we should hold on to this or that or deny the Lord this part of our lives or that part of our lives. We can give Him a little and keep the rest.

Today, across the world, many theologians speak of and speak about common grace, electing grace, irresistible grace, persevering grace, prevenient grace, pursuing grace, and saving grace; but to the sinner, it has always been amazing grace! And there was grace at work in Bethany: Grace for Lazarus that brought Him back from the dead. Grace for Mary that welcomed her joy and love. Grace for Martha by choosing her home for dinner when there were so few nights left and so much left to say and do. And if you are acting like Judas today, there is grace for you too. It is not too late to take hold of the hands that were nailed for you.

And there is grace for us too. A grace that forgives, welcomes, and receives us. A grace that invites us to come by the Lord's side for a while and simply be still. It is always about grace. And grace will lead us home.

DAY 76

When we read John 13:21–32, two words stand out for us in this Gospel reading—*betrayal* and *denial*. They are siblings. They are two roads that take you to the same place. Jesus was on the receiving end of betrayal and denial—by two men He had personally called, known, and loved for three years. Today is the midpoint of Holy Week. It is the time when we think about our personal acts of betraying or denying Jesus. Most of us have accumulated a lifetime of such deeds and debts.

We often betray Jesus by choosing our ways above His. We betray Jesus when we live bitter, angry, petty, and even selfish lives. We betray Jesus when we put a price or even limits on how much we will do, give, or serve. We often deny Jesus when it is convenient or when faith becomes inconvenient. We deny Jesus when we refuse to let Him be the Lord over certain things or even certain sins we would prefer to keep.

Peter and Judas were ordinary men. They were a complicated combination of good/bad, strengths/weaknesses, highs/lows. We tend to be aghast when Peter denied Jesus, wondering how this lovable fisherman could have ever stooped so low. We tend to be less surprised when we read about Judas's conspiracy to betray Jesus and hand him over to an overeager lynch mob. We think there was a mean streak, an ugly character flaw in Judas that anybody should be able to see a mile away. But the reality is both men are flawed—deeply so. And so are we. We dare not cast too many stones against these men for we may find the stones ricocheting back on us.

At any moment in time, we could sink so low as to betray or deny Jesus. We have sold him out for much less than thirty pieces of silver. We have rejected him when it was easier than standing for Him. So today, we can and frankly should feel badly—guilty, remorseful, and even regretful over the volume and depth of our sins and depravity. It is only when we recognize, own, and name our sins that we can confess them and receive forgiveness from the One we have too often betrayed and too easily denied. This Wednesday is the time when we take our place with Paul and declare we are the chief of all sinners. It is where we stand with David and say, "Create in me a clean heart O, God" (Psalm 51:10).

We begin to gain a glimpse of the cross that will dominate the landscape and sight lines in just two days. The cross of Christ reveals our sin at its worst and God's love at its best. The cross is where Jesus was crushed and crucified for every betrayal and denial we have ever uttered or committed.

Researchers at the University of Virginia conducted a fascinating study to answer the question of whether having a friend nearby makes the pain more bearable. They wanted to see how the brain reacted to the prospect of pain and whether it behaved differently if a person faced the threat of pain alone, holding a stranger's hand, or holding the hand of a close friend.

Researchers ran the test on dozens of people and found consistent results. When a person was alone or holding a stranger's hand while anticipating pain, the regions of the brain that process danger lit up. But when holding the hand of a trusted friend, the brain relaxed. The comfort of a friend's presence made the pain seem more bearable.

Too often we have pushed aside and pushed away the hands of Christ—the only One who can save us. We have tried to go it alone. We have turned to idols. We lived isolated and selfish lives. We have filled our hands with other things—lesser things. Today, we come face-to-face with the reality that at differing times we have all been Judas and Peter. We have all pushed away, in hate and anger, the One who died for us. We have turned from the only One who can save us.

DAY 77

Acts is a fascinating book in the New Testament. We have a front-row seat to the early growth and expansion of the Church that Luke recorded for us. Acts often carries the additional title "Acts of the Apostles." A more accurate title might be "Acts of the Holy Spirit through the Apostles." For the Spirit was working to call people to Christ beyond the early and narrow cultural and geographical origins of the Gospel's first launch. Early in Acts 2, the promised Holy Spirit came on the day of Pentecost. In fulfillment of prophecy and the promises of Jesus, the Holy Spirit was poured out upon believers. Luke recorded the Holy Spirit's coming in this way: "Suddenly a sound like the blowing of a violent wind came from heaven and filled the whole house where they were sitting. They saw what seemed to be tongues of fire that separated and came to rest on each of them. All of them were filled with the Holy Spirit and began to speak in other tongues as the Spirit enabled them" (Acts 2:2–4). A few lessons stand out for us about the Holy Spirit.

First, the Spirit is real and alive. The Holy Spirit is not the stuff of science fiction or fantasy. He is not a mysterious force or phantom that inhabits places. The Spirit is God. The Spirit is the third member of the Holy Trinity. We are not to reduce the Spirit to a ghostlike creature that lingers in the shadows or dark places of life. Second, the Spirit is personal and inhabits the people of Christ. We are filled with the Spirit at the moment of conversion when Christ forgives our sins and applies His cross and blood to remove our guilt. The Spirit takes up residence in our lives. The Spirit remains with us forever. There is never a second of time when the Spirit has abandoned the people of Christ or vanished from them. He remains with us through the totality of life. Third, the Spirit empowers and enables us. With the help of the Spirit, we are able to do and say things we could never possibly undertake with human power alone. The Spirit inspired the preaching of the early Church but also the preaching of Spurgeon, Tozer, Billy Graham, and the finest preachers in the world today. The Spirit produces fruit in and through us that we could not produce by ourselves. The accomplishments of the early Church that we read about in Acts are really accomplishments and victories that the Spirit won through willing apostles, disciples, and servants who looked to Him above all else.

The Spirit will always bear witness to Christ and draw us to the Son of God. There is no competition within the Trinity. The Son glorified the Father. The Spirit draws the lost to the Son. We walk with the Lord and lean upon Him with the help of the Holy Spirit. The world does not understand the Spirit and cannot receive the Spirit. In Acts 2:13, scoffers believed that the believers who had been filled with the Holy Spirit were actually drunk from too much earthly wine. The world often dismisses and discredits what it cannot comprehend. Just as the numbers and ranks of believers swelled during the time of Pentecost, so is the Holy Spirit still at work today bearing witness to the work of Christ and drawing believers to Him for grace and forgiveness.

Give thanks today, as a believer, that the Spirit is God in *you*. The Spirit has taken up residence in your life to comfort, counsel, console, and even intercede for you when your weary mind and heart cannot form the right words even to pray. The Spirit is faithful to fulfill His work in every believer. The power witnessed at Pentecost is still present today. The Spirit that indwelled Peter and Paul indwells believers like us today.

DAY 78

Romans has been called the Magna Carta of the Christian faith and the constitution of our faith. Practically all of the great doctrines of our faith are explored and addressed by Paul in this seminal letter. Indeed, in Romans 1:1, Paul identified himself in three distinct ways that we would want to say about ourselves. He wrote, "Paul, a servant of Christ Jesus, called to be an apostle and set apart for the gospel of God." Paul called himself a servant of Christ Jesus, an apostle, and one who has been set as part for the Gospel. To be a servant is generally not a title that most of us would pursue for ourselves. Yet to be a servant of Jesus Christ is high praise and a lifelong honor. May we never despair of the joy we possess in both knowing and serving the Lord Jesus.

The word *apostle* means "sent one" or "one who is sent." Paul was a sent man. He had been saved by Christ and sent by Christ to make the Gospel message known. And he lived out this life as an apostle. His missionary journeys, church planting, New Testament–letter writing, and preaching all bore witness to the faithful way that he embraced the title of "apostle." We may not engage in the same kind of work that Paul did, but we are sent as well. We are sent to bear witness to the Gospel and to declare what the Lord has done for us. Family, neighbors, and friends are waiting to hear from you!

Paul was happy to say that he was "set apart for the gospel of God." To be set apart is the essence of holiness. This old apostle was set apart and made holy through his trusting and saving faith in Christ Jesus. The Gospel calls us away from fruitless, trivial, and frankly, sinful pursuits in life. We are set apart for better pursuits and better ways of life. The Gospel is a clear and uncompromising call to leave behind the old for the new, what is wrong for what is right, and what separates us from the Lord for what draws us faithfully to Him. When Paul was saved on the Road to Damascus, he left behind the old life totally and fully. He unhesitatingly reached out for Christ and held on to Him alone.

Perhaps the Lord calls you today to be set apart—to let go of old things and sinful things and the things that keep you from holding on to the Lord as well or as tightly as you could. We cannot be set apart for the Lord unless we are set apart from sin, evil, and wickedness. We cannot live for Him if we are living for the flesh and to satisfy ourselves. Much of what follows in Romans hearkens back to these early identifiers that Paul used to describe himself as he attempted to serve the Lord and live out his faith in Christ Jesus. In Romans 1:11–12, Paul wrote, "I long to see you so that I may impart to you some spiritual gift to make you strong—that is, that you and I may be mutually encouraged by each other's faith." As we live, our mission is to bless one another mutually in the faith and our daily discipleship. We are to live so that we might be an example and encouragement to others. And we are to draw into our lives those other believers who might be examples and encouragement to us. Living as a servant, as one who is sent to declare the Gospel and set apart for the Lord alone will leave a lasting impact and influence.

DAY 79

Near the end of Romans 2, Paul addressed the matter of circumcision. While not a pressing or even often-mentioned matter in twenty-first-century Christianity or churches, this matter of circumcision was one that Paul and the early first-century church often had to address. Some teachers in the days of Paul and Peter emphasized the importance of circumcision and even its necessity for salvation and being able to relate rightly to the Lord. And some would insist that circumcision imparted degrees of grace and righteousness to its recipients. Paul battled this almost constantly as he emphasized the superiority of Christ and His cross to the physical acts and results of circumcision. He wrote, "A person is not a Jew who is one only outwardly, nor is circumcision merely outward and physical. No, a person is a Jew who is one inwardly; and circumcision is circumcision of the heart, by the Spirit, not by the written code. Such a person's praise is not from other people, but from God" (Romans 2:28–29).

The only circumcision that makes a difference is the circumcision of the heart. And Christ alone is able to perform this one. The surgery that Christ performs removes the sin of the heart and its callousness, harshness, and guilt. There is often this belief that humans can do something to affect their sinful state and plight. Surely, there is some human solution or recourse to sin. But Paul teaches us that only Christ can deal with the sins of humanity that cling like barnacles to the heart, mind, and life of all who dwell in and inhabit sin. The most significant circumcision is performed not by human hands or tangible instruments. Rather, this circumcision is performed by the Lord through His grace and cross. We cannot remove our sinfulness or the stains of such sins because we are deeply flawed and broken. As fallen sinners, we are seduced by sin and not separated from it.

As Paul wrote, "There is no one righteous, not even one, there is no one who understands, no one who seeks God" (Romans 3:10–11).

The righteousness that we find and gain in Christ alone is not obtained by human ways or deeds. It comes through faith alone, not by human works, but by faith in the final and finished work of Christ. We read, "But now apart from the law the righteousness of God has been made known, to which the Law and the Prophets testify. This righteousness is given through faith in Jesus Christ to all who believe. There is no difference between Jew and Gentile" (Romans 3:21–22). Both Jew and Gentile can enjoy this righteousness that comes by faith—a righteousness that circumcision could never supply or produce.

As we think about these things, we must ask whether we place faith in the finished work of Christ or our own abilities. Do we magnify our goodness at the expense of the perfect righteousness of Christ received by grace through faith? Do we even believe that we can make an argument for our goodness and righteousness? While we might not put much (if any) faith in circumcision today, we can easily make the mistake of trusting our works to gain us credit before God. Volunteering, charitable giving, activism, serving, and self-improvement ventures have all become human ways of making ourselves good, right, and even acceptable. But apart from Christ and the completed work of the cross, such things are merely more barnacles on the human heart that demand the Lord's attention and forgiving grace. Give thanks today for the gifts of salvation and righteousness experienced as expressions of God's grace and received through our faith in Him. Our forgiveness and salvation depend not on our feeble and often failing attempts at being right or good. We can, thankfully, lean upon and lean into the righteousness and merits of Christ. "It does not, therefore, depend on man's desire or effort, but on God's mercy" (Romans 9:16).

DAY 80

As he opened Romans 5, Paul paid tribute to some of the many blessings that believers enjoy through justification. He wrote, "Therefore, since we have been justified through faith, we have peace with God through our Lord Jesus Christ, through whom we have gained access by faith into this grace in which we now stand. And we boast in the hope of the glory of God" (Romans 5:1–2). A few important truths stand out for us to consider and, more importantly, remember.

First, Paul wrote about an accomplished event. "We have been justified." This justification occurred at the moment of our conversion when the work of Christ at the cross was applied to us. Justification is a one-time event or action where God looks at us and pronounces us "not guilty" of our sins and wickedness. This not-guilty verdict is rendered because of Christ's willingness to take sin's penalty for us. Recall for a moment the truth of Romans 5:8, which says, "But God demonstrates His own love for us in this: while we were yet sinners, Christ died for us." The innocent died for the guilty. The only One who was not guilty took our guilt while willingly giving us His innocence. We can take joy today in being declared "not guilty" if we have placed full trust and faith in the debt payment made on our behalf at the cross.

Second, Paul wrote we are justified, or declared not guilty, on the basis of faith. We do not work for this reality. We do not buy it or inherit it. We receive it through faith. We place our faith in the sufficiency of Jesus's death and the promise of the Father to apply that debt-satisfying death to us. Scripture teaches us more than once that it is impossible to please God apart from faith. We take God at His Word and trust that He will faithfully bring to completion the good work that He started in us. When we trust God, we live that way.

Third, Paul wrote about the consequences of justification. We have peace with God. We are no longer at war with our Maker. We are not separated from Him because of our sinfulness. We can walk with the Lord in fellowship and friendship. We are His, and He is ours! This peace that we enjoy inspires us to live for Him, seek Him, pursue Him, and choose righteousness above wickedness and evil. We are now free to live for greater things since we are no longer participants in a full-blown war of rebellion and discontent against our Creator.

And fourth, we enjoy all blessings through "our Lord Jesus Christ." Remember what Paul wrote in 2 Corinthians 1:20, "For no matter how many promises God has made, they are 'Yes' in Christ." Christ is the mediator and deliverer of all the good things that the Father has made available to His people. Consider how many times we read the expressions "in Christ," "by Christ," and "through Christ" in the New Testament. Paul's reaction to the wonders that we enjoy in Christ was expressed in Romans 5:11 when he wrote, "Not only is this so, but we also rejoice in God through our Lord Jesus Christ, through whom we have now received reconciliation." To rejoice is our response to what God has done for us. We have paid for nothing, yet we have been graciously given all things. May we savor today the power and blessings of justification.

DAY 81

The chances are good that you remember when you were baptized. Baptism is an outward and public sign that confirms what God has done inwardly and privately in the heart and life of a person who has responded to the Gospel of Jesus Christ. Paul used the image of baptism in the opening of Romans 6 to help us understand what God has done for His people. The Bible says, "Or don't you know that all of us who were baptized into Christ Jesus were baptized into his death? We were therefore buried with him through baptism into death in order that, just as Christ was raised from the dead through the glory of the Father, we too may live a new life. For if we have been united with him in a death like his, we will certainly also be united with him in a resurrection like his" (Romans 6:3–5). For Baptists, baptism involves believers being immersed in the water fully and completely. This act of baptism represents or symbolizes our dying to the old ways of life and leaving them behind while, at the same time, being born again in Christ and taking up the new life that He alone promises to us. There are a few truths that Paul named that we need to see in these verses from Romans 6. These truths help to frame some central pillars of our faith.

First, baptism represents our death to sin and our identification with the death of Jesus. The Gospel says that Jesus died for us (while we were yet sinners). To be baptized in the name of Christ means that we have applied His death to ourselves so that we do not have to die for our sins. We accept the payment that Christ made on our behalf. Going into baptism waters in a church baptistry or even the Jordan River does not save us or gain us any grace. Water is only water. But identifying with Christ means everything. And to be baptized acknowledges that we have died to all the old things and the old order so we could be born again in Christ and through Him. When one emerges from the water of baptism, one symbolizes that he or she has risen to this amazing new life in Christ.

Second, a new life in Christ is real. "Born again" is not a work of fiction. It is not some whimsical hope or fantasy. By faith, we trade our old and sin-marred life for the new life that Christ won for us by His death and resurrection. And we know that new life continues into eternity as we go to be with the Lord. Satan would love to convince us that we are victims of our sins, captive to those sins, and forever lost. These lies deceive many people. But the words of Romans teach us about a very different reality. There is victory and deliverance in our Savior.

Third, we live in anticipation of our resurrection. Baptism symbolizes and reminds us of the day when the grave cannot hold us. God calls us to His side through our faith and trust in His Son. The resurrection of Jesus guarantees our personal resurrection one day. Because He lives, we too will live through Him. Jesus said at the graveside of Lazarus that He is the resurrection and the life. All who believe in Him will live even though we may die physically (John 11:25–26).

And fourth, take note of the certainty with which Paul wrote. There were no doubts, no ambiguity, no wavering, and no posturing. Paul wrote with the conviction of one who knew the truth that he recorded. The Holy Spirit had clearly revealed to Paul all that the Son had accomplished for our salvation and for the glory of the Father. We build our faith on this kind of certainty and assurance. We never have to worry about the changing and unpredictable world scene when we have the unchanging and certain Word of God that tells us what God has done for us. Scripture never stumps us or misleads us.

DAY 82

God has blessed us with five senses—seeing, smelling, tasting, touching, and hearing. Each one is a gift and plays an important role in helping us to navigate the activities of each day. In Romans 10:17, Paul wrote about the relationship between hearing and faith. We read, "Consequently, faith comes from hearing the message, and the message is heard through the word about Christ." Faith comes by hearing the Word of God. Listening to the reading of scripture is a faith-building exercise. Occasionally, if we read scripture aloud, we are able to understand simple truths that we might otherwise miss if we are reading silently. Early Christians certainly read scripture. Israel in the Old Testament lived in an oral tradition culture where truth and stories were often transmitted by telling them aloud often to new listeners and repeating them for the sake of old hands.

How often do you listen to scripture being read? Whether listening to someone else or yourself, there is power in hearing the Word of God read. I have read stories of different youth groups doing marathon readings of scripture such as all the Gospels, the entire New Testament, all of Paul's letters, or in one case, a group reading the entire Bible from Genesis through Revelation in only one sitting! Remarkable! God uses the hearing of His Word to build our faith and deepen our walk with Him. A sermon or a Sunday school lesson is an amplification of the Word itself. No sermon or study can ever take the place of reading scripture or hearing scripture. And any good sermon or study wants to be and must be grounded in scripture.

Often, when you read the Old Testament, you will find occasions where Israel did not listen to the Word of God or heed the demands of it. Occasionally, Jesus called out to an audience for failing to listen to the truth of God's Word or put it into practice. Paul even took his readers to task for not knowing the truth of God's message to them. You may recall how Paul even said the Galatian Christians had been deceived, tricked, and bewitched by false teachings. The Berean Christians knew to search the scripture to confirm the accuracy of teachers and their teachings. They trusted what they read and heard from God's Word. When we have heard the Word of God, then we know how to navigate our way through the challenges and minefields of the day.

Paul began Romans 10 by stating his desire that Israel be saved. But this salvation that Paul hoped for was gained only by hearing and acting upon the Word of God—not human efforts, traditions, or man-made customs. When we learn and know the truth of God's Word, then we can confess with our mouths that Jesus is Lord and we can believe that the Father raised Him from the dead (Romans 10:9–10). Protestants have historically valued and placed great emphasis upon the preached Word—believing that the saving grace and faith that lead to salvation are experienced by hearing the Word of God. Faith comes by hearing. Consider what you are hearing. Look for ways to increase your intake of scripture and watch your faith soar.

DAY 83

As a missionary, Paul always maintained a passion for the Jewish people to know Jesus as their Messiah. He preached often at synagogues and labored to show his listeners that Jesus was the Savior anticipated by the law and the prophets. Near the end of Romans 10, Paul quoted from the prophet Isaiah as he addressed the sad plight of Israel. "But concerning Israel he says, all day long I have held out my hands to a disobedient and obstinate people" (Romans 10:21). The words *disobedient* and *obstinate* might speak to folks today as much or more than they did to biblical Israel. Stubbornness is not a virtue to be celebrated or pursued. It is not to be confused with perseverance or endurance, which are spiritual virtues. Stubbornness is a consistent dismissal or rejection of what is plainly right or true. It is a state of contention with God. Hearts can be stubborn when called to repent and return to the Lord. We can often prefer our sins to the freedom that God offers us in Christ.

To be obstinate is to live in contradiction to truth and goodness. Obstinate living is a rejection of what God offers and a decision to remain in what is wrong and sinful. We can all be obstinate. Frankly, our obstinacy was an original reason for our need for a Savior. We could not save ourselves. We had little, if any interest, in the things of the Lord and the new ways of life that God called us to embrace. We needed a Savior to rescue us from our attraction to sin and our obstinate living apart from God. We can often make light of things like stubbornness or living obstinately. We can even subtly make these qualities sound virtuous, heroic, or quaint. We can smile and nod and even think such behavior is becoming or endearing.

Yet scripture takes a different view. Stubbornness or resistance to God and His ways is not quaint, heroic, or endearing. It is sinful. It is a vice that needs to be shattered and abandoned. If we choose to hold on to ourselves or our sins more than the Lord, then something is significantly and seriously wrong. On more than one occasion, God saw Israel as a "stiff-necked" people. Could the same be said about us today? Are we more interested in being right or being righteous? Would we rather win an argument with someone else, or fight the good fight of faith and discipleship against the enemy? God sent the law, prophets, John the Baptist, and even His Son to break through the walls of stubbornness and obstinacy, but stiff-necked people held on to their ways and their wishes.

The solution to stubbornness is humility before the Lord and His Word. Let scripture read your life as you read it. Listen to the conviction that the Holy Spirit may bring to you when He reveals your sinfulness or stubbornness. Let the Lord examine your life as you worship Him. Turn to a trusted and beloved fellow believer if you need help in the battle with stubbornness. Ask for prayers from fellow believers that you can trust to lift you up to the Lord. The ultimate act of stubbornness or defiance is making the terrible decision just to stay where you are. You can change, and the grace of God can set you free.

DAY 84

In Romans 12, Paul wrote about a "surrendered life." As followers of Christ, we surrender ourselves to Him in faith, trust, and discipleship. To live a "surrendered life" means that we submit ourselves to the Lord and pursue His ways above our wishes. Romans says, "Therefore, I urge you, brothers and sisters, in view of God's mercy, to offer your bodies as a living sacrifice, holy and pleasing to God—this is your true and proper worship. Do not conform to the pattern of this world, but be transformed by the renewing of your mind. Then you will be able to test and approve what God's will is—his good, pleasing and perfect will" (Romans 12:1–2). When we consider Paul's words, we see a few lessons that speak to us as we live in a surrendered way.

First, surrendering ourselves to Christ is a form of worship. We elevate Him above ourselves. We exalt His ways above our ways. We make it clear that He is Lord and we are His people. Worship involves bringing everything to the Lord and holding back nothing. We acknowledge that life is best lived through a trusting relationship with the Lord. Second, when we surrender ourselves to the Lord, we are not living in conformity to the ways of the world. We live in stark contrast to the world. We choose the Lord above the treasures of this world. You may recall when Satan tempted Jesus that the enemy offered our Lord the kingdoms of this world if only our Lord would bow before the enemy. But Jesus refused. The best treasures and most valuable possessions of this world can in no way exceed our relationship with the Lord. At times, we simply have to draw a line and declare that we belong to the Lord and we will yield to Him.

Third, to be surrendered involves a change in the mind or in the way we think. Because we are sinners by nature and choice, our minds will pursue that which is sinful and wrong. The mind has to be changed and transformed by God's grace. We want to fill our minds with good things like God's Word. Remember how Paul instructed us to renew or change our minds: "Finally, brothers and sisters, whatever is true, whatever is noble, whatever is right, whatever is pure, whatever is lovely, whatever is admirable—if anything is excellent or praiseworthy—think about such things" (Philippians 4:8). When we surrender to the Lord, we begin to see the world as He sees it. We begin to look for Him each day rather than the things that could capture, control, or tempt us.

And fourth, to be a surrendered follower of Christ means we are going to look for and choose His will. Even when it is difficult, unpopular, and demanding, we will choose His will above our will. Making this choice is not always easy. And often, we fail to make that choice. So we repent, we confess, and we seek His will as we should. Remember how Jonah ran from God's clear directive to him. But then Jonah came back to do what was the right thing in the first place. We have all had our "Jonah moments." Pray today for God's grace and strength to live a surrendered life and to leave at His feet the things that are not worth pursuing, chasing, or attracting into your life. Give up all that is wrong, and exchange it for the joy the Lord offers when we surrender to Him.

DAY 85

We often encounter evil in the world today as we experience the sinfulness of others. There is the natural and human tendency to want to lash out at or against evil and injustice. If we are not careful, however, we might engage in evil ourselves in response to others and what they have done. Twice in Romans 12, Paul offered a warning to anyone who might be tempted to respond to evil by doing evil. He wrote, "Do not repay anyone evil for evil. Be careful to do what is right in the eyes of everyone. If it is possible, as far as it depends on you, live at peace with everyone" (Romans 12:17). And he wrote, "Do not be overcome by evil, but overcome evil with good" (Romans 12:21). The mandate is clear. We are to confront evil with goodness and righteousness. We are not to be "overcome by evil." The idea is we are not to allow evil from others to push or prod us into evil behavior of our own. Acting sinfully in the face of sin is not a solution. Likewise, acting unjustly in the face of injustice is not a solution either. God's people are to be different. Indeed, the world has a right to expect God's people to act like Jesus Christ. We are His. We are to follow Him. We are to make His ways our ways. We are to behave like Him. It is not a burdensome expectation for the world to expect God's people to act like His Son.

Paul gives us a word about how to respond to evil or injustice and those who commit such things against us. We read, "On the contrary: If your enemy is hungry, feed him; if he is thirsty, give him something to drink. In doing this, you will heap burning coals on his head" (Romans 12:20). Repaying injustice with compassion and repaying evil with goodness is God's way. And since this is God's way, it must become our way too. We gain nothing by going toe to toe and blow by blow with those who do evil.

We are to rise above such things and live with grace. Grace is the response of the believer toward those who are hard-hearted and bitter. Kindness is the response toward those who rail against us. To be sure, these responses are hard. But we respond with the help of Christ and the strength He supplies.

If we needed any more clarity, God tells us that He will personally deal with the evil and injustice that we encounter. His response will be perfect and decisive. Paul wrote, "Do not take revenge, my dear friends, but leave room for God's wrath, for it is written: 'It is mine to avenge; I will repay,' says the Lord" (Romans 12:19). We trust God to settle scores and accounts that others may have run up against us. When we repay evil with evil, we likely only escalate the situation and make matters much, much worse. Escalation usually leaves behind a trail of brokenness and pain for all. The Bible says we are to fix our eyes upon Christ. Why? If we make a priority out of seeing Christ and serving Christ in all matters, we are not likely to get sidetracked by fruitless battles and petty squabbles. Leave the big things and small things to God as we make a point to live like His Son.

DAY 86

There is much conversation about the end of time and the end-times. And frankly, this topic has been a popular conversation for a long, long time. People often wonder about how to get ready for the end. Well, one way to be ready for the Lord's return is simply to stay ready for His return. We do not have a specific or definite date given to us in scripture, so the best way to live is to assume the Lord could come at any time for His people. In Romans 13, Paul addressed the matter of the Lord's return and the end of time. We read, "And do this, understanding the present time: The hour has already come for you to wake up from your slumber, because our salvation is nearer now than when we first believed. The night is nearly over; the day is almost here. So let us put aside the deeds of darkness and put on the armor of light. Let us behave decently, as in the daytime, not in carousing and drunkenness, not in sexual immorality and debauchery, not in dissension and jealousy. Rather, clothe yourselves with the Lord Jesus Christ, and do not think about how to gratify the desires of the flesh" (Romans 13:11–14). A few lessons stand out for us as believers who anticipate our Lord's coming.

First, we should not slumber or sleep. We should be awake. Keep your faith awake and alive. Do not slip or slide into cruise control or just drift along. Read scripture, pray, worship, and live an anticipatory life where you look for the Lord's return. We want to stay ready to keep from getting ready. Each day that we live brings us one more day closer to being with the Lord forever. What a joy!

Second, make sure you are living rightly and righteously. Put aside any sin or darkness in your life. Pursue the Lord. Live your life in such a way that you can draw others to Jesus based on what they see and find in you.

Create a hunger for the Lord in others by living distinctly and differently. If we know the Lord is coming back, we have no need to waste time on sinful things or trivial and fruitless pursuits. Invest your life and days in the things that truly matter.

Third, Paul said we are to behave "decently" in verse 13. The idea is we are to exercise self-control and to channel our lives and energy in the direction of honoring the Lord. In fact, he gave some opposing examples of what living "indecently" looks like. We should ensure that we are living worthy lives and not living to please ourselves. *No* is a good biblical word. And simply saying no to certain things is the right step to take. The modifier "as in the daytime" means that we are to live as if our lives are in the full view of others. Certainly, God sees how we live. And likely, others observe us as well. Put forth a worthy example for others to see. You may inspire someone else.

And fourth, make Christ your passion. Paul commanded to "clothe yourselves with the Lord Jesus Christ." Seeing Christ, leaning on Christ, and abiding with Christ are the passions we are to cultivate. We are not to think about how we make ourselves happy or how we flirt with sinful pursuits and ways. Strike a Christlike posture in every situation where you find yourself. If we make Christlikeness our highest pursuit, we can ensure that we are staying ready for His return.

DAY 87

We do not know everything there is to know about heaven in perfect detail and understanding. Indeed, we, as humans, are not going to possess that kind of perfect understanding in this world or these mortal lives. But Romans 14 does say there are two certainties about heaven that we can count on and look forward to experiencing. The Bible says, "It is written: 'As surely as I live,' says the Lord, 'every knee will bow before me; every tongue will acknowledge God.' So then, each of us will give an account of ourselves to God" (Romans 14:11–12). Paul points us to a coming day when we find ourselves in the presence of the Lord. He makes it clear that two things will happen. First, we will bow before the Lord. We will acknowledge that only God is God. Some may not give much thought to God moment by moment, but the time is coming when we will acknowledge His greatness, majesty, and presence. Paul added in Philippians that every knee will bow and every tongue confess that Jesus Christ is Lord to the glory of God the Father (see Philippians 2:10–11). Since the day is coming when we will bow before the Lord, we should prepare by practicing here and now.

We can bow before the Lord today in worship and prayer, in humility and trust, in surrender and submission. There could be any number of ways and places in your life where you could bow before the Lord today and honor His greatness and majesty. Often today, even God's people have extended seasons of indifference toward God or even an outright ignoring of Him. When we know that we will one day bow before the Lord in heaven, then the earth becomes a good place to prepare for that moment.

Second, Paul assured us that we would give an account of ourselves to the Lord. We will speak about what we have done with our lives. We will address what we have done with the blessings and opportunities entrusted to us. We will not be able to fake it or shade the truth in any way. All will be revealed before the Lord's perfect vision and wisdom. Since we know there will be an accounting to come, it makes sense to live in anticipation of such a time. God has told us what is coming. May we live in ways that honor Him and bring glory to Him. May we live in ways that are generous, devout, and humble. May we live as vessels who reveal His light and deflect glory back to Him.

How would you live today if you knew you would have to explain your actions and words to the Lord at midnight? The reality is you and I will do that one day. The accounting may not take place today, but it will happen in eternity. When we know that the Lord is expecting an accounting of our lives, that reality definitely impacts how we live now and the choices we make. Paul gave us a recipe for worthy living in Philippians 2:14–15, "Do everything without grumbling or arguing, so that you may become blameless and pure, children of God without fault in a warped and crooked generation. Then you will shine among them like stars in the universe." Take time to bow today and think of the record you will present to the Lord.

DAY 88

The Kingdom of God is a prominent concept in the New Testament and especially in the teachings of Jesus. You may recall that Jesus said that His kingdom was not of this world (John 18:36). He ushered in a very different kind of kingdom because He was and is a very different kind of King. Rather than gathering prestige and fame, He chose a cross. Jesus is the King of kings. In Romans 14, Paul addressed the idea of the kingdom of God. The apostle wrote, "For the kingdom of God is not a matter of eating and drinking, but of righteousness, peace and joy in the Holy Spirit, because anyone who serves Christ in this way is pleasing to God and receives human approval" (Romans 14:17–18). In just two verses, Paul told us what the Kingdom of God is and what it is not.

We are not to think of God's Kingdom in normal ways and terms. It is not a kingdom where the accumulation of power and possessions is paramount. It is not a kingdom where one is consumed by pleasure and living as one pleases. It is not a place or kingdom that lacks boundaries and borders where we can engage in any kind of conduct or behavior that we might wish. Those who possess earthly means and power may see the idea of the kingdom in those terms. But we are not to see it that way. Paul said that God's kingdom is primarily understood as a matter of righteousness, peace, and joy. We are to see this kingdom as the way we serve God and extend His goodness and holiness into a dark and fallen world.

God's kingdom is about changing us and changing our perspective. We are to see His Kingdom from His perspective. We are changed from the inside out. When the Lord has come to change our hearts, minds, and lives, we then in turn change how we engage the world around us. We look for ways to serve and not be served. We look for ways to live righteously and refrain from sinful patterns and habits. In Luke 17:21, Jesus taught that the Kingdom of God is within His people. It is Jesus sitting on the throne of the human heart and life more than occupying a palatial throne in some far-off and distant place. Christ came to change hearts and lives and through those changed hearts and lives to extend the good news of His righteousness, peace, and joy.

Paul's passage in Romans calls us to examine whose kingdom we serve today. Do we serve ourselves and embrace power and possessions as the world teaches? Do we embrace the kingdom that is within—gained and enjoyed by a personal relationship with Christ and our walk with Him? The best way to answer is to examine how and where you spend your time, money, thoughts, energy, and pursuits. Are you kingdom-minded and kingdom-living, or have you settled for the lesser kingdoms of this world? Perhaps you are ready for a new King to sit on your heart's throne. Jesus stands at the door and knocks. All we have to do is invite Him to come in and change the things that belong to the kingdoms of this world into things that belong to His kingdom.

DAY 89

We know Paul as a missionary, a preacher, a church planter, a writer of much of the New Testament, and probably Christianity's finest theologian. Following his very intense and powerful conversion experience, Paul knew his mission. He knew where God wanted him to go. His plan was to plow the new ground for church planting and the sowing of gospel seeds. He stated his mission clearly in Romans 15:20-22, "It has always been my ambition to preach the gospel where Christ was not known so that I would not be building on someone else's foundation. Rather, as it is written: 'Those who were not told about him will see, and those who have not heard will understand.' This is why I have often been hindered from coming to you." There is a message in Paul's mission that can speak to us too. We can see at least four things that might empower how we serve the Lord and represent Him today. Paul's standards remain the same for us today.

First, we are to develop an ambition to make the Lord known and honored. Some Christians will live decades without ever sharing their faith, inviting someone to worship, or speaking about Jesus. Some will never speak about Jesus to anyone else. That approach is a failure. We have daily opportunities to speak about Christ, but we need the ambition to match. Be eager to talk about the Lord and what He has meant to you. Share the Gospel with those who are simply floating through life lost and aimless. We usually speak about the things that matter to us. Speak about the Lord today. Proclaim His greatness and Gospel.

Second, there are people you could reach for Christ that no one else can. There are people who would listen to you that might never listen to a sermon, follow a Christian podcast, or read a Christian book. You may call these people members of your family or some of your closest friends.

You may work alongside them. You may share other hobbies or interests with them. Speak up. Talk about the Lord. Build on this foundation that no one else has ever built before. Seize the moment to make a difference for the Lord. There are huge numbers of husbands, wives, parents, children, and homes that have never heard a clear and simple presentation of who Jesus is. You may be just the one the Lord counts on to present it.

Third, perhaps God has already opened a door of service for you, but you have failed to walk through it. God has clearly identified what He has given you to do, but you have resisted. Delays, excuses, and disobedience have kept you from enjoying the chance to see God work through you to change someone else's present and future. Look at the ways and places where you have said no. Could God be calling you, at last, to walk through this door that He has opened?

And fourth, our actions or inactions can have eternal consequences. People will die today. People die every day. That is the reality of this world. We may not have the luxury of limitless time to reach others with the Gospel, but we do have it now. May we not waver or wait while others need to hear a message of hope and encouragement that is found in Christ alone. Paul knew his mission and pursued it passionately and eagerly. Be a voice for Christ while you can. Tomorrow may never come, and for some people in this world, it will not come. Their clock runs out today. Take time today to speak about Christ in the openings and opportunities that He has created for you.

DAY 90

Gratitude is part of the Christian life. We are often moved to gratitude by the blessings of God. We can be moved by the generosity and thoughtfulness of others as well. Often, God blesses us through other people so we have the occasion to be grateful for God and those folks who are His hands, heart, and voice to us. In 1 Corinthians 1:4, Paul began his first letter to the Corinthians with a grateful voice. He wrote, "I always thank my God for you because of his grace given you in Christ Jesus." Paul was never reluctant to express humble gratitude to those who had blessed him. A commitment to gratitude should be a mainstay in a believer's life. There should be consistent and faithful gratitude for what we have been given and the way God keeps watch over us.

We can often identify very particular and specific ways that God has blessed and enriched us. The evidence of His abundance is visible for us to see. We see answers to prayers, unexpected blessings, and opportunities that only God could have orchestrated or granted to us. Consider the changing of summer into fall and the dazzling gift of color and beauty that we find in nature at this time of year. The approaching months of November and December give us opportunities to see the abundance and blessings of God in Thanksgiving, Advent, and Christmas where we celebrate the greatest of all gifts—His Son Jesus.

Paul was thankful for the evidence of God that He saw in the Christians to whom he wrote in Corinth. We can also take joy in those where we see clear and even unmistakable evidence of God being at work. A child who professes faith in Jesus Christ is a reason for giving thanks—God has been at work in that child to bring His love and grace. We take joy in the counsel of a trusted Christian friend who speaks to us from the heart and takes the time to invest in our lives in some special way. We give thanks to those through whom God teaches us. A Sunday school teacher or a beloved author may be just the one God uses to bring a word of instruction or encouragement to us.

If you read Paul's letters, you find that he often singles out and names people who have been a blessing to him and for whom he is profoundly grateful. Romans 16 reads like a "who's who" from Paul's life as he made connections with believers in Rome. 1 Corinthians 1:4 teaches us to recognize occasions to be grateful. This passage helps us to recall that God is always at work to bless, encourage, comfort, counsel, or correct us. And we give thanks for each expression of His fatherly love and kindness to us.

In this single verse from 1 Corinthians, Paul reminds us that God's gifts are always grounded and centered in His grace. The gifts are undeserved. Nonetheless, they are given and provided. And God knows how to bless and honor us. He is fully aware of what we need and precisely when we need it. We give thanks for this faithfulness that we encounter each day. Consider some ways you can be grateful today. Voice your praise and thankfulness to God and acknowledge what He has done for you and in your life.

DAY 91

There is no comparison between the wisdom of God and the wisdom of the world. While we may know some really smart men and women, all human wisdom is limited and finite. No one knows everything. And not one person possesses perfect recall of the past, flawless knowledge of the present, and keen insight into the future. At best, we have some memories of the past, some understanding of the present, and little more than dreams or hopes for the future. In 1 Corinthians 1:18–20, Paul wrote about God's wisdom and carefully contrasted it with man's wisdom. We read, "For the message of the cross is foolishness to those who are perishing, but to us who are being saved it is the power of God. For it is written: 'I will destroy the wisdom of the wise; the intelligence of the intelligent I will frustrate.' Where is the wise person? Where is the teacher of the law? Where is the philosopher of this age? Has not God made foolish the wisdom of the world?" Paul gives us four lessons about wisdom.

First, the world often regards God's wisdom as foolishness or worthy of dismissal. As an example, Paul pointed to the cross. Most people in his day would have seen death on a cross as demeaning and demoralizing. "What good could come from a cross?" many would ask. But the cross was where God satisfied His justice and extended His gracious love to a lost and dying world. The cross was where God's eternal plan for salvation found fulfillment and completion. Those who know Christ know what incredible power and wisdom are found on the cross. But to those who are lost, the cross possesses no power or wisdom. The cross teaches us to see the world from God's perspective and through the lens of His wisdom.

Second, God promises to frustrate or confound the "wisdom" of the "wise." That is to say, God will deal with those who profess or believe their wisdom is unimpeachable or unassailable. God will expose them for their pride and selfishness. Our wisdom must always be checked by humility and by comparing what we may think to what scripture declares to be right. We can easily find ourselves in conflict with what God has determined to be right or wrong. If our wisdom stands in contrast to God's wisdom, we must humbly repent and submit to Him.

Third, God's wisdom possesses the power to save. Human wisdom cannot make such a boast. Human views on salvation often conclude that we are saved by good works, everyone will be saved, the good we do must outweigh the bad we have done, or that God may favor one category of people above another. God's wisdom teaches us that everything depends upon the cross—not good works or anything else humans may think or do. Salvation was (and is) God's idea. We are simply invited to receive what He has conceived. We welcome what He first offers and calls us to take.

And fourth, humans have much to learn from God and His perfect wisdom. We can read God's Word and take in valuable lessons about life, faith, parenting, prayer, and how to use our blessings. We will never fully draw out all the wisdom there is for us to discover in God's Word. Reading one chapter per day in Proverbs alone would be a graduate-level education in God's wisdom. We can learn practical lessons about money management, marriage, friendship, forgiveness, and making good choices in life. God has not left us alone to figure out life by ourselves. He has blessed us with all we need to know to be what He wants us to know so we can be who He wants us to be.

Joni Eareckson Tada turned seventy-three years old on October 15, 2022. She has been a quadriplegic since the age of seventeen when a diving accident left her paralyzed from the neck down. Her life mission, in her words, is "I want to be God's best audio-visual aid of how His power shows up best in weakness." Now that is a mission! May we be people who tap into the wisdom and power of God so that through us, He is glorified and magnified to a world that desperately needs to know Him.

DAY 92

In his first letter to the Christians in Corinth, Paul wrote, "For no one can lay any foundation other than the one already laid, which is Jesus Christ. If anyone builds on this foundation using gold, silver, costly stones, wood, hay, or straw, their work will be shown for what it is, because the Day will bring it to light. It will be revealed with fire, and the fire will test the quality of each person's work" (1 Corinthians 3:11–13). Paul wrote about the disciples of Christ as being builders. The foundation is provided for us. Christ Himself is the foundation. There is no greater foundation. Our faith is in the person and finished work of Christ for a worthy foundation in life. Just like there is more to a house than the foundation, we have to build on what Christ has done for us and given to us. We are not to abandon the foundation or leave it unadorned and unbuilt.

Paul says we are not to spend our days accumulating ordinary things, such as wood, hay, or straw. These things are a little better than a sugary snack that is tasty for a moment and then quickly gone. But we are also not to reduce life to gathering extravagant things made from gold, silver, or precious stones. If we build a life defined by what we have made or collected, then we are building the wrong kind of life. We are to build a life marked by worship, service, faith, trust, faithfulness, gentleness, and self-control to name just a few things. A life surrendered to Jesus, day by day and moment by moment, is the kind of thing that will last.

The Bible teaches that one day we will present our lives to the Lord and give an accounting for what we have done with what we were given. We are to be faithful in small ways and with few things so that we can be equally faithful when bigger ways and more opportunities are given to us. As Jesus taught, we are not to bury our talents or blessings. We are to use them—multiply them, grow them, deploy them, and put them to use for His glory and His mission. Could it be that you spend a lot of time dabbling in the things that will not matter or last? Time itself is a gift, and we are to make the most of every single opportunity entrusted to us. A prayer, a conversation, and a note shared with others may be a good way to redeem the time the Lord has given to you.

Sometimes children or grandchildren will present us with a work of "art" that we ooh and ahh over. The truth is, we do treasure such things because they were given in and made by love. We cherish what they have made or done because we love them. We may often think that we have little to offer to the Lord or the cause of Christ. But faithful offerings and devoted service are welcomed and embraced by the Father and duly noted in heaven's recordkeeping. He loves us and welcomes what His children bring to Him. Building a life worthy of the foundation we have been given begins by giving the Lord our mind, heart, and body. Think on what is good and fill your mind with His Word. Let truth occupy a place in your mind and respond to the deceptions of the world and the enemy with truth. Harbor what is gracious and loving in your heart. Fill your heart with grace, generosity, patience, and perseverance. Let your body be a vessel for service. Abstain from what is evil and engage in what is righteous and good. Do not act out of pride, resentment, anger, or selfishness. Think before you act or unload.

If you remember what it is like to build with Legos, Lincoln Logs, or just a good set of colorful building blocks, then you know that you can easily scrap what you have made and start over. The same principle works with faith too. If you are saddened, sickened, or sullen about the life you have built, it may be time to start over. You already have your foundation in Christ and Christ alone. With His grace, power, and forgiveness, you can start over and begin to build the kind of life that you would like to present to Him one day.

DAY 93

Paul ended 1 Corinthians with some personal requests and remarks. He named some people and offered some admonitions. In 1 Corinthians 16:13–14, the apostle wrote, "Be on your guard; stand firm in the faith; be courageous; be strong. Do everything in love." We find five simple and direct commands that help to frame how we can live as followers of Christ. The first command is to be on guard. On guard against what? we might ask. Guard against sin and yield to temptation. Guard against bad influences entering your life. Guard against false teachings and bad theology taking hold that leaves you doubting the truth of scripture. Satan has a multitude of things and ways that he can come against us. So the message is to be on guard or to stay watchful. Do not allow yourself to be led astray by the cunning and trickery of the enemy. Do not let the enemy infiltrate your mind or heart.

Second, Paul said that we are to stand firm in the faith. If we are to resist false teachings and sin, then it makes sense to stand firmly in and among what is right, true, and good. We hold on to the cross, the Gospel, the promise of salvation in Christ alone, and God's promises to be with us always, even to the end of the age. To stand firmly means we also resist what is evil or wrong. We push back against the enemy's efforts to confuse or deceive us or others.

Third, Paul says be courageous. Be bold when it comes to speaking about your faith and inviting others to know the Lord Jesus. Do not fade away from your commitment to follow Christ without reservation. We often sing that we will follow Jesus, no turning back, no turning back. To be bold means we live that way in addition to singing about it. You may decide to take the courageous step of tithing and letting the Lord be the God of your finances. You may need to speak about Christ to a child or grandchild. Christ courageously went to the cross. Maybe there is a courageous step you can take for His glory.

Fourth, Paul says to be strong. We build physical strength by exercising, eating right, getting proper rest and sleep, checking in with our doctor for annual physicals, and paying attention to anything that is not right with our bodies. Staying strong spiritually is important too—and more so. We stay spiritually strong with a diet of Bible reading and prayer. We worship, we tithe, we serve, and we live humbly before the Lord. We build our faith as diligently as we would build a home or garden.

And fifth, we wrap everything in love. We love the Lord, and we love others we may encounter. Love becomes our motivation for the previous four steps. Because we love the Lord, we take His admonitions seriously and follow them obediently. Our love for God makes us want to walk and fellowship with Him. Our love for others makes us want to share Christ with them. Some of the Bible's simplest verses can make a huge impact on how we live. Today's verses are two such examples. These simple and short commands can build a steady and sturdy faith.

DAY 94

Paul continued his dialogue with the Corinthian Christians by writing his second letter to the believers in that part of the Roman Empire. As he often did, Paul began by connecting his identity to Christ. "Paul, an apostle of Christ Jesus by the will of God, and Timothy our brother, to the church of God in Corinth, together with all his holy people throughout Achaia" (2 Corinthians 1:1). He took joy in being an apostle, a brother, and a partner with those who belong to Christ as holy and separate people. It is not often today that we hear people ground their identity in Christ. People will often identify by name, place of birth, vocation, age, or address. But it is not often that a person leads by saying, "I am a follower of Jesus Christ." Why not?

In 2 Corinthians 1:3–4, Paul spoke about some of the practical gains and joys that we experience from our relationship with the Lord. We read, "Praise be to the God and Father of our Lord Jesus Christ, the Father of compassion and the God of all comfort, who comforts us in all our troubles, so that we can comfort those in any trouble with the comfort we ourselves receive from God." A few joys stand out for us to see that Paul also experienced through His relationship with Christ.

First, we enjoy a faithful and unfailing Father. Twice, Paul used the word *Father* when he wrote about God. Jesus, God's Son, made it possible for us to know His Father as our Father. We can come to the Father through the Son and only through the Son. You may be fatherless today or have grown up fatherless. But the greatest of all fathers loves you and calls you to know and enjoy Him now and forever. As Father, God is both our provider and protector. He gives us what we need. Nothing approaches us that evades His watchful eye and hand. He can protect us when battles rage around us and exceed our human power to manage them.

Second, we are assured of God's compassion or love. We do not work for it or earn it. But we rest confidently in the knowledge that God does love us. And that love does not change contingent on our age or behavior. Even when we act sinfully or shamefully, God's compassion does not recede or fail. His compassion remains consistent and unwavering. Human love can often change like shadows change as sunlight moves and changes. But God's love does not fade from reality.

Third, we enjoy His comfort. In our grief, confusion, or anxiousness, the comfort of God remains with us. Through His Word, prayer, worship, or even fellow believers, God delivers His comfort to us—in the right measure and at the right time. This comfort can be a peace that passes all understanding that Paul addressed in Philippians 4:7. Or this comfort could be an abiding confidence that God will sustain and steady us, come what may.

And fourth, this comfort that we experience from God can flow through us to comfort others. Often, our troubles and the comfort we experience can become occasions where God uses us to comfort others who may be hurting in similar ways. We often serve God by serving and encouraging others who are going through trials or battles from which we may have recently emerged. Grace can flow from God through us to bless and comfort others. We often sing, "Make me a channel of blessing." Paul says that is a distinct possibility as God works through His people to confer His blessings to others. Perhaps God is leading you to be just such a channel for someone else today. These verses in 2 Corinthians call us to praise God for His Fatherhood, compassion, and comfort. Take confidence in knowing that these unchanging gifts from God are yours today and always.

DAY 95

I recently had my annual eye exam. My optometrist asked me to fix my eyes on certain locations as he conducted the exam to test my vision and the health of my eyes. Where I fixed my eyes made a difference in how my doctor could determine the well-being of my sight. In our faith, we are asked to fix our eyes as well. Scripture tells us exactly where to look and focus our gaze. Paul wrote in 2 Corinthians 4:18, "So we fix our eyes not on what is seen, but on what is unseen, since what is seen is temporary, but what is unseen is eternal." This wise apostle was calling us to see the Lord and the things of faith more than we see our circumstances and the temporary things in life that can easily dominate our field of vision and even our lives. There are some excellent life lessons we can easily glean from this one verse.

First, we have to decide what we focus on. The choice is ours to make. We cannot blame others for what we choose to see or to dwell on. We can fix our eyes on the unsettled and changing world scene, or we can fix our eyes on the Lord. We can allow ourselves to be disturbed and frustrated, or we can look to the One who has conquered every kind of temptation or trial we might be experiencing in life. It has been often said that we cannot always control the things that happen to us. But we can certainly control our response or reaction to those things. The way we respond rests squarely in our hands and heart.

Second, we are to look for the Lord each day and not be obsessed with or blinded by the things we see. School, your job, a health matter, or a family crisis can easily dominate your thinking and capture your peace of mind and heart. Such things can rob you of sleep and contentment. It can be good to have some Bible verses memorized that can reshape and reframe your thinking when those occasions occur. You want to be able to see the Lord and His Word each day more than you want to see the things that oppress you or disturb you.

Third, remember that everything we experience in this world or life is temporary and not everlasting. You might be familiar with the well-worn cliché that says, "This too shall pass." Such a line might be a cliché, but it does contain a lot of truth. We do not want to be dominated and captured by things that have no eternal command or control over us. And troubles do tend to pass after a season. Just one verse earlier, in 2 Corinthians 4:17, Paul wrote, "For our light and momentary troubles are achieving for us an eternal glory that far outweighs them all." Did you see what Paul wrote about earthly and temporary things? They are "light and momentary." These things will pass, and we will be fine. God remains in control, and we are still yielded to Him. Make sure you place the temporary and earthly things where they belong—at the feet of Christ who is God over them and you.

These words from 2 Corinthians have much to say about balance in life and keeping one's heart and head in the right place. That can be hard to do when the battles come at us so quickly and so unrelentingly. But the Lord supplies the grace and guidance we need to refocus and reshape.

DAY 96

Splinters can be aggravating and annoying. And so too can briars and thorns. Paul suffered with something he called "a thorn in my flesh" (2 Corinthians 12:7). We do not specifically know what the thorn was that afflicted Paul. It could have been some physical illness or discomfort. And frankly, knowing the answer would not make that much difference to us. Perhaps God led Paul to conceal the identity or nature of the thorn so we could apply the truths He has for us to see to our situations when we face "thorns" in life. If Paul had named the thorn, we might miss the way God's grace can be experienced when we deal with thorns.

Paul said that he prayed three times and "pleaded with the Lord to take it away from me" (2 Corinthians 12:8). Maybe you have had some situations in your life, thorns if you will, where you prayed for God to remove them. There are certainly times when we pray, and God does not answer the prayer as we prayed it or as we might have wished. But God did give Paul an answer. The Lord did not ignore Paul. Paul wrote, "But he said to me, 'My grace is sufficient for you, for my power is made perfect in weakness.' Therefore, I will boast all the more gladly about my weaknesses, so that Christ's power may rest on me" (2 Corinthians 12:9). Rather than removing the thorn, the Lord gave Paul the grace to handle the thorn and whatever outcome might result from the thorn. And God gave Paul a testimony that he could freely share and proclaim.

The lesson for us to see is the reality of "sufficient grace." When God does not act in ways that we request, we are not to be too quick to suggest that He hasn't answered us or that He's forgotten us. The answer is often the gift of sufficient grace. God does occasionally allow us to go through trials, thorns, and testing. Jesus was tested and tempted by Satan.

Job suffered through significant trials. John was exiled to Patmos as he approached his later years. In those times of testing, we rely on grace to see us through.

Thorns can teach us something about God. Thorns can introduce us to grace as we have never experienced. Thorns can turn our attention away from ourselves and toward the Lord. Thorns can keep us humble and rely totally and fully on God for daily needs and even the big needs that come along at times. Those thorns can always be met with grace. Honestly, at times, thorns are necessary to break through the stubbornness and hardheadedness we can all be guilty of suffering. I know that more than once, God has convicted me of stubbornness. Thorns often direct us to see God more clearly and to hear Him more intently.

Paul said that this thorn he dealt with and the grace that the Lord supplied gave him the opportunity to boast about God's greatness or to brag about what the Lord has done. We often brag about accomplishments, our kids, our favorite team's championship, and many other things. But do we brag about what the Lord has done? Do we brag about what God has given to us? Do we brag about the way the Lord has seen us through a trial or a thorny situation? Paul said that he would boast about his weakness so that the power of Christ would rest upon him. May we be the same way. May we speak more about our weaknesses and thorns so that we have the occasion to brag about God's grace and magnify His power and His goodness. We often sing that we love to tell the story. What story could you sing or tell about the Lord? Where has His grace been sufficient for you? What thorn has His grace enabled you to endure? Be courageous and boast in the Lord!

DAY 97

Ephesians is Paul's letter to the church located in the city of Ephesus. You may recall that Jesus sent a letter to the same church as part of the seven letters to the seven churches in Revelation 2–3. This church in Ephesus had been blessed by the influences of Paul, Timothy, and John. In his opening chapter, Paul wrote the following message: "Praise be to the God and Father of our Lord Jesus Christ, who has blessed us in the heavenly realms with every spiritual blessing in Christ" (Ephesians 1:3). Imagine being a Christian in Ephesus who received such a message. The grandeur and confidence of this message would have been hugely inspiring to anyone receiving it in the first century. Paul made a few lessons abundantly clear.

First, note that Paul wrote in the past tense: "Who has blessed us." He wrote about an accomplished reality. These Ephesian believers already possessed these blessings or gifts. They were custodians of them. We often have to take inventory of what God has already given or provided. We might find ourselves longing or wanting a blessing, only to realize that God has already blessed us and He has done so in ways far, far greater than we could have asked or imagined and greater than our longings could have secured. Remember the confidence with which Paul wrote in Ephesians 3:20, "Now to him who is able to do immeasurably more than all we ask or imagine, according to his power that is at work within us." God can grant blessings that we cannot even begin to imagine or expect.

Second, Paul wrote that we have already received every spiritual blessing. He has provided all that is necessary for us to live as followers of Jesus Christ. Nothing is lacking. Jesus described His death on the cross with these words: "It is finished" (John 19:30). And it was. The Son of

God had done everything that needed to be done for our salvation and eternal life with Him. We cannot add anything to the Gospel events that Jesus carried out on our behalf. Likewise, God has available all that we could ever need to be His people and to live as His people. Every spiritual blessing we could need, want, or crave is abundantly available to us. There is nothing that we could want or desire that we do not already possess.

Third, Paul reminded us about our new identity. We are "in Christ." We are grounded, rooted, situated, and identified in Him and by Him. We belong to Him. Our old identity and old ways of thinking have died with Christ. We now live for Him and by His power. We are new people, and we have let go of the old ways and the old lifestyles. To be "in Christ" means we are never alone and we are never without His presence with us. He promised His disciples (and us too) that He would be with us always, even to the end of the age. We should live and act like we believe that promise.

Have a great day as you enjoy the blessings that God has prepared for you to enjoy. Walk confidently with Him.

DAY 98

Anger can be debilitating. And anger can be dangerous. And the Bible contains many warnings against letting anger take control of your life. Psalm 37:8 says that we are to refrain from anger and turn from wrath. Colossians 3:8 says we are to rid ourselves of anger if it is a problem in our lives. James 1:19 says we are to be quick to listen, slow to speak, and slow to become angry. Maybe the most significant teaching about anger in the Bible comes from Paul in Ephesians 4:26–27. We read, "'In your anger do not sin': Do not let the sun go down while you are still angry, and do not give the devil a foothold." In just those two verses, the Bible gives us some helpful guidance about anger. First, we can be angry without sinning. For example, Jesus was angry when he cleansed the temple of money changers and those who saw prayer and worship as for-profit activities or ventures. There will be times when we are angry at sin and sinful behavior. But we are not to be sinful in expressing our anger. We never confront sin with more sin. We can be angry at the same things that make the Lord angry—sin, wickedness, injustice, exploitation of others, and evil. But we are not to sin when we feel anger. Control your anger rather than letting anger control you.

Second, the Bible warns against lingering anger. A good motto to follow is not going to bed angry or, as the Bible says, not to "let the sun go down while you are still angry." Lingering anger can very quickly turn into bitterness, resentment, and even hatred. If we stew in anger, we can easily say things that we will regret or destroy relationships that may not be easily fixed or repaired. Many families have been devastated by anger that has persisted for years or decades. Anger that lingers can easily consume and infect us much like a wound that has become infected because it has gone untreated for too long.

Third, anger can become a foothold for the devil's work or activities. Satan loves to establish strongholds or anchors in our lives from which he can go to work in even more sinister ways. Lust can lead to slavery to pornography. Greed or the love of money can easily lead to stealing what belongs to someone else. Anger can easily lead to us engaging in even worse behavior. Anger can create ill feelings in your life where you are eager to take advantage of others or to pay back someone for what they have done. You would never want to let a couple of cockroaches into your home. Two roaches can easily become two thousand, and soon your home is infected. Likewise, anger can become a foothold for Satan to infect your life in more dangerous and disturbing ways. Guard against anger! The Lord warns us because He knows what the consequences can look like.

Fourth, remember that anger can be treated by the grace of God. Anger can be left at the cross for the Lord's blood and forgiveness to cleanse. Anger can be healed when we give it to the Lord and His power. You may have a history of being a hothead or one who has a hair-trigger temper. But that old way of living does not have to define you or remain with you. God can change an angry man or woman just as much as He can change any other kind of sin, lifestyle, or habit. Extended time in God's Word and prayer can be two excellent ways for managing your anger and seeing it less as an influence in your life. We are not to tell ourselves, "Well, that's just the way I am." We may be that way, but we do not have to stay that way. And if we stay that way, it is by choice and not necessity.

DAY 99

The work of Jesus at the cross is beyond total human comprehension. It is nothing short of extraordinary to consider what Christ did for us by paying the debt of sin. We do not treat this lightly. As one song puts it, "You are amazing God." We remember and honor the work of Christ at the cross with reverence as we observe the bread and the cup in the Lord's Supper. We do not take this communion worship lightly or whimsically. It is a holy moment whereby we remember the death of the Son of God and anticipate the day when believers will enjoy life with Him forever. Paul wrote about the transformation that we experience through Jesus's finished work at the cross. In Ephesians 2:13–14, we read, "But now in Christ Jesus you who once were far away have been brought near by the blood of Christ. For he himself is our peace, who has made the two groups one and has destroyed the barrier, the dividing wall of hostility." A few important truths about salvation stand out for us to see.

First, salvation is only "in Christ Jesus." Our Lord said He is the way, the truth, and the life. There is no salvation apart from Him. We cannot enjoy salvation and a living relationship with the Father unless we are "in" the Son. We cannot walk with the Father unless we are positioned "in" the Son. We might think it is repetitive or small-minded to emphasize the significance of that small word *in*, but it is crucial in today's world to understand the greatness and preeminence of Christ Jesus. He is not one choice among many. He is the only way we can be saved from sin and secure with the Father. To be "in Christ" is everything!

Second, believers were once far from God—separated, estranged, cut off. Our sinfulness had driven a wedge between a holy God and sinful men and women. But Christ removed that wedge of separation by His death at the cross. There is a bridge that spans the great divide between God and us caused by our sins. And that bridge is the cross that makes it possible for us to know, to access, and to walk with the Father. Paul wrote decisively, we "have been brought near." The separation ended the moment we took our place, by faith, at Calvary's cross.

Third, Christ is our peace. He not only brings peace, but He is also the embodiment of peace. Christ is the living peace treaty between the Father and believers. He experienced the judgment, justice, and wrath of God so that we might enjoy peace, reconciliation, and reconnection with the Father. There are, on average, about 106 deaths per minute around the world. Many of those who perish each minute will enter into a Christless eternity. If you are a believer, you can approach death with the peace you have in Christ. For those who do not know Christ, call on Him now. Confess your sins. Believe that He died for those sins and rose again and call upon His name alone, the name of Jesus, for your forgiveness, salvation, and eternal assurance.

And fourth, Christ destroyed the barrier between the Father and us. We can approach the Father directly through the Son. We do not have to satisfy God by keeping the law, making sacrifices, or hoping our good outweighs our bad. The sin barrier was judged and removed. By His blood, we are cleansed, forgiven, and made new. The old self has been crucified with Christ, and the new self, the born-again believer, comes as a gift from the Father. Give thanks today for what Christ has done. Worship Him in wonder and joy for His accomplished and completed work.

DAY 100

October 31 is Reformation Day. Every year, we recall the actions of a priest named Martin Luther who nailed ninety-five theses or protests to the door of the Catholic church in Wittenberg. He led the way in the rediscovery of salvation by grace through faith—not by works or papal prerogative. This basic gospel message remains under assault today by opponents who would seek to add to it or detract from it. When thinking about Luther and salvation by grace through faith, we can think of Paul's words in Galatians 2:20, "I have been crucified with Christ and I no longer live, but Christ lives in me. The life I now live in the body, I live by faith in the Son of God, who loved me and gave himself for me." And therein lies the Gospel. Christ gave Himself for us, and we receive that offering and gift by faith.

The great themes of the Reformation are worth remembering on a day such as this—grace alone, faith alone, Christ alone, scripture alone, and the glory of God alone. These five pillars allow us to build a sturdy house of faith that can withstand the winds and trials of life. Faith and belief are how we receive God's gift of grace and acknowledge what the cross means for us personally. Paul wrote, "So also Abraham "believed God, and it was credited to him as righteousness" (Galatians 3:6). God calls us to believe in Him and to take Him at His Word. He desires obedience above sacrifice. And Luther's rediscovery of biblical truth continues to bless believers like us even to this day.

The Gospel calls for clarity in understanding and in the proclamation. If the enemy can deceive us into losing sight of the Gospel, then we are in a troubling place. Remember the price that was paid for salvation and the power of the cross. Do not depart from these essential values and truths. In

Paul's day, he was baffled by the tendency of the Galatians to turn from the Gospel and embrace the latest fad that came their way. This conundrum was not unlike the circumstances that we face today. Paul wrote, "I am astonished that you are so quickly deserting the one who called you to live in the grace of Christ and are turning to a different gospel—which is really no gospel at all. Evidently some people are throwing you into confusion and are trying to pervert the gospel of Christ" (Galatians 1:6–7).

May we recognize that Satan is the author of confusion, chaos, and disorder. He would be happy for you to settle for almost anything other than the Gospel. He often whittles away at the Gospel—a little at a time until we are deceived into both believing and living in ways that are at odds with the Gospel. Whenever we observe Reformation Day, be clear about what the Gospel says and is. Refresh your mind and heart by reading Galatians and Ephesians (and if you are really ambitious today, give Romans another read). Luther considered Romans a "gospel of iron or steel." And base your Gospel on the inspired text of scripture and not whatever the enemy happens to be peddling or selling.

DAY 101

Near the end of Galatians, Paul wrote in a rather tongue-in-cheek way. He wanted to call emphasis to the importance of the message that he was sending to the Galatian believers. This message could not be dismissed or delayed. These Christians were being besieged by false teaching that sounded so smooth and credible but was dangerous in both content and influence. Paul wanted there to be no doubt that he was writing to the Galatians at the prompting of the Lord and under the inspiration of the Holy Spirit. So we read his message, "See what large letters I use as I write to you with my own hand!" (Galatians 6:11). Paul wrote in large letters. Today, large letters can be used to express emphasis, urgency, or even anger. A text or email that comes in large caps could be the written equivalent of a verbal scream.

But Paul wrote in large letters for emphasis—to call attention to some truths that were imperiled in some way. He wrote to capture the attention of Christians who could easily fall prey to smooth, slick teachings that did not honor the Lord or advance the Gospel message. If the Lord sent you a message in large letters today, what would it be? What would it say? What wall does the Lord seek to break down in your life? Have you ignored the Lord's large letters in the past? If so, it is not too late to pay attention now.

Occasionally, pride can get in the way of becoming what God wants us to be. We can easily, stiffly, and tightly hold on to old ways that seem right and comfortable to us. It is always easier to remain in the same ways and the same place than to take a step of courage and faith and walk where the Lord could be leading. Fear can get in the way too. God often has to break through our fears and worries to deliver to us a message that has the ability to transform us into greater Christlikeness.

God wrote in large letters at the cross and the empty tomb. He wanted us to know that the work of salvation had been completed by His Son. There was nothing left to do or to pursue. The finished work of Christ deserved to be written in large letters. Jesus's death was real, and so too was His resurrection. There can be no mistaking that these events really did occur. God wrote in large letters in the creation. There is enough evidence of God in the creation for us to know that He is real and the maker of all that exists today. Consider God's handiwork in the heavens as His glory is written in large letters that span the course of the universe.

Large letters. Maybe there are some things that you would say or write to yourself using large letters. Maybe there are some sins that need to be confessed. Maybe there are some places from which you need to turn away. Maybe there are some old ways of life that need to be dropped or left behind. Maybe there is some anger that has been allowed to linger for too long. Paul wrote in Galatians 5:7, "You were running a good race. Who cut in on you to keep you from obeying the truth?" Large letters were necessary to redeploy believers back into the race of faith. These believers had lost their way or had been deceived into running the wrong race. It was time to turn around and pursue a different pathway.

When the truth is hanging in the balance, large letters are essential and necessary. And when life and faith have gone off the rails, large letters are important too. You might want to ask a trusted friend to speak to you in and with large letters whenever necessary. Someone could be a real brother or sister to you if they speak with large letters at crucial times.

DAY 102

One of the themes found in Philippians is joy. As you probably know, joy is a fruit of the Holy Spirit. Biblical joy or the joy of Philippians comes from the Lord and is rarely, if ever, contingent upon external happenings or circumstances in life. The joy we read about in Philippians (or elsewhere in Paul's letters) is a creation of the Holy Spirit. He is the architect or designer of joy. And the Holy Spirit does not work in ways that depend on what is or is not happening in your life. If your joy is running low, winning a lottery probably will not increase your joy level. And there is a big difference between happiness and joy. Early in Philippians, Paul wrote about the joy that the Philippian believers brought to Him. Indeed, even the mere memory or recollection of his relationship with them brought him great joy and satisfaction. Paul wrote, "I thank my God every time I remember you" (Philippians 1:3).

Are there people in your life for whom you give God profound thanks and praise? Is there anyone in your life whose mere presence is a blessing to you? God often blesses us through the lives and contributions of others. God graciously gives us shared experiences with others and memories that endure. When we enjoy conversations, experiences, opportunities to serve, and amazing God moments with others, we often grow to cherish and savor those times. Indeed, we look forward to them!

Every year, we celebrate Thanksgiving. It is a defined day on the calendar but every day can be an occasion for thanking God. God often works in us and blesses us through the presence of other people. Family, friends, neighbors, and even strangers can be carriers and conveyors of God's richest blessings. Take time during these days of Thanksgiving to remember those who have shared your life with you or poured blessings into your life.

One way to express your thanks for the gifts of others is by telling them what they have meant to you and how they have blessed or encouraged you. You could speak with them directly over lunch, coffee, or a chance to catch up. You could bless someone else with a card, email, or text. Generally, if we make thankfulness and gratitude a big part of our lives, we will find that stress, anxiousness, and disagreeable behavior begin to recede. Living in conflict or contention with others can easily rob us of the joy that comes from living thankfully and gratefully.

DAY 103

Confidence is a quality that many good athletes possess. They are confident in their abilities or their teammates or their coaches. And possibly all three. If you thought today of where you place your confidence, you might name the Lord, family members, some friends, scripture, and possibly some other places. Just six verses into Philippians, Paul picked up the theme of confidence. He had an unreserved and unhindered faith in something. "Being confident of this, that he who began a good work in you will carry it on to completion until the day of Christ Jesus" (Philippians 1:6). Paul was confident in the Lord. He knew that he could trust the Lord to begin and finish any good work. God's purposes, plans, and promises would never fade or fail.

Paul likely based this confidence on his relationship with the Lord. He had experienced the faithfulness of God in the circumstances of his daily life. He knew he could trust God in a prison cell, on a missionary journey, or while preaching the Gospel to a group of listeners. He knew that he could count on the Lord. He also knew that he could count on the promises of God. God's reliability and trustworthiness in the past were great encouragements as this apostle looked to the future. One of the best predictors of the future is the past. We can base our confidence in God in the future on how He has provided for us and blessed us in the past. Paul likely had a lengthy list of the many ways that he had experienced God's power and provisions as he preached, wrote, traveled, and taught the Gospel.

This passage in Philippians teaches us that God is at work in us to make us more like His Son Jesus. One aspect of salvation is sanctification. Even though it is a big word, we have a simple way to understand it.

Sanctification is becoming more like Christ every day and in every way. This process occurs over a lifetime. We all have moments and days where we do not feel or even act very Christlike. The old self pushes through in what we say or do. But over the span of a lifetime, God is at work to increase our likeness to Christ and decrease the amount of old self that pushes or breaks through us. The Christian life can often be compared to a mountain chain where there are peaks and valleys, but the general trend is upward until one reaches the summit. For believers, the summit is the day that we go to be with the Lord and enjoy the eternal dwelling that He has prepared for us. We call that summit glorification.

We do not know when the end of life will be, but we can stand confident that God will welcome us into His company and into what He has prepared for us. God is perfect and the only One worthy of full trust, faith, and confidence. God cannot improve and cannot become better. He is perfect and will always remain so. Like Paul, we can take great joy in knowing that we walk with One who is perfect—perfect in position, power, and purpose. Live with confidence today—the confidence that you have in the Lord God! He will complete and conclude all that He has ever started.

DAY 104

Paul's letter named Colossians was intended for the Christians in the city of Colosse. This city was located in what we know as modern-day Turkey. The apostle greeted his readers as "God's holy people" and faithful "brothers and sisters in Christ" (Colossians 1:2). Clearly, the believers in that city meant so much to him and had a special place in his heart and ministry. He began his letter to the Colossians with a stirring offer of thanksgiving and an opening prayer. We read, "We always thank God, the Father of our Lord Jesus Christ, when we pray for you, because we have heard of your faith in Christ Jesus and of the love you have for all God's people" (Colossians 1:3–4). A few lessons stand out for us to see in this simple prayer.

First, Paul said that the mere memory of these Colossian believers moved him to give thanks to God. Are there people for whom you profess profound gratitude and thankfulness? God often places people in our lives that move us to heartfelt thanks and deep appreciation. The Thanksgiving season is where we take a more careful look or accounting of where God has blessed us and provided for us. One such source of blessing could be the people that God sends into your life. You might be thankful for a teacher, a neighbor, your doctor, a coach, or an employer who blessed you in some lasting and special way.

Second, Paul took note of the faith of the Colossians. Their confidence and trust in God stood out for Paul to see. He prayed for God to continue to fill the Colossians with the knowledge of His will and wisdom. Do you admire someone's faith? Is there a person you would single out for possessing an amazing and inspiring faith? Learning to trust God more profoundly and more consistently is a lesson that many of us would love to master. We can pray for the Lord to increase our faith. The disciples did. We can ask God to help us develop a deeper faith that can glorify Him and encourage others around us.

Third, Paul acknowledged the love of the Colossians (for Him and for other believers). Their fellowship was sweet and endearing. One aspect of their love might have been their willingness to root out false teaching and immorality. They loved truth and righteousness more than deception and sin. These two sins were consistent challenges and threats to churches and believers in the first century. It has been said that the church that corrects is the church that loves. The Colossians could have been aggressive in addressing false teachers and wolves in sheep's clothing that threatened the truth and harmony of the church. Paul gave a stern warning about the dangers of worldly wisdom in Colossians 2:8, "See to it that no one takes you captive through hollow and deceptive philosophy, which depends on human tradition and the elemental spiritual forces of this world rather than on Christ."

To counteract "hollow and deceptive philosophy" as Paul stated, we are to continue in Christ and to hold fast to Him and in Him. Live with gratitude, faith, and love in the face of the world's assaults and traps. Paul wrote in Colossians 3:15, "Let the peace of Christ rule in your hearts since as members of one body you were called to peace. And be thankful." A spirit of gratitude often turns our thoughts to the Lord. And when we think of the Lord, we express gratitude. Gratitude pays huge dividends as it builds our faith and love and opens us to what God is doing in our lives and all around us.

DAY 105

In our Bibles, we have two letters that Paul wrote to the Christians in Thessalonica. Paul had likely founded this church during his second missionary journey. Paul's message to the Thessalonians in his first letter was not as concentrated or focused on doctrine as much as some of his previous letters like Galatians, Ephesians, and Romans. He wrote 1 Thessalonians in a more personal way, seeking to encourage and exhort his readers in their Christian living.

In 1 Thessalonians 1:6–7, Paul encouraged his readers to be models or examples for Christ that their neighbors could see. He wrote, "You became imitators of us and of the Lord, for you welcomed the message amid severe suffering with the joy given by the Holy Spirit. And so, you became a model to all the believers in Macedonia and Achaia." Christians can be examples and models for an unbelieving world to see and observe. Our lives can often draw others to Christ. Perhaps you could name some people in your past or present whose lives were instrumental in you personally coming to faith in Christ. It could be a family member, a teacher, a coach, or a fellow employee whose life was a compelling argument for Christ. You simply could not dismiss it.

Paul would later write in 1 Thessalonians 1:9 that believers there had turned to the one true God from idols and paganism. As they left their sinful past and disobedience behind, they became examples to others who might have wished to leave a life of idolatry and immorality. Courageous decisions of faith, boldness in living your faith, and consistently seeking the Lord are all ways that God can work through your life and witness to reach others with the same Gospel message that changed and transformed your life.

There is an expression called "divine appointments." This expression means that God has been at work to orchestrate encounters, conversations, and exchanges where He can work through a believer to impact or influence another person, a home, or a situation for His glory. God may well have orchestrated a divine appointment in your life where you had a chance to declare the Gospel or offer a word of faith to another person. Never discount such an opportunity. The Bible is full of examples of God sending people on a mission to speak about His grace, the Gospel, or Christ Himself. David Platt has written that "God in His providence has not called us to watch history but rather to shape history for the glory of His great name." Be a shaper of history whenever God gives you an occasion to glorify His name and ways.

One of the first places you can be a model or influence is the home itself. Be proactive in making your home a place for Christ and where conversations about Christ and faith can be conducted and shared. Consider serving as a family in one of the many ministries, mission trips, and projects that we offer through our church. Shop for and fill a couple of shoeboxes for Operation Christmas Child. Let your home be a place where Christ is an honored guest and a frequent subject of conversation. Just as Paul took note of the influence of the Thessalonians, may others see that in you as well.

DAY 106

Paul's second letter to the Thessalonians cleared up some misconceptions that the believers in that town had about the Lord's second coming and how they were to prepare for such an event. He began by encouraging the believers in Thessalonica not to be "unsettled or alarmed" that they had in some way missed the Lord's coming (2:2). They were not to allow themselves to be deceived "in any way" (2:3). Through the generations, some misguided individuals have attempted to assign dates and times to the Lord's coming, and each one has been completely wrong—all the while, thousands of believers have been duped and deceived. Be careful about gullibly falling for deception, false teaching, and smooth-sounding tall tales. Theories about the end of the planet are a dime a dozen and easily peddled by those looking to make a name or a buck.

The antidote to deception is the truth and thinking clearly and soberly about important matters of faith. Paul encouraged the Thessalonians with these words about standing firmly on truth alone. "So then, brothers and sisters, stand firm and hold fast to the teachings we passed on to you, whether by word of mouth or by letter. May our Lord Jesus Christ himself and God our Father, who loved us and by his grace gave us eternal encouragement and good hope, encourage your hearts and strengthen you in every good deed and word" (2:15–17). Keep scripture's commands and teachings about the Lord's return at the forefront of your thinking. Do not be deceived by questionable bestsellers, slick teachings, and people who may claim to have all the answers. We trust that the Lord will come again at a time of the Father's choosing. Our mission is simply to stay ready.

Paul prayed that his readers in Thessalonica might be encouraged "in every good deed and word" (2:17). They were to continue doing what was right. They were to press on in their service to the Lord. They were to continue to share the Gospel. They were to continue to grow in their faith and understanding of God's Word. A bit further in chapter 3, Paul encouraged the Thessalonians not to become idle or passive. "Now may our God and Father himself and our Lord Jesus clear the way for us to come to you. May the Lord make your love increase and overflow for each other and for everyone else, just as ours does for you" (3:11–12). There is no need to drop out and look to the sky waiting for the Lord's return.

We are to press on with whatever God has given us to do. We are to work at our jobs, engage in family life, worship, serve the Lord, and share the Gospel. Paul challenged his readers to resist urges to drop out and drop off and live in an idle and passive way. Stay on target, and stay focused on the work the Lord has entrusted to you. Paul even went so far as to warn the Thessalonians not to associate with those who made a mockery of the Lord's second coming or marginalized the daily work of serving, worshipping, and making the Gospel known. The apostle did not want to see believers corrupted and misled by false teachers who simply were wrong in their beliefs and behavior.

To prepare for the Lord's return, we stay focused on loving Him, serving Him, making the Gospel known, and living as salt and light in the places and situations where God may call us to be or place us. God does not expect us to abandon the daily ways that we have to serve Him. Be not anxious about the Lord's return but rather be at peace. Indeed, Paul ended his letter by saying to his readers (and us), "Now may the Lord of peace himself give you peace at all times and in every way" (3:16). We can confidently trust God to manage both the present and the future while we serve Him in the ways that He has given us.

DAY 107

Paul and Timothy shared a special relationship. They were more like a father and son than merely co-laborers or coworkers in the Gospel. They were bound together in Christ and their shared faith in the Lord Jesus. Indeed, Paul referred to Timothy as "my true son in the faith" (1 Timothy 1:2). Later, in 1 Timothy 1:18, Paul again referred to Timothy as "my son." The older apostle was even brutally honest about the way he regarded himself. He wrote, "Here is a trustworthy saying that deserves full acceptance: Christ Jesus came into the world to save sinners—of whom I am the worst" (1 Timothy 1:15). Not many of us would share so honestly and candidly about ourselves. Yet Paul possessed the kind of relationship with Timothy where he was completely comfortable in doing so. They knew each other, trusted each other, and loved each other in Christ.

It is good to have a friendship (or maybe two or three) where you can share freely, openly, and candidly with someone and know that they have your best interest at heart and will hold confidentially and discreetly to whatever you share. While Paul's first letter to Timothy was similar to a father writing to his son, it was also a correspondence between two Christian brothers who shared a common faith in the Lord Jesus. While Paul could counsel and instruct Timothy, he could also lean on him for spiritual support and encouragement. What a blessing to have someone in your life whom you can trust in such a way!

Near the end of this letter, Paul gave Timothy some guidance that speaks to us today. We read, "Timothy, guard what has been entrusted to your care. Turn away from godless chatter and the opposing ideas of what is falsely called knowledge, which some have professed and in so doing have departed from the faith" (1 Timothy 6:20–21). There are at least two good life lessons that stand out for us. First, Paul says that we are to be good guardians of what has been entrusted to us. If someone shares a battle or struggle with you, guard what has been shared. Maintain discretion and prudence. Often, a trusted ear and closed mouth are the best gifts you can offer to someone who may be going through a battle in life. Likewise, if you are entrusted with property, a responsibility, a task, or practically anything you can imagine, demonstrate that you are worthy of such trust. Treat what has been entrusted to you as if the Lord Himself placed it in your care.

Second, never waste time with godless chatter or endless and aimless arguments and battles. You do not always have to participate in the fruitless divisions and conflicts that some people enjoy perpetuating. Stay focused on what God has given you or called you to do. The enemy can easily distract us and divert our attention away from the things that matter and require the best we can muster. You can pray for the misguided, but you do not have to let them hijack your mission or the work of the day. We have no obligation to be the stone upon which someone chooses to grind his or her axe.

Paul gave Timothy (and us) something better to consider and to pursue in 6:11. We read, "But you, man of God, flee from all this, and pursue righteousness, godliness, faith, love, endurance and gentleness." These six verses are worthy pursuits for us. They have more to offer others and us. Give thanks to the special person or persons that God brings into your life in a special friendship or way. Guard what they mean to you and bless them as they bless you. Together, like Paul and Timothy, you can both encourage each other for the glory of God and the greater work of Christ.

DAY 108

Paul wrote a second letter to Timothy. Some people believe this was either Paul's final letter that we have in our Bibles or at least one of his last letters. He gave some parting words to his "son" in the faith. He quickly made clear how he felt about Timothy. He wrote, "I thank God, whom I serve, as my ancestors did, with a clear conscience, as night and day I constantly remember you in my prayers" (2 Timothy 1:3). There may be someone now for whom you would offer an immediate prayer of thanks. This person may have blessed you in some way recently or their mere presence in your life remains a blessing to you. They have stood beside you for years and you love and trust them. The apostle Paul was never reluctant about identifying the people that the Lord had used to bless him in his journeys and preaching. Timothy was one such man. And early on in this second letter, Paul wanted Timothy to know how special he was.

Paul gave Timothy some fatherly advice in 2 Timothy 1:7. We read, "For the Spirit God gave us does not make us timid, but gives us power, love and self-discipline." With God's power and help, we can live courageously. The Lord gives us the strength that we would otherwise be lacking by ourselves. This strength comes to us in the midst of trials and adversity. We experience this strength when we serve the Lord or speak up for Him. We also possess the power we need to root out sin, defiance, and disobedience from our lives. God gives us the strength we need to practice the basic Christian disciplines like worship, personal Bible reading, prayer, tithing, serving, and spending time in silence before the Lord. These practices are not ordinarily what we might pursue, so we must "discipline" ourselves to pursue them. But the blessings are ours when we practice the great disciplines of the Christian faith.

One of Paul's themes in 2 Timothy is faithfulness. Generally speaking, he issued a call to Timothy (and to us) to be faithful in all things. We read in 2 Timothy 3:14–15, "But as for you, continue in what you have learned and have become convinced of, because you know those from whom you learned it, and how from infancy you have known the Holy Scriptures, which are able to make you wise for salvation through faith in Christ Jesus." The keyword is *continue*. The Christian life is a marathon. We are running to the finish line, which is eternity with the Lord. We want to prove ourselves faithful with the blessings, opportunities, and avenues that the Lord has given to us. The keyword *continue* implies uninterrupted, ongoing action. We do not succumb to weariness, and we do not leave the race. We press on.

It could be that God is encouraging you to continue in your faith in some way. Maybe you have recently felt some sense of discouragement in your faith. Maybe you have battled the temptation to quit or to drop out of your race. Perhaps trials or battles have left you feeling weary and worn down. Maybe your walk with the Lord has not gone very far recently. You feel like you are walking in mud or even sinking in quicksand. It could be time to come back to where you once were, to embrace the key spiritual disciplines of faith we named a bit earlier, and to trust God to provide you with the power and strength that you need. Paul reminded us in 2 Timothy that God uses His Word to equip us for every good work. We can count on this promise and for God's Word to do what He has promised it will do. Continue on today! Do not grow weary, and do not let the enemy sideline you. Reach out to the Lord who will equip you for every good work.

DAY 109

Titus was a young pastor who had been charged with spreading the Gospel and building disciples for Christ on the island of Crete. Paul wrote a three-chapter letter to Titus to encourage him in the work that had to be done. One of Paul's main themes was doing good works. To be sure, Titus does not teach or embrace a message of salvation by good works. For example, Paul wrote, "He saved us, not because of righteous things we had done, but because of his mercy. He saved us through the washing of rebirth and renewal by the Holy Spirit, whom he poured out on us generously through Jesus Christ our Savior, so that, having been justified by his grace, we might become heirs having the hope of eternal life" (Titus 3:5–7). Though not saved by good works, we are saved to do what is good and to serve the Gospel. We often have the ability to introduce others to Christ because we have been able to bless their lives in some sort of tangible way through what we have done.

In Titus 2, Paul wrote about the roles and duties of various groups of individuals like older men and women, younger men and women, and slaves. The principle behind this instruction was doing what was good. Good was defined as being self-controlled, maintaining order and godliness in the home, having integrity, sound speech, purity, kindness, embracing the Word of God, and rejecting ungodliness and worldly passions. A well-timed word for us today is Titus 3:9. We read, "But avoid foolish controversies and genealogies and arguments and quarrels about the law, because these are unprofitable and useless." We can easily get drawn into foolishness—foolish conversations and controversies that are not worth the time or breath that we spend pursuing them. These fruitless endeavors can easily draw us away from the greater things that God would have us pursue.

We all have a relatively short period of time on earth to live and serve the Lord as He calls us to do. That time is running out as the days go by. We want to ensure that we are using our days to do what is good and to bless those God may put before us. Paul gave a final admonition to Titus in 3:14. We find, "Our people must learn to devote themselves to doing what is good, in order to provide for urgent needs and not live unproductive lives." Paul says we have to learn to devote ourselves to what is good. By nature, we usually do not do such things. We have to learn how to devote our time and lives to the things that matter most in life. Influence others in a godly way, be eager to share the Gospel, do what is good, and lean on the Lord. Again, these activities are not naturally wired into us. But the Holy Spirit can help us to make them mainstays in our lives each day.

While we wait for Christ, Titus shows us the good and worthy things that we can do. Waiting for the Lord's return is not a navel-gazing or sky-gazing endeavor. We are to do what the Lord has given us to do so that when He does come again, He finds that we are faithful to Him and His assignments.

DAY 110

Philemon is a personal letter from Paul to an individual. The apostle wrote to make a personal appeal to Philemon to receive back Onesimus who was once a slave. This once runaway slave had been converted to faith in Christ through the preaching and influence of Paul. There is an inference or suggestion in verse 18 that he might have robbed his master and fled to Rome to go into hiding. Paul even offered to pay back and settle any outstanding debts that needed resolution (verse 19). Paul asked Philemon to receive Onesimus back as though he were receiving back the apostle himself.

There certainly are times in faith when we have to do the hard thing. It might be easier to look away or even to run away (as Onesimus did). But the Lord calls us to do the right thing, and the right thing may often be very hard to recognize and even harder to bring into reality. God often closes certain doors so that we have only the right door to open or the right pathway to pursue. It could be that God is closing some doors in your life at this moment. Maybe God is directing your steps in a new and different way. It can be frightening to move in new directions. And complacency can often be a tempting alternative.

God often works in ways that seem inconceivable or incredible to us. Paul pled with Philemon to welcome back Onesimus not as a slave but as a brother in Christ. That's a substantial upgrade in a relationship. Paul wrote, "Perhaps the reason he was separated from you for a little while was that you might have him back forever— no longer as a slave, but better than a slave, as a dear brother. He is very dear to me but even dearer to you, both as a fellow man and as a brother in the Lord" (Philemon 15–16). God was at work to change the dynamics from slave/master to brothers in Christ. Only God could do something that extraordinary. Only God could make that transformation happen.

But in Christ, all things are possible. We can enjoy new life and renewed relationships. We can enjoy new doorways and pathways that take us from where we are to where we could be—an experience of life in a new and amazing way. The enemy often deceives us into thinking that we are simply stuck—stuck in a place in life from which there is little hope and no discernible means of escape. The enemy would have us believe that we have no other recourse or plan to follow. But Paul's letter shows us that God can overcome obstacles and barriers to set us on a new course that leads to a better place. The journey may not be easy, but it will be right.

DAY 111

As we approach the end of the New Testament, we find the book of Hebrews. The primary theme of this book is the superiority of Jesus and the work that He completed through His life, death, and resurrection. There is no real consensus about who wrote this book. People have suggested the author could be Paul, Barnabas, Apollos, Luke, and a host of other first-century Christians. Rather early in this book, the writer makes an argument for the superiority of Christ to Moses or any other luminary or leader from the Old Testament and Israel's history. "Jesus has been found worthy of greater honor than Moses, just as the builder of a house has greater honor than the house itself. For every house is built by someone, but God is the builder of everything. 'Moses was faithful as a servant in all God's house,' bearing witness to what would be spoken by God in the future. But Christ is faithful as the Son over God's house. And we are his house, if indeed we hold firmly to our confidence and the hope in which we glory" (Hebrews 3:3–6). A few lessons or truths about Christ stand out for us to see.

First, we can see Christ as a builder. He is the foundation for the house of faith that God has created the finished work of the Son at the cross and the empty tomb. There is no greater foundation for faith than the one we find in Christ. As amazing as the Church may be through the centuries, the builder is of even greater acclaim and esteem.

Second, Christ did greater work than Moses. The venerated leader of the Exodus did the work of God in rallying and leading Israel out of Egyptian slavery and captivity. He received the law of God. He pleaded with God to be gracious and kind to Israel even when the nation was in rebellion and defiance against him. Though Moses did not enter the promised land, he led the people to the frontier of it. But Christ did even more. Christ satisfied the justice and wrath of God and made the way to God open for all—Jews and Gentiles alike. Christ canceled sin's penalty and made the way open for resurrection and everlasting life.

Third, we are the new creation that Christ has made. In Christ, the new has come and the old has departed. As this new creation, we live in new ways, and we live in ways that serve as examples of the power that Christ has at work in us. Hebrews 3:15 says, "Today, if you hear His voice, do not harden your hearts as you did in the rebellion." When we see that we have grown hardened, bitter, or jaded in some way, the Lord calls us back to His healing and purifying grace. The old battles and scars do not need to linger in us or on us. They do not need to turn us into something we will likely regret. These old scars do not need to carry us back to a time of division and discord from which Christ has freed us. We are to live into the new life that the Lord has bought and won for us through His death and resurrection.

And fourth, we hold on to the hope and confidence that we have in Christ. He is Lord of all—life, battles, trials, the present, and the future. We place our faith in Him to protect us and to fight for us. Moses told the people of Israel that the Lord would fight for them and that they only needed to be still and behold His glory. We trust that the Lord is our warrior and champion today as He wins the battle for us.

DAY 112

Many sports, professions, organizations, and pursuits have a "hall of fame." and to be enshrined in a hall of fame is usually a high honor. An inductee into a hall of fame has reached the pinnacle of success in a chosen field. You may be surprised to learn that the Bible has not a hall of fame but a hall of faith. Hebrews 11 is often called a "hall of faith." We learn how God sees faith and what His expectations are of us. The opening two verses give us a wonderful summary of what faith is and how it works. We read, "Now faith is confidence in what we hope for and assurance about what we do not see. This is what the ancients were commended for" (Hebrews 11:1–2). A few lessons stand out for us about faith.

First, faith "is." That might sound or look confusing. But faith is. Faith "is" means that faith is something we do. It is an action that we undertake. We place our faith in someone, something, or somewhere. Faith is not passive; it is not idle or whimsical hoping or wishing. Faith is leaning upon something or someone. Faith is resting one's full weight and trust in something that is reliable and trustworthy. For us, faith is best placed in Christ. We trust in Him and His finished work at the cross for our salvation and forgiveness.

Second, faith is "confidence in what we hope for." We know that God will work on our behalf for His glory and to bring about what He has promised to do. We can be confident that God knows our situation in life. We can be confident that God will take action on our behalf. We are not alone, forgotten, or forsaken. God is not weak or impotent. God is a bulwark that never fails. He is our anchor in storms and our rudder through turbulent times and waters.

Third, we have assurance about what we do not see. We cannot see God, yet we trust in Him. We cannot see the future, yet we trust that God will meet our needs and provide for us. We cannot see the way the world will end, yet we trust that God is writing the final words of history and will bring His creation to the end that He wishes to see. We wake up each day not knowing what the day will hold, but we have the firm assurance that God knows the future, has already seen the day that is unfolding and will provide for us throughout the circumstances of the day.

The Bible teaches that we live by faith and not by sight. Living by sight can be confusing and even frightening. We can be sidelined and tripped up by what our eyes behold each day. It is much better to trust what we see and what we cannot see to the Lord and trust Him to bring life and faith to completion. This week would be a good time to celebrate the victories that God has brought to you by faith. Remember and recall where God has been at work and what He has done. When you express your thanks to God, you are even acknowledging by faith that you believe He will continue to work in your life and continue to provide for you. Let faith be your compass and heading. Let faith be the steering wheel of your life. Let faith be your windshield.

DAY 113

The Christian faith has often been likened to a race. Indeed, Paul sprinkled his letters with a variety of sports metaphors with running or racing being one of them. Hebrews 12 borrows from the sport of running to teach us some important faith lessons. We read, "Therefore, since we are surrounded by such a great cloud of witnesses, let us throw off everything that hinders and the sin that so easily entangles. And let us run with perseverance the race marked out for us, fixing our eyes on Jesus, the pioneer and perfecter of faith. For the joy set before him he endured the cross, scorning its shame, and sat down at the right hand of the throne of God" (Hebrews 12:1–2). A few lessons stand out about faith and how we run our race of faith.

First, we are not alone. We are running with other believers from across the world and the span of nations. We have to run our race. No one can do that for us. But we are not running alone. We have the company or fellowship of other believers. We also have the example and model of biblical characters that we can follow. The men and women of the Bible were not perfect humans. Like us, they were sinners and often failed the Lord. But we can find examples in their lives of how we are to live and what we are to do. We can be encouraged by the example of ordinary believers and the way they ran their race.

Second, we are to cast off or toss aside anything that may hinder us in our race. We are not to entertain sin or wickedness. We are not to keep company with temptation. We are to remove influences and impediments that might trip us up or keep us from running with the kind of stamina and endurance that God would like to see us produce. Some matters may not be sinful, but they simply slow us down or capture our energy and focus. All things that keep us from running a good race of faith must be pruned away.

Third, we are to fix our eyes on Jesus. Any runner knows that the quickest way to lose a race is to look at other runners or to turn one's head. Running requires that we focus straight ahead and pay little mind to what is happening around us or behind us. In faith, we are to look squarely at Jesus. We trust Him to provide for us. We trust Him to show us the track where we are to run. We trust Him to lead us to where we need to be. We lean on Christ and cast on Him any cares or burdens that might keep us from running as we should.

Fourth, we run the race that is marked out for us. God has a pathway for us to follow. That pathway is for our good and His glory. We cannot run someone else's race. We have to run "the race that is marked out for us." God may be working to produce patience in your life or to chip away at hard feelings and a calloused heart. We trust that God will finish what He has started in us if we will faithfully run for Him.

And fifth, we run with endurance. We are not to pick certain days to serve the Lord and forget about Him at other times. We are not to fight temptation only when we may feel like it. We build endurance through Bible study, prayer, worship, serving, and leaning into the Lord much as a runner would develop his skills through training, diet, and preparation. We lean into the Lord like a runner leans forward as he approaches the finish line. One quality often lacking in God's people today is endurance. Believers often take themselves out of the race or beat a pathway to the sidelines. Do not drop out from the race of faith. Run with endurance and finish each day as strongly as you can as you live in anticipation of the crown of life.

DAY 114

Most of us would likely say that trials are not fun. Life's battles are usually not enjoyable. We might compare trials and battles to some of our most dreaded experiences or encounters in life. But we can count on the reality of trials and battles. No one is immune. There is no shield that will insulate us from battles or trials. James wrote about trials in the opening chapter of his New Testament letter. He said that trials have some value and pay some good dividends. We read, "Consider it pure joy, my brothers and sisters, whenever you face trials of many kinds, because you know that the testing of your faith produces perseverance. Let perseverance finish its work so that you may be mature and complete, not lacking anything" (James 1:2–4). James helps us to reframe our perspective about trials. We learn some important truths to remember when we go through trials.

First, we will face trials. James used the word *whenever*. Trials are a matter of "when" and not "if." Most folks fall into one of three camps—going into a trial, in the middle of a trial, or emerging from a trial. We live in a fallen world. We are sinful ourselves. Life is not an exercise in fairness or goodness. We are often surrounded by trials that trip us and ensnare us. So James wants us to be prepared.

Second, trials can lead to joy. How? Well, trials can lead to some good things in life—perseverance, faith, maturity, completeness in your walk with the Lord, and your service to Him. God works in trials and through trials. We often learn more in and through adversity than prosperity. Trials often put a spotlight on our hearts and minds so we can see where we stand and where God might like us to go. We can look back after a trial has passed and celebrate what we have gained and where God was at work.

Third, we can experience God in richer ways through trials. Let's face it, if life were perfect, we would probably not seek the Lord very often or walk with Him very closely. We can take huge steps forward in our relationship with God through trials and battles. We delve into His Word. We fall before Him in prayer. We ask others to pray for us, and we welcome their intercessions. Trials can reveal the kind of root system that our faith has and whether we are building and living on the right foundations.

Fourth, trials lead to perseverance. You develop some spiritual toughness and tenacity. This perseverance to the end enables you to share what you have learned with others. You can testify to God's goodness and power. You can tell others about how God provided for you and led you through the trial. Sadly, the sidelines of life are littered with believers who have been tripped up by the enemy or who have dropped out of the race of faith. Do not join them. Trust God to see you through these trials and battles. Let him be your strength. Perseverance leads to maturity and completion in faith. When we press on, we are blessed by all that God has for us. We never want to miss a single blessing or expression of grace that God has for us. Do not let the enemy trick you into thinking that sitting down or leaving the race is the way to go or the easy way out. Stay in the race, and let God show His power in the midst of your trials.

DAY 115

Wisdom is a virtue that we all need. But we often find ourselves lacking wisdom. We can lack wisdom about any number of things—finances, family, faith, or failures we have suffered. God's wisdom is perfect—about anything at any time. Indeed, the Bible is a collection of wisdom that can be applied to real life and real circumstances here and now. The book of Proverbs alone is a graduate-level education in practical wisdom. James wrote, "If any of you lacks wisdom, you should ask God, who gives generously to all without finding fault, and it will be given to you" (James 1:5). We find six good lessons that James has for us in this one verse.

First, we all lack wisdom at times. No one knows everything. And nobody handles every situation in life perfectly and without fault. Frankly, we often gain wisdom from bad decisions and bad experiences. Failure can be a good teacher. But if you think you lack wisdom, you are not alone. We all share that frustration and find that wisdom can often be in short supply. We have to acknowledge those times when we lack wisdom or certainty. When we admit what we are missing, we are ready for what God can supply.

Second, God possesses complete and full wisdom. He knows everything there is to know at the same time and all the time. God never has to learn anything. Nothing is ever new to Him. God was "in the beginning." And God will be alive for eternity. It is rather mind-blowing to consider that God has always existed. Wow! How do we even begin to imagine that? Humanly speaking, we cannot get our finite minds wrapped around it. The One who has always had perfect wisdom and guidance on any matter we wish to take to Him. In so many instances, God has already revealed in His Word exactly what we need to see or do.

Third, God is the giver of wisdom. We have His Word. We have His Holy Spirit living in us and with us. We have His assurance and promise to be with us always—even to the end of the age. We have His commitment to hear us when we pray—ask, seek, or knock. So yes, we can ask God for wisdom. We can ask for guidance and godly understanding when we need it. We can ask Him to open our eyes, supply us with grace, grant us patience, give us endurance, and show us what we could not see by ourselves.

Fourth, God's wisdom can change our perspective. We often ask God to change situations or outcomes. A better prayer might be for God to change us. It may be that God wants to use a situation to sharpen our faith, teach us humility, show us how to forgive, or prepare us for service. We can easily think only about the present moment at hand and change it to something far better. But God acts with eternity in mind. He works to change character and perspective when we might prefer a shortcut or two.

Fifth, we need to embrace God's wisdom when He provides it. His answer might be 100 percent different from what we would have thought or expected. But when God shows us His way, it is our responsibility to follow it and pursue it. If we are not prepared to act on the wisdom that God gives us, then we should not ask for it.

And sixth, wisdom is an exercise in living by faith and not by sight. To us, it might not make sense to forgive, to hold our tongue, to avoid that social media post, to hold our fire when someone has hurt us. But divine wisdom might suggest we choose a different way to live or to act. God does not promise that we will always see the outcome in advance when we choose to trust Him. Rather, He calls us to trust Him first and promises that we will have the light and grace we need to move forward.

The best way to encounter God's wisdom, and to embed it into your life is reading His Word. There is no substitute for scripture reading and thirsting for God's Word. Time in His Word will exchange human wisdom for Godly wisdom, our ways for His ways, and frustration for faithfulness.

DAY 116

Christmas is the season of gift giving. Children share gift requests with Santa while sitting on his lap. Some retailers allow you to sign up for a gift registry. Some online sellers even allow you to compile a wish list. There is a popular Christmas song about a grown-up Christmas list. And remember that the wise men brought gifts to Jesus as they recognized who He truly was. Gift giving was originally God's idea. He gave us life. He gave Adam and Eve a perfect garden to call home. And at Christmas, we celebrate the greatest of all gifts—the birth of Jesus. Indeed, scripture reminds us that God's love is so great and so strong that He gave us His one and only Son. James is careful to remind us of the origin of the gifts we enjoy. James wrote, "Every good and perfect gift is from above, coming down from the Father of the heavenly lights, who does not change like shifting shadows" (James 1:17). A few lessons stand out about God for us to see.

First, God is the source or originator of every gift. Grace itself is a gift. James wrote comprehensively. "Every" gift, James wrote, comes from God. Not a few gifts but all gifts. By His perfect nature, God is a giver. Salvation itself is a gift. We do not work for salvation or try to earn it by our best efforts. We might receive gifts through people, organizations, or places, but God is the originator of all gifts that we possess.

Second, God knows how to bless us and provide for us. He knows what we need before we even ask for it or receive it. God does not randomly or haphazardly send blessings to us. He is aware of our situations in life and what we most need to have and when we need to have it. God is not limited to blessing us in only one particular way. Not every blessing is financial or material in nature. Some of God's greatest blessings are beyond human sight or hearing. We may not even be able to touch or handle them.

Third, God does not change. He is a giver and a provider. Like a loving earthly father knows what his children need or require, God does too. God does not play games with His blessings. He does not dangle them in front of us like we might dangle a string in front of a cat or something shiny in front of a baby. God's gifts are always better than we could have imagined or gained by ourselves. We can trust that God's gifts are exactly what is needed and when they are needed.

Fourth, God expects us to use the gifts that He provides. God blesses us so we can in turn bless others. God gives to us that we might give freely to others. One of God's greatest blessings is turning a clenched hand into an open hand or turning a miserly heart into a gracious and generous one. God once told Moses to look at what he already had in his hand. We can easily serve God with what we have now. We do not have to wait to be blessed before we can bless others. We already possess some blessings that can be turned into gifts that we offer to others.

James bids us to be both hearers and doers of the Word (James 1:22). He also instructs us to demonstrate or to show our faith by our deeds and the things that we do (James 2:18). In this season of gifts and gifting to others, look at what you already have and use it for His glory and the good of others.

DAY 117

Boasting is not something that most people enjoy hearing. Bragging and braggarts can become trying and tiresome before long. The Bible warns against boasting many times. In James's letter, we find a warning about a particular kind of boasting. James's concern was boasting about tomorrow or future events. He cautions us to be humble about the future and to seek the Lord before we get too far down the road in planning for what we might do tomorrow. We read, "Now listen, you who say, Today or tomorrow we will go to this or that city, spend a year there, carry on business and make money. Why, you do not even know what will happen tomorrow. What is your life? You are a mist that appears for a little while and then vanishes. Instead, you ought to say, if it is the Lord's will, we will live and do this or that" (James 4:13–15). There are some lessons for us to consider in these practical verses.

First, we are called to be humble about the future. We cannot see the future. And we want to be cautious about making bold and brash statements or plans for the future. When we are busy making plans, we can easily push God to the margins. Each day that God gives us is a gift. Why not seek His guidance for how we use the days we are given? As followers of Christ, our days are to be about serving Him and leaning on Him. Let God be part of your plans and dreams for the future. Why would we even want to consider a future where God is not part of it?

Second, we have to recognize our humanity. Life is compared to a mist or a vapor that vanishes quickly. A life that spans one hundred years is brief when compared to the scope of eternity. Even the longest-living human leaves just a trace behind when compared to the endless eternity that awaits. We can get so caught up in the future that we miss where God is at work in the present and what God is doing in our lives here and now. We want to be careful not to trade the joys of today for an uncertain and not even promised tomorrow. One way we can remember the brevity of life is to compare a day to the vastness of the universe. We may think a day or a week is long and just grinds along. But remember, space is measured in light-years or the time it takes from light to travel from one point to another.

Third, we recognize how fragile life is. Tomorrow certainly is not promised to anyone. We could find ourselves in the presence of the Lord at any moment. May we invest fully in the opportunities the Lord gives us today—in family life, on the job, in our relationships with others, and in our service to the Lord. We want to be careful not to leave behind unfinished business in our walk with the Lord.

Fourth, approach tomorrow with faith. Trust that God will lead you as you lean on Him. Let Him open doors rather than push through in human power and with human motivations. Much of life can be about waiting—waiting on the Lord and letting Him work on you in the meantime. We often enjoy holidays like Christmas and Easter and special days like baptisms, anniversaries, birthdays, and Sundays. But much of life is lived in the meantime between special days and special celebrations. Commit each day to the Lord shortly after waking up and ask Him for the grace, patience, and strength to live out whatever He has chosen for you.

As we think of the future, we can always draw strength from Romans 8:28 and remember that God is working all things together for the good of those who love Him and who have been called according to His purposes. We do not or cannot always see the work that God is doing, but we surely trust Him. There is an old cliché that says while we may not always see God's hand, we can always trust His heart. And indeed, we can. We know that His heart is good.

DAY 118

We know Peter as a fisherman turned disciple. We know him as an apostle and a missionary of the Gospel message in the early church of the first century. We know him as one who cut off the ear of Malchus who was the servant of the high priest at the time of Jesus's arrest. We know him as the disciple who swore that he would never abandon Jesus, only to deny Him not once or twice but three times.

Peter was one of the better-known figures of the New Testament and early Christianity. Two letters in the Bible bear his name. He wrote a combined eight chapters about Christian living and the hope that we possess in Christ. While we can identify and define Peter in a variety of ways, it might be best to let him speak for himself and identify himself as he chooses. Well, the old fisherman did that in 1 Peter 1:1. He gave the following personal introduction: "Peter, an apostle of Jesus Christ" (1 Peter 1:1). He connected his identity to Jesus.

How would you define yourself today? Husband, wife, father, mother, grandparent, child? Maybe you would open by identifying your current vocation or what you once did for a living. Some people might choose a title by which to identify themselves. But Peter chose Jesus. The Lord cast such a large shadow over Peter's life that there was no way he could choose anyone else. Now that says much about Peter's walk with Jesus! Does the Lord cast a greater shadow over your life than anyone else? To be sure, Peter was not perfect. He was impulsive, quick to anger, and unreliable, and his mouth tended to make claims that his life could not back up. He did not always stand up for Christ as he could or should have. If I am honest, I can say that I have a lot in common with Peter. There's evidence of Peter's faults that can be found in me every day.

One good way we can be like Peter is to identify with Christ. We can see ourselves first off as followers of Jesus. We may not be perfect and we may fall down a lot in our walk, but we can still say we are unapologetically followers of Jesus. There may be times when it does not look as solid or as shiny as we would like, but we still cling to the Lord. Near the end of his first letter, Peter gave a message that should remain with us forever. His words are a great comfort in those moments when we struggle and fail in our walk with the Lord. We read, "Humble yourselves, therefore, under God's mighty hand, that He may lift you up in due time. Cast all your anxiety on Him because He cares for you" (1 Peter 5:6–7). The cares, burdens, and even anxiety that may cause us to fall can be cast upon Him and released to Him. Indeed, we may stand for Christ in direct proportion to how much we cast upon Him.

To be a follower of Jesus means that we are casters of care—cast not to the wind but to Christ. You may feel like you fall down and fail more than you succeed in your walk with Christ. I know that feeling too. The more glorious vision that I have of Jesus often leads to an incredibly sober and humble vision of who and what I am. But we can take joy in knowing that just as Jesus was not finished with Peter even after Peter denied Him, our Lord is not finished with us yet either. There is still work to be done. And our Lord graciously does that work as we turn to Him.

At Christmas, we can give thanks for an amazing gift—a Lord who is still not finished with us even though we have given Him every reason to turn us away. Christmas is about Immanuel—God with us! A disciple of Christ is not perfect but persevering, not finished but following, and not stubborn but surrendered.

DAY 119

In 1 Peter 2:6–7, Peter the disciple spoke of Christ as the cornerstone or capstone of our faith. He wrote these words: "For in Scripture it says: See, I lay a stone in Zion, a chosen and precious cornerstone, and the one who trusts in him will never be put to shame. Now to you who believe, this stone is precious. But to those who do not believe,

The stone the builders rejected has become the cornerstone." The Lord Jesus is the cornerstone upon which we build our house of faith. We all know how critical the foundation is to the building of any home. A poor or unstable foundation calls into question the very sturdiness and safety of the entire home. We can easily make a comparison between home construction and faith construction. In faith, we are only as good as our foundation. Everything rests on the foundation that we select. This cornerstone that Peter had in mind held or tied together the whole structure (house or building). And Christ is the One who ties both life and faith together for us. He is the stone upon which we rest our faith and lives. He is the stone that does not fracture or fail.

Peter's use of the word *cornerstone* borrows from a tradition that in the building of the temple, the builders had dismissed or rejected an unusually shaped stone as being unsuitable for the temple, only to discover later that they needed just such a stone. People today reject Christ, only to discover that there is no other Savior or Lord available to forgive their sins and assure them of a new life. Like builders who rejected a stone for the temple, Christ too had been rejected by the people of His day—indeed His own people rejected Him and called for His crucifixion when given a choice.

This image of a cornerstone offers some faith lessons for us. First, Christ is our anchor. Much like a stone can be used to hold down something or to hold it in place, Christ holds us in place too. We have all that we need in Christ. We have no need to pursue another master or the trivial things in life. Christ balances us and stabilizes us when the winds of life beat against us. Second, Christ is everlasting and unchanging. A rock that you place on a table in your home will be there long after your life has come to an end. Stones are enduring. Christ endures as well. He is unchanging—indeed the same yesterday, today, and forever. He will neither fail nor fade away. We never have to worry about Christ failing us or defrauding us. He is everlasting. He does not enter and exit our lives based on whims or feelings.

Third, Christ brings the different parts of life and faith together for us. He can bring fulfillment to families, marriages, careers, relationships, and the way we spend our time. Like a cornerstone that ties a building together and makes the collective structure stronger than the individual pieces, Christ does the same for our lives. He holds us together and brings us together so that our one mission in life is to bring glory to Him and to live for Him. As Lord, Christ casts a wide shadow over all that we are. We leave no compartment or cubicle in life unyielded or unsurrendered to Him. We bring everything to Him.

A poor foundation calls into question the viability, safety, and stability of the entire structure. Likewise, the wrong cornerstone in life can lead us down dangerous and even deadly roads as we look for fulfillment and meaning in all the wrong places. Peter calls us to Christ—to his Savior and Lord with whom He walked and behind whom He followed. In these days, think about whether Christ is your cornerstone or just another rock. There is time to make the baby who was born in Bethlehem your firm foundation and your cornerstone.

DAY 120

In 2 Peter 3, the disciple wrote about God's way of measuring time. We do not possess God's perspective on time. Past, present, and future are all the same to the Lord and plainly in view before Him. While we cannot see the future, we also do not possess a perfect recall of the past or a perfect perspective on the present. Rather than the ticking away of seconds, minutes, or hours, God tends to see time from the perspective of accomplishing His purposes and divine will. Time is not something that God charts or counts. It is the environment where He does His work. We read in 2 Peter 3:8–9, "But do not forget this one thing, dear friends: With the Lord a day is like a thousand years, and a thousand years are like a day. The Lord is not slow in keeping his promise, as some understand slowness. Instead, he is patient with you, not wanting anyone to perish, but everyone to come to repentance." Two important perspectives stand out for us to see in Peter's words.

The first perspective is God's purposes. God is at work to bring forgiveness, salvation, and reconciliation to the world. Indeed, Christmas is the story of God's redemptive work. He sent forth His Son to do for us what we could never do for ourselves. He sent His Son to pay a horrible penalty for the sins we have committed. God's purpose is salvation—every day, all day, any day. Through the Son, the Father has ransomed us from Satan's captivity and clutch. We are no longer under the dominion of the evil one. We have been saved by the work of Christ at the cross—saved by grace through faith. God sees time as the forum for fulfilling His purposes. Think of it in this way—God worked in the past at the cross: He convicts us of our need for a Savior in the present, and He will welcome us into His heaven in the future. The past work of Jesus on the cross still applies to sin and sinners today. And what happens today impacts our eternal destiny. Again, time is the forum or the arena for the work of God to unfold.

The second perspective is patience. God is calling people to Him. His patience keeps people from perishing here and now. God is not slow. He is never late in doing His work. But He is patient. He operates by His standards and not the expectations of the world. God is not late in answering prayers. He does not procrastinate like we might be tempted to do. Because the past, present, and future are all plainly visible to God at the same time, He is able to craft the perfect answer to any prayer and the perfect response to any battle or challenge we face in life. God does not act impulsively or reflexively. He is not in reaction or response mode. He does not have to adjust and react to headwinds or circumstances. It stands to reason that we should place our faith in the One who shapes history rather than simply watching it happen.

Scripture says that God sent forth His Son in the fullness of time. That is to say, the Father chose the right time to bless Bethlehem with the birth of His Son and the whole world through His Son's life, death, and resurrection. We can wake up each day and patiently acknowledge that we already have all that we need to live through this new day. We can patiently navigate through the channels and corridors of the day as we meet them because we know God's purposes will provide all the light and grace we could possibly need. Give thanks today that God acts with purpose and patience. Long ago, the purposes of God led to an out-of-the-way town called Bethlehem with His Son entering the world at just the right time. And now, with patience and grace, God is still at work redeeming and reconciling all who believe in Him and look to Him in faith and trust.

DAY 121

Henry Wadsworth Longfellow was fondly called "America's Poet." He regaled nineteenth-century Americans with works such as "Paul Revere's Ride," "The Song of Hiawatha," and even a poem set to music that became the Christmas carol "I Heard the Bells on Christmas Day." Perhaps you have sung that carol many times yet never really knew the story or the power behind it. Here is a portion of how that song came to be part of our Christmas tradition. Longfellow was suffering from despair and depression over the loss of his wife Fanny to burns suffered in an accidental fire when her dress was consumed by flames. His heart was broken to learn that his son Charlie had been wounded in battle in the Civil War.

Longfellow had shut down—physically, emotionally, and spiritually. He had become a recluse in his own house—rarely venturing out and even then, only to purchase ether to help relieve and anesthetize the pain he carried. For a long time, he did not write anything. His pen was silent, and the inkwell was dry. His desk gathered dust and cobwebs. He was a tragic shell of the man, writer, and father that he had once been. A poet's once creative voice had been silenced by incredible and unresolved grief that seemed to multiply but never go away. On Christmas in 1863, he spoke with his minister who assured him that whatever he carried could be left with Christ. Longfellow may have lost his way, but Christ had not given up on Longfellow.

And then Longfellow wrote again, "I heard the bells on Christmas Day, their old familiar carols play, and wild and sweet the words repeat, of peace on earth, good will to men." And then, as he stumbled into the third verse, the grief and depression suddenly seized him and tormented him once again. He wrote, almost confessionally through the tortured pain of a broken heart, "And in despair I bowed my head, there is no peace on earth I said, for hate is strong and mocks the song, of peace on earth, good will to men." He stopped. The pen would not write anything else, and his heart was devoid of anything to say.

But then upon hearing the Christmas bells ring at the nearby church, Longfellow was gripped by God and the joy and hope that always reside in the arms and power of Christ and His birth. He remembered the laughter, innocence, and squeals of delight that accompanied the sound of those bells when his children were younger and the imagination and magic were still real to him.

The now-rejuvenated poet summoned the courage to write the fourth and fifth verses. "Then pealed the bells more loud and deep, God is not dead, nor doth He sleep, the wrong shall fail, the right prevail, with peace on earth, good will to men. Till ringing, singing on its way, the world revolved from night to day, a voice, a chime, a chant sublime, of peace on earth, good will to men." My friends, God always has the last word—not the earth, the grief, the circumstances we face, the sorrow we may carry, and the battles we often fight.

My friends, we may not think as often as we should about the simple lessons of Christmas and the simple images and symbols of Christmas like bells, manger scenes, carols, Christmas Eve worship, and the rare Christmas Day on a Sunday; but these simple things matter deeply and profoundly. They change lives. They change homes. They change nations and history. While earth may be unsettled and raging, there is power and Kingdom authority on the throne in heaven. Be gladdened and joyful for Christ has come. The goodwill of God has been poured out for us to see. May the familiar traditions and symbols of Christmas renew you and enliven you. May the small things that you see, touch, hear, and speak bring the reality of Christ into the troubled places that you might be carrying. May this Christmas renew you like no other one ever has.

If you are looking for something special to add to your Christmas journey, I encourage you to see the movie *I Heard the Bells*. It is playing in theaters now and tells the story of Henry Wadsworth Longfellow and his journey from despair to faith and from grief to joy. You will be blessed and moved to tears by this amazing story of faith and triumph.

DAY 122

John is a standout figure in the New Testament. He was a fisherman prior to hearing the Lord's call to become a fisher of men. His Gospel is distinctly different from the way Matthew, Mark, and Luke present the good news of Jesus. The way John introduces us to Jesus stands in contrast to Matthew's genealogy, Luke's story of the birth of Jesus, and Mark's starting point at the baptism. John unapologetically presented Jesus as God—God in the flesh.

John also contributed three letters and the book of Revelation to the New Testament. He casts a large and looming shadow over the Gospel message. In 1 John, we find an opening that is similar to the way John opened his gospel. We read, "That which was from the beginning, which we have heard, which we have seen with our eyes, which we have looked at and our hands have touched—this we proclaim concerning the Word of life" (1 John 1:1). Jesus did not come into existence in Bethlehem. Not at all. The birth of Jesus in Bethlehem was not His "beginning." As John pointed out, Jesus was from "the beginning." Our Lord has always existed. He is the Son of God who has revealed Himself as Father, Son, and Holy Spirit.

We also learn from John that Jesus was real—fully human in addition to being fully divine or fully God. John wrote that he had heard and seen Jesus. He had looked at Him and touched Him. There was no doubt that Jesus was real and walked among John and others in the first century. He was not a ghost or phantom. Equally, there was no doubt about His resurrection on Easter morning. The Lord walked out of the tomb and lives to this day.

In 1 John, the apostle made it clear that he would speak about and testify to the reality of Jesus so that others would know the Lord too. John wrote, "The life appeared; we have seen it and testify to it, and we proclaim to you the eternal life, which was with the Father and has appeared to us. We proclaim to you what we have seen and heard, so that you also may have fellowship with us. And our fellowship is with the Father and with his Son, Jesus Christ" (1 John 1:2–3). John shared what he knew and believed. We are called to do likewise—to speak and to declare how we have met the Lord and how He has entered our lives.

These opening three verses teach us four truths that we can apply to our lives today. First, we are not to be silent about the Gospel or our faith in Christ. We are to speak about the Lord and to make known how He has changed us. Just as you might talk about your favorite movie, team, or concert, talk about the Lord. Engage others in a conversation about the Gospel and God's love. Second, we need to invest in our faith. We want to grow in Christ and in our knowledge of Him. We do not want to meander through life in a stagnant way. May we live with a passion to grow in our faith. Third, we enjoy fellowship with other believers. We worship together. We serve together. We celebrate our faith with other brothers and sisters. I have had the chance to worship in many different places where I did not understand the language but felt a connection with my fellow believers. That connection was our fellowship in Christ. And fourth, John challenges us to be bold and courageous in sharing Christ. Share what He has done for you. Seize the opportunities that the Lord may give you. Never neglect a single chance where you can talk about the Lord and your faith. Trust that Christ will give you the courage to testify and to make Him known. After Jesus healed a blind man, this grateful man simply said, "I was blind but now I see" (John 9:25). A testimony does not have to be a book in length or deeply complicated with big words. We just confidently talk about how Christ has changed us.

DAY 123

Luke presents the beautiful Christmas story in chapter 2 of his Gospel. It is a familiar account to most of us. We read this story every year during the Christmas season. It is a story of majesty and simplicity. Luke told an amazing story of love in a way that even a child could understand. When we think of Luke 2, we may fondly remember the way Linus shared the Christmas story with Charlie Brown and the rest of the Peanuts gang. When *A Charlie Brown Christmas* originally aired in 1965, network executives were not happy about the inclusion of scripture in the script. But Charles Schultz, the creator of *Peanuts*, insisted that the Luke account remains in the show. And as they say, the rest is history. Today, it is hard to imagine not recalling the way Linus shared the Christmas story from Luke when Charlie Brown was at his wit's end.

In Luke 2:15, we read, "When the angels had left them and gone into heaven, the shepherds said to one another, 'Let's go to Bethlehem and see this thing that has happened, which the Lord has told us about.'" The first recorded example of people being excited about Christmas was not young children on Christmas morning in search of gifts. Oh no, it was these shepherds. Upon hearing the news, these shepherds dashed off to Bethlehem to see what the big fuss was all about. They did not wait. They took flight and left probably everything behind—including the flock over which they were keeping watch. But when the Lord calls, what else can you do?

Do we share the excitement of these shepherds today? Does Christmas still hold some special power over us? We know the story so well that we can easily take it for granted or underestimate it. We grow so accustomed to hearing the story that we can run the risk of reducing it to something ordinary or even pedestrian. We would do well to have the excitement of these shepherds and to revel in the majesty of what God has done in providing a Savior for us.

What gets you up and moving? What kicks you into higher gears and stokes a passion within you? Hopefully, your relationship with the Lord brings some joy and passion to your life each day. While Christmas can be one of the busiest and most consuming times of the year, it can also be a time of wonder and awe as we reflect on what Luke has to tell us. May we never lose the childlike or shepherd-like awe and wonder that we find in the Christmas season. May the coming of Jesus rouse us from our boredom, lethargy, laziness, and indifference. May we step up to see the Lord with greater vision and serve Him with greater passion. May we desire to know Christ and to enjoy Christ.

In the days to come, maybe there is something that will compel you to get up from where you are to see what the Lord is doing and to find where you can join Him. You might be able to share the Christmas story with someone who knows only bits and pieces of it. Perhaps there is someone you could serve with your blessings. Perhaps there is someone you would vow to pray for and to encourage with your words and life. These first shepherds recognized something awesome when they heard and saw what the Christmas angel and the heavenly host had to say. No way would they stay in the fields even one second longer. They got up, they got going, they got moving. May we be just as passionate about the Lord today and get moving ourselves. What if you decided to make this Christmas better than all the ones before—not because of what you gained but because of what you gave? Not because of what you watched happen but because of what you stood up and did. The Christmas story has been entrusted to us. May we share it, live it, and be energized by it.

DAY 124

Luke 2:8–9 says, "And there were shepherds living out in the fields nearby, keeping watch over their flocks at night. An angel of the Lord appeared to them, and the glory of the Lord shone around them, and they were terrified." The shepherds were part of the Christmas story and are generally part of any nativity scene or Christmas pageant. In the first century in Israel, shepherds were held in extremely low regard. They occupied a place at the bottom of society's class or pecking order. Generally, only lepers were below the shepherds in class standing. The fact that God would break the news of His Son's birth to shepherds is extraordinary—a feat that we might not fully recognize or appreciate today or ever. Because they spent most of their time with animals, shepherds were not allowed in the temple areas. They usually worked on the Sabbath and were regarded as ritually unclean 24-7. Few people, if any, would have placed a bet on shepherds' first hearing the good news of the Messiah's birth.

We know that Jesus was born in Bethlehem, so the Christmas shepherds were in that area of Israel when they heard the good news. Bethlehem was not far from Jerusalem where worship and sacrifices routinely took place at the temple. Over time, a rule or law was established that decreed Bethlehem was to be the holding place or the storehouse for animals that were destined to be sacrificed for the sins of the people. Thousands of sheep were slaughtered every year as offerings, atonement, and sacrifices for the sins of the people. Isn't it amazing that the *Lamb*, Jesus, would be born in a town known as a holding place or dwelling place for animals who were destined or bound to end up as sacrifices and offerings for sin and disobedience?

Consider what happened in Bethlehem—the *Lamb* of God, or Jesus, was born to pay the price for sin's penalty. It made perfect practical and theological sense that the greatest sacrifice of all—the very Son of God—would be born in a place known for supplying sheep for sacrifice. It also makes sense that God would announce the birth of the perfect *Lamb* to shepherds who knew all there was to know about sheep, sacrifices, and the way to Jerusalem from Bethlehem. God announced the birth of His sacrificial *Lamb* and Son to men who were responsible for keeping watch over the supply of sheep bound for sacrifice. The angel of the LORD appeared to the men in this field who were discarded as sinful, unclean, and separated from fellowship with God. The Christmas angel announced to these shepherds that the final and ultimate Passover Lamb had been born at last and that His perfect and innocent blood would cleanse sinners and bring those same sinners into intimate fellowship with God. Only God could do this!

These shepherds were the first to hear that God was making things right once again. In a field and village full of sheep, at last, the perfect *Lamb* had been born. And God declared this news not to the Roman emperor or any of the high priests but to the humble and lowly shepherds who knew all the details about sheep, sacrifices, and the way to the temple from Bethlehem. Just as the way to the Father was open at last to everyone—including shepherds, the way to the Father is open to us now. Jesus, the *Lamb* of God, is the way, the truth, and the life. And maybe today, you are ready to walk with God in new ways and richer ways. If you're feeling a bit lowly or down, you can't possibly be any lower than these Christmas shepherds were considered to be. And God appeared to them in one scintillating and unmatched night. Give thanks today that the good news of Christmas is for you too. And the Lord is now open for you to receive and embrace.

DAY 125

It is almost impossible to imagine what Mary must have been thinking as the day of her son's birth drew near. Any mother-to-be is thrilled with the first sight and touch of her baby boy or girl. Mary would have been no different. Yet she carried a very different baby boy in her womb. Jesus was not only her son but God's Son too. What raced through Mary's young and innocent mind as the days to Jesus's birth counted down? What would it have been like to make about a ninety-mile trip from Nazareth to Bethlehem while on the edge of giving birth at any possible moment? Some of us traveled between Nazareth and Bethlehem back in September in the comfort of a motor coach—imagine making that journey by animal or on foot! And pregnant too!

Near the end of Luke's Christmas account, we read the following comment about Mary: "But Mary treasured up all these things and pondered them in her heart" (Luke 2:19). To ponder means to consider, to reflect upon, to work through, or to work out in one's mind. Mary surely had much to ponder. She was a new mom, a soon-to-be-newlywed, a woman who had just given birth, and she was far from home. And by the way, she had just given birth to the Son of God—the second member of the Holy Trinity. Yes, there was much to work through and much to ponder. What dreams did she have for her son? What thoughts raced through her mind as she wrestled with whether or not she was up to the task? She must have had the same worries and anxieties that all new moms and dads go through. But she likely also pondered the joys of all that had just happened in her life—and the joys that would follow too.

What do you ponder at Christmas? What captures your thoughts and feelings as you read the Christmas story? Maybe you ponder the enormous grace and love that God expressed to the world by sending His Son to be our Savior. Maybe you are captured by the way God chose to save the world—not by armies or empires but through a baby born in a stable in a backwater town. Much to ponder. What do you pray for at Christmas? Where do you seek the Lord in your life? Where can God comfort, forgive, heal, or renew you?

Christmas is about God breaking into the affairs of the world—to shatter all that we think we know with His undeniable truth. Perhaps you are crying out for God to break into some aspect of your life. Maybe there is a place of ache or longing that you carry. Maybe you have carried this ache for longer than you would care to admit. But maybe as you ponder what God has done, you find that you can release this ache or burden to Him once and for all. I suspect Mary cast many cares upon the Lord as the majesty of Christmas night turned into the ordinariness of the next day. Raising the Son of God never got any easier. A few days remain before Christmas comes once again. Take time to ponder—your life, God's gift of His Son, where you have been, and where you are going. It has been said that an unexamined life is not worth living. Perhaps that is one person's way of saying we need to ponder more so we roam less.

The Advent season is all about waiting, anticipating, and yes, pondering. God gives us time to get ready for His Son's coming (the first coming and the second coming). Use the time well—ponder and pray. Read the Christmas story today or the prophecies of Isaiah and others who tell of that history-altering night in Bethlehem. And as you read, ponder, savor, and cherish every word. Let the Word capture you. And let the Word drench the words you speak and the thoughts that you entertain. May you treasure this Christmas that is coming. And may you carry forward a new experience with the Lord as you ponder His coming.

DAY 126

We might not expect to find much about Christmas or the Christmas story in 2 John, but we actually do. There is an important truth to be gleaned from this small one-chapter book near the end of the Bible. In his Gospel, John introduces us to the reality that Jesus is eternal. His birth in Bethlehem was only the beginning of His earthly existence. Jesus is eternal and everlasting—the Ancient of Days and the Word of God. He has always existed. In Revelation, John depicts Jesus as the Victor and the worthy Lamb of God who will come again one day. In 2 John 7, we find another glimpse of Jesus. John wrote, "I say this because many deceivers, who do not acknowledge Jesus Christ as coming in the flesh, have gone out into the world. Any such person is the deceiver and the antichrist." John made it clear that Jesus came in the flesh. The Son of God was born as the Son of Mary. Do not be deceived by those who might deny the human or fleshy side of Jesus. He had a real, physical body with bones, organs, and muscles that function just like yours or mine. John wrote that if we deny the humanity of Jesus, we are "antichrist."

To say that Jesus came in the flesh is an important article of faith. We are to acknowledge that God became man in the person of Jesus. We call this the incarnation where God took human form in the fullness of the Son. John wrote in his Gospel, "The Word became flesh and made his dwelling among us. We have seen his glory, the glory of the one and only Son, who came from the Father, full of grace and truth" (John 1:14). Because Jesus came in the flesh, He could live the perfect and righteous life that we have not lived and cannot live. By coming in the flesh, Jesus became the perfect and innocent sacrifice—the sinless Lamb of God who gave His life for the sins of the world. It is important to acknowledge that Jesus came in the flesh—vitally so.

Early Christianity often had to contend with opponents and heretics that wanted to deny or dismiss the reality of Jesus being God in the flesh. But the Church insisted that Jesus was and is fully God and fully man—not one or the other but both. So what does this mean for us? Since He came into the world as a man and was tempted in every way that we are, He can provide us with help and strength to resist temptation. We are never tempted beyond what we can bear and withstand with His help. Also, once more, Jesus lived the life we have not lived. Our lives are wrecked by and wretched with sin. Saturated by sin and deeply stained with sin. But Christ was perfect. His righteousness is credited to us as we surrender our sins to Him and His cross.

As a perfectly lived life in the flesh, Jesus could be the Lamb of God who removed the sins of the world. Indeed, John wrote, "The next day John (the Baptist) saw Jesus coming toward him and said, 'Look, the Lamb of God, who takes away the sin of the world!'" (John 1:29). There had to be a perfect sacrifice to cover the sins of humanity. Jesus paid a debt that He never incurred and died a death that He did not deserve to die to satisfy the justice of God and to remove the consequences of sin. To say that Jesus came in the flesh was and is a big deal. And this reality of His coming in the flesh is at the heart of the Christmas message. The first cry uttered by Jesus at His birth was a most welcomed sound to a lost and dying earth. Hope had come at last, and this home had come in the form of a baby named Jesus who grew to be a man and took His place on the cross to die as a man for all who believe in Him. Give thanks for what God has done and for the many places in the Bible where we find the Christmas message.

DAY 127

Not long after Jesus was born, Mary and Joseph took Him to the temple to comply with the purification rites that the Law of Moses required. Upon arriving at the temple, they met a "righteous and devout man" named Simeon and a "prophet" named Anna. While these two individuals, Simeon and Anna, appear after the birth of Jesus, their role in the Christmas story should not be minimized. Anna, we are told, "never left the Temple but worshiped night and day, fasting and praying. She gave thanks to God and spoke about the child (Jesus) to all who were looking forward to the redemption story" (Luke 2:37–38). Simeon had the following to say, "This child is destined to cause the falling and rising of many in Israel, and to be a sign that will be spoken against, so that the thoughts of many hearts will be revealed. And a sword will pierce your own soul too" (Luke 2:34–35). Consider for a moment what this man and woman have to teach us about the birth of Jesus.

First, they realized that Jesus was not an ordinary son and that His birth was not just another happy moment for a mother and father. They recognized what had taken place. They knew the Messiah had come at long last. Likewise, we want to be sure that we do not miss the lead story at Christmas—our Savior has come. We do not want the trappings of Christmas to blind us to what God has done by sending His Son. Christmas is always, first and forever, about the birth of Jesus in the fullness of time. Christmas is not just another December day or just more of the same. It is a divinely ordained day when God took active measures to defeat the evil one.

Second, they knew that Jesus would redeem all who believe. *Redeem* or *redemption* is one of the more powerful words we find in the New

Testament. The origin comes from the practice of slavery whereby someone could purchase a slave for the purpose of granting the slave his freedom. The purchaser would be said to have redeemed the slave by setting the slave free. The purchaser bought the slave out of captivity and into freedom. God redeemed us in and through His Son. We are bought out of sin and separation and set free in Christ. We no longer serve the enemy or sin or find ourselves hopelessly cut off from God. We are redeemed by Christ who paid for our forgiveness and freedom with His life.

Third, Christ became the dividing line in human history. When we are "in Christ," we have been saved, forgiven, and made new. Those who are apart from Christ or separate from Christ remain in slavery to sin and Satan. The world changed at three distinct locations—Bethlehem, the cross, and the empty tomb. Christ was born, Christ died, and Christ rose again. These events orchestrated by the Father make it possible for us to be on the right side of history and the dividing line—in and with Christ forever.

And fourth, as Simeon noted, many have spoken against Christ and continue to speak and work against Him. The enemy will do anything to draw glory away from Christ and His cross and resurrection. The enemy whispers that we are okay as we are, and any path or way we may choose to live is okay. But the Lord Himself said that small is the gate and narrow is the way that leads to life (Matthew 7:14). May we never be seduced and misled by arguments against Christ and those who would minimize His birth, life, death, and resurrection. May we grow in boldness and courage to live for Him and to renounce anything that keeps us from Him or draws us away from Him. Eternity hangs in the balance based on what we have chosen to do about Christ. We are either for Him or we oppose Him. There is not a third way that He offers us. He is either the Lord of us or something starkly less to us. And if He is less than Lord of all, He is not Lord at all. May you be encouraged by where God is at work and all that He is doing in your life.

DAY 128

3 John is a small letter. This letter is tucked away almost at the back of the Bible. It can be easy to miss or overlook. It is rarely read or studied by individuals or classes. It could be that Christians look at the maps in their Bibles more often than they read or study 3 John. This letter can be read in less than five minutes. In verse 11, John gave us a word to consider as we start another new year in 2023. He wrote, "Dear friend, don't be like those who do evil. Be like those who do good. Anyone who does what is good belongs to God. Anyone who does what is evil hasn't really seen or known God." His message is simply "do good." That is a wonderful resolution for the year that lies ahead. Maybe that is a resolution you would make here and now—"I will do what is good."

Make "doing good" a priority in your life. You can do what is good in relationships, the workplace, your family, and practically any other place where the Lord may have you serving and working. To do what is good, John wrote, means that we resist what may be evil or sinful. The enemy often gets us to rationalize or justify the evil that we might do. We can convince ourselves that evil is the payback someone else deserves or the only possible response we could muster. But doing what is evil is not something that we can quickly justify. Evil is, well, evil. And doing what is evil originates with the enemy and not with the Lord. Evil is wrong, no matter how hard we might try to argue otherwise.

If we are quick to do what is evil or we react in an evil way, John said we do not know God. We cannot entertain desires to do both evil and good. As Jesus noted, we cannot serve two masters: "No one can serve two masters. Either you will hate the one and love the other, or you will be devoted to the one and despise the other" (Matthew 6:24). As followers of Christ, we want to make doing what is good and the pursuit of what is good our passion in life.

We can practice well in anonymous ways without really calling attention to ourselves. We can pay it forward when someone does something good for us or blesses us in some way. We can practice random acts of kindness without informing the recipient of what we did for them. Some counselors and therapists suggest that practicing goodness, generosity, and kindness are ways we can shake free from despair or depression. Indeed, turning your attention toward something that blesses others is certainly a way that allows you to focus less on what may be happening in your life or circumstances. Doing good can help us to shake loose any struggles or personal slumps we may be going through.

Doing what is good does not have to cost a lot of money. A brief note, email, or text might do wonders to lift someone else's day. A small and costless or inexpensive gift might be a way to start a habit of goodness and kindness each day. Think of those simple ways that others have blessed you, and begin with them. You could easily share those same blessings with others. If you read Paul's letters, you can see that he often singled out men and women who had blessed him in some way or enriched his faith. You could set aside time to pray for someone and then follow up, letting them know that you carried them to the Lord's presence and prayed over their lives and their needs. Goodness never goes out of style or fashion. And goodness is often in short supply. Perhaps as you step into a new day, you will be inspired by the words of this small third letter from John and incorporate goodness into your life.

DAY 129

Jude is another small one-chapter book found near the back of the Bible. He identified himself as "a servant of Jesus Christ and a brother of James." His purpose in writing was to encourage and warn believers against falling for immoral teachers and the heresies they teach. He issued this warning, "They said to you, 'In the last times there will be scoffers who will follow their own ungodly desires.' These are the people who divide you, who follow mere natural instincts and do not have the Spirit" (Jude 18–19). Though issued in the first century, his warning is worth considering and remembering even today. The enemy does seek to deceive us. He is by nature a liar and deceiver. The word *scoffer* (some Bibles say *mocker*) refers to those who ridicule God or misrepresent God. In Old Testament times, these individuals would have been false prophets. In Paul's days, scoffers were those who preached to itching ears and said what others wanted to hear or paid to hear (see 2 Timothy 4:3) but not necessarily what they needed to hear.

We have to be careful not to be duped into feel-good teachings or feel-good messages. Scriptural truth is not always easy to hear or easy to follow, but it is truth. God's Word is His Word. Some preachers and writers today can easily strike a bargain to trade truth for a large and captive audience or deal away God's Word for the lesser feelings and impulses of humankind. As Jude noted, "natural instincts" can be dangerous and deceptive. If we followed our instincts alone, we would end up in some terrible situations. I am not a fan of red lights. And I would love to barrel through everyone that I see—that would be a natural instinct. But that kind of behavior could result in someone's injury or death and possibly the same for me.

Following our natural instincts is not a recipe for discipleship or a way to bring glory to God each day.

Jude gave us a better way. In Jude 3, we are told to hold on to (or contend for) the faith that has been entrusted to us through God's Word and God's messengers. "To contend for" means we will not settle for anything less. We will not bargain or barter away what we know to be God's ways, Word, and truth. You would probably contend for a number of things—your family, your health, your pictures, and your home. Likewise, Jude is saying to contend for the faith you have in Christ. Do not settle for watered-down and warmed-over feel-good messages that have little to do with scripture and a lot to do with making some profits for preachers and writers. If Christ is not glorified as the Son of God who died, lives again, and is coming again, be careful with what you are reading or studying. If God's Word is devalued, dismissed, or demoted to just another book, watch out for where you are. The pathway that you are walking on is not a good one.

Grace is never a license to sin (Jude 4). Truth is not fluid and constantly changing to fit one's mood or situation. Be wary of those who might try to convince you that God's Word can be carelessly or dismissively handled like a beanbag. The enemy would be happy to offer you any number of options so long as you stray from Christ and truth. At the end of Jude, he prayed that God would be honored for His authority, majesty, and power (Jude 25). May that be true in our lives each day.

DAY 130

In Matthew 6, Jesus gave us a lesson on prayer. We commonly call His teachings "The Lord's Prayer." And the prayer that Jesus gave is a perfect example for us to study and follow as we seek to pray each day. No book you read will ever give better guidance for praying than what Jesus offered in His model prayer. Near the beginning of the prayer, Jesus said, "Your kingdom come, your will be done, on earth as it is in heaven" (Matthew 6:9). The King James Bible reads, "Thy kingdom come, thy will be done on earth, as it is in heaven." The expression "thy will be done" is a powerful one! And frankly, I'm not sure there is much else for us to pray—thy will be done. Say it now, "Thy will be done." I have found myself, in recent days, praying "thy will be done" maybe more than ever. Often, we lack clarity or discernment about what to do or how to proceed. When the road ahead is unclear, praying for "thy will to be done" is a statement of faith and trust in God and His providence and sovereignty over all things.

When we commit something to the Lord's will, we release our control and anxiety to Him. We trust all to Him. We often sing "I surrender all." When we ask for His will to be done, then we have truly surrendered all to Him. "Thy will be done" is incredibly simple to read and say. But it is a profound statement of trust! When we pray "thy will be done," we are asking for God's ways and path and nothing less. We are willing to let go of control, our agendas, our wishes, and even our dreams. There could be areas of your life where you simply need to pray "thy will be done" over them. What would your life look like on December 31 if you cultivated the spiritual discipline of praying "thy will be done"?

When we pray "thy will be done," we are acknowledging that God has the help, provisions, and power that we need. We are recognizing our total dependence upon Him. He gives us His Word. We enjoy the company of His Holy Spirit each day. We have the assurance of the cross and empty tomb. We know He will work all things for His glory and our good (Romans 8:28). We are already far richer than we often realize. To pray "thy will be done" means we are letting go of our feeble power and resources and trusting His almighty power.

We cannot see the future in any way—not tomorrow, next month, or even the next minute. We navigate our way into the future knowing that He will be with us. When Moses stared at the Red Sea before him and the Egyptian army behind him, he said to the people, "The Lord will fight for you; you need only to be still" (Exodus 14:14). Another "thy will be done" moment. Today, we can get lost in battles and trials—even to the point we feel like we can't swim or breathe our way to safety. The solution lies in being still and knowing that God is still a fighter for His people. We are not alone. Calm your anxiousness by praying, "Thy will be done." Trust the battle or the struggle to Him and watch in amazement as He parts the waters that you are swimming against or protects you against the enemies and trials that you are facing. J. B. Phillips warned many years ago that most believers hold to a view of God that is way too small. May your view of God not be small today or ever. May you see the greatness of God and His will as you seek Him.

DAY 131

Working through the last book of the Bible—the book of Revelation—can be a daunting challenge. Broadly speaking, Revelation shows us how God will restore what was lost in Genesis when the fall of Adam and Eve took place. As God makes all things new (Revelation 21:5), He sets right every wrong and puts an end to the sin, rebellion, and defiance that have characterized history from the moment of the first sin all the way to now. At the end of Revelation, John wrote, "He who testifies to these things says, 'Yes, I am coming soon.' Amen. Come, Lord Jesus. The grace of the Lord Jesus be with God's people. Amen" (Revelation 22:20–21). The Bible makes it clear that Christ is coming again. The Lord Himself made that promise at the end of Revelation. The last thing the Lord Jesus left for His people in His Word was His unchanging promise to come again. He left us with this amazing assurance.

When will the Lord return? We do not know the specific day and time. Have people made attempts to know? Yes, most certainly. Some have engaged in assigning dates to the Lord's return. I used to have a book in my office entitled *101 Reasons Why Christ Returns by 1988*. The book clearly did not age well. And frankly, it was wrong and deceived people badly. The same author later corrected himself and stated that Christ would return on October 28, 1992. Yet here we are still. There is almost nothing to be gained by projecting a day, date, or time for the Lord to return. Jesus said in Mark 13 that only the Father knows such things. Jesus even issued this warning, "At that time if anyone says to you, 'Look, here is the Messiah!' or, 'Look, there he is!' do not believe it. For false messiahs and false prophets will appear and perform signs and wonders to deceive, if possible, even the elect" (Mark 13:21–22).

Knowing that the Lord is coming again should offer us at least three practical blessings. First, we can be comforted by this certainty. The Lord keeps His promises and remembers His people. The battles we face today are temporary in nature and short-lived in comparison to eternity. The Lord will make right every wrong and bring justice to every injustice. Second, we should be compelled to serve the Lord. Knowing that Christ is returning should motivate us to live every day for Him and to serve Him fully with all that He has provided to us. Share your faith. Pray for others. Serve Him with joy and gladness. Whenever the Lord does return, may He find us doing what He has given us to do and being faithful to the gifts and blessings He has provided to us.

Third, we should be convinced that God's Word is true and His ways are right. We should not worry much about those who make end-time forecasts and predictions like a weatherman may do. Frankly, a lot of people just want to sell books or make a name for themselves and they take advantage of others in doing so. Hold on to what God says He wants us to know. His Son is coming again. And just as Jesus was born in Bethlehem in the fullness of time, He will return in the fullness of time when the Father says it is right. If we are ready to meet Him every day or any day, then we have nothing to do to get ready. We can simply say, as Revelation says, "Come, Lord Jesus."

Do not be fearful; rather be faithful. Do not be anxious; rather be at peace. Do not be doubtful; rather be confident. Place your hopes in the Lord who has kept every promise and does everything just as it should be done. Be joyful with each passing day because we are one day closer to beholding the most beautiful sight we could ever see—the face of our Lord coming triumph and glory! Great things await us. A great moment is on the way. Live each day in anticipation of this moment.

DAY 132

One thing that is immediately clear in Revelation is how much we do not know. For example, we do not know when Christ will return to His people. Even Jesus said that He did not possess that knowledge. Only the Father knows. Jesus said, "But about that day or hour no one knows, not even the angels in heaven, nor the Son, but only the Father" (Mark 13:32). As we have said as we make our way through Revelation, we always want to avoid setting dates and times for events or moments that we do not know. We do not want to speak decisively and definitively about that which we do not possess perfect knowledge or insider knowledge.

But there is an even larger lesson that we can draw out of Jesus's words. God knows everything, and we clearly do not. Compared to God, we know terribly little. We can see the present moment (though not perfectly). Our knowledge of the future is limited and almost nonexistent. We might have some general inklings about the future but nothing written in certainty. Our knowledge of the past is tainted by poor memories and incomplete recall. So, Jesus's words teach us to be humble about what we do and do not know. We trust Him to work out details that are beyond our understanding or strength to change.

When it comes to the future, we can approach it with three guiding principles. First, we can be confident that God will work out His purposes in our lives as we trust Him and look to Him. We do not have to be captured and controlled by the events of the world. God's ways are not impacted by the actions of nations, governments, financial markets, or businesses. His ways are eternal, and He will see them through to completion. If we trust the Lord and seek His purposes in life, we know we are in a safe place (Proverbs 3:5–6).

Second, God calls us to be faithful a day at a time and often a moment at a time. We are not to be stressed or strained by what might be coming tomorrow, next week, or next year. We are to be faithful to what God has given us to do at this moment in time. Paul wrote about God's sufficient grace. And the old apostle knew that grace and experienced it personally more than once. He will always grant the grace that we need to serve Him in anything that has been entrusted to us. Set your face and heart on what God has for you today. And if tomorrow comes, do likewise. Jesus modeled this kind of resolution for us to see. On the night before His crucifixion, Jesus prayed with fervency and asked if "this cup" (the cross) might be taken from Him. But Jesus prayed, "Not what I will, but what you will" (Mark 14:36).

Third, be grateful that God is in charge and in control so you and I do not have to take the reins of the universe. It is good to know that the Father is on the throne and will reign forever and ever. The Bible says that a day with Him is like a thousand years (2 Peter 3:8). The small things that might trouble or puzzle us can always be released to Him to take control. Faith and spiritual maturity often involve recognizing the majesty and magnificence of God over all things. His kingdom is forever, and we can be grateful that we live in that kingdom. Or as Paul put it, "Our citizenship is in heaven" (Philippians 3:20). To be citizens in His kingdom means we can relax and let Him be in control and trust all things to Him.

DAY 133

The first word in the book of Psalms is blessed (1:1). The last word in Psalms is LORD (found in Psalm 150:6). The reality is we are blessed. We are blessed people. We are blessed by the LORD. Blessed is a word that figures prominently in the Bible and in many places besides Psalms. We find this word in both the Old and New Testaments. Throughout the Bible, we learn the ways we are blessed and the means by which God blesses His people. We often recognize some of the obvious blessings that God provides to us (food to eat, a home where we live, family, friendships we can trust, healing, forgiveness, salvation). But we can easily overlook or simply miss many of the ways God blesses His people. Our busyness and humanity often get in the way of clearly seeing all that God is doing in and for His people.

I read a story recently about an older gentleman well into his nineties who had developed a practice about seventy years earlier in his life. He simply writes down at least three blessings every day that God has given to Him. As you might imagine, he has filled quite a few notebooks through the decades naming what God has given to Him. But this gentleman is on to something important. We want to be able to name, identify and acknowledge what God has done and how amazingly blessed most of us can say that we are. Living with an awareness of our blessings and in a state of gratitude is a healthy choice for us emotionally, mentally, and physically.

Paul commanded us in I Thessalonians 5:18 to give thanks in ALL circumstances. While circumstances can and do change for all of us, and often quickly so, there is one constant linear thread that does not have to change. We can maintain a state of gratitude and an awareness of the ways we are blessed. Indeed, we might be better at handling some of the circumstances we face if we began with an awareness of our blessings and gifts.

A goal for all believers is spiritual maturity or, put another way, growing up in Christ. Recognizing how we are blessed is one step on that continuous journey and process known as maturity. Looking for the ways we are blessed is a rewarding exercise in discernment or sharpening our spiritual vision and eyesight. In 2 Timothy 4, Paul gave some valuable life instructions to his beloved spiritual son. In 4:15, Paul wrote about how to handle or live out these instructions. Paul wrote, "be diligent in these matters; give yourself wholly to them, so that everyone may see your progress." Many things in faith require diligence and devotion. Recognizing our blessedness is one such thing. Human nature often tends toward envy, jealousy, and pettiness. We can be captured by small, trivial things yet miss the huge matters that God has for us to see or to learn. Be diligent in seeing, naming, and acknowledging the way God has blessed you. Perhaps a running list of daily blessings is the discipline you need to sharpen your vision and discernment.

Perhaps you establish an agreement with a good friend that you will mutually text each other three blessings you have experienced each day. You could hold each other accountable in doing that. After about forty days, that practice will likely become part of your life and you will be experiencing the joys and maturity that it brings to you. Blessed! The word alone brings a sense of peace and contentment. Perhaps even a smile begins to form on your face. It is hard even to say the word "blessed" without a smile forming on your face and a warm feeling rising in your chest. Remember today that you are blessed. And that the LORD is the author and maker of all blessings.

DAY 134

We have probably all heard the expression that "we reap what we sow." Indeed, it has a biblical origin. Galatians 6:7 says, "a man reaps what he sows." Generally speaking, this verse is saying we tend to get back what we give. If we engage in dangerous or destructive behavior, we will likely suffer the consequences from it. We could think of this as a boomerang effect. Just as a boomerang is designed to return to the user or sender, sin tends to come back against us. Harmful behavior that we inflict upon others can land on us too.

Proverbs 26:27 says, "If a man digs a pit, he will fall into it; if a man rolls a stone, it will roll back on him." Solomon is helping us to realize that we can become captive to our own sinful ways and schemes. These things can easily blow back against us. There is a cause-and-effect relationship in the spiritual world. The antidote to this boomerang effect is seeking to do good and to sow seeds that are good. We want to invest in good things for our lives and, likewise, we want to sow good things into the lives of family, friends and others we meet. We want to uplift and encourage them by offering good seeds and not bad ones.

You can proactively sow good in the lives of others with a warm text, an encouraging letter or card, a hug when someone is hurting or an email that offers your prayers at a challenging time. Some of the people who do the best job of sowing good seeds into the lives of others are usually people who are below the radar. They are not making a big deal out of what they are doing. They are simply, quietly, and graciously sowing and planting good into the lives of others.

There is a man in the New Testament named Barnabas who was known for his encouraging capabilities. He was among the first to extend a hand of brotherhood and friendship to Paul following his turn away from being a terrorist and turn toward trusting in Jesus Christ. Barnabas took a risk by sowing good seeds into the life of a man whose mere name raised fear and trembling among Christians across the Middle East. To be a man or woman who sows what is good, we often have to take a risk.

In the Old Testament, we read about the friendship enjoyed between David and Jonathan. Remember Jonathan was Saul's son. And David was God's chosen replacement for Saul after God had rejected him as king. Jonathan could have stewed in a soup of bitterness and resentment. But he did not do that. He kept his friendship with David and always acted in ways that were in David's best interest. As Proverbs tells us, we never want to set traps for others and we never want to roll a stone on someone to crush him. We want to offer an open hand of friendship and good seeds that we can plant for God's glory.

Today, take a look at the seeds you are sowing. Pray for someone. Send a quick text or email to brighten someone's day. Give a pat on the back to a friend whose love and support have meant the world to you. Bless someone with a small gift that simply says I love you and I appreciate you. Be the one who sows good today so the harvest you reap is good as well. Have a great day being a blessing to others!

DAY 135

It has been said that we can enjoy as much of God as we wish. Think of these words in terms of a relationship with a spouse or child. You may have some casual contact and a few perfunctory words here and there but there is not much depth. You live in the same house but share few of the same joys, interests, or pursuits. You know each other but, well, all you can say is you know each other. We can often adopt the same stance toward the Lord. We want salvation, forgiveness, and grace but we have little interest in pursuing the Lord and devote little time to walking with the Lord. We make our faith "one more thing to do." One of my favorite preachers from the nineteenth century is A.W. Tozer. He once wrote, "we have been snared in the coils of a false logic which insists that if we have found Him, we need no more to seek Him." Sadly, that logic prevails today in many hearts and minds of people who believe themselves to be followers of Christ and profess that faith openly and confidently.

We can easily become complacent and think that a conversion experience is both the starting line and the finish line of faith. It may be helpful to think of the salvation experience in three ways. First, we are justified. That means God declares us not guilty of our sins based on what Jesus did for us at the cross. We exercise belief in the death and resurrection of Jesus and the power of His cross for our forgiveness. Nothing else! We are justified by God's grace and our total surrender to Him in faith making no pretense that we can save ourselves, forgive ourselves or earn any special favor or standing. Second, we are sanctified. God is making us more like Jesus every day and in every way. Through reading the Bible, prayer, worship, life situations and the work of the Holy Spirit in us, God is making us increasingly into the likeness of Christ. Unlike justification, which is a one-time event, sanctification is a daily process that extends over the life of our faith and existence. If we live as a Christian for 100 years, sanctification lasts for 100 years. Third, we are glorified. Glorification happens at the moment of death when God calls His people to be with Him forever, to enter into His presence and to enjoy what He has prepared. Glorification does not happen in this lifetime or this world. It awaits us.

Based on these three ways of seeing salvation, we can say that God is faithfully at work in the past, present, and future. He has worked. He is working. He will work. We never want to strike a posture that says we know all that we need to know and we are satisfied in our faith. We always want to continue to grow...in grace, truth, love, faith, and fellowship. We will never exhaust the riches of God's grace, wisdom, and truth. May we always be wanting more of God in our minds, hearts, days, and lives. May we never think that we have no need to pursue Him or to deepen our relationship with Him. Paul wrote in Romans 11:33, "Oh, the depth of the riches of the wisdom and knowledge of God! How unsearchable his judgments, and his paths beyond tracing out!" You might think the wisdom and ways of God are as plentiful and rich as the grains of sand on the earth. Wrong! The grains of sand, though numerous and many, are a finite number. There is a sum or finite total. That is not the case with God. He is infinite and unending in greatness, glory, wisdom, and truth. We will never reach a boundary with God where we have gone as far as possible. May we wake up each day and ask, "Lord, what do you have to teach and show me today?" And may we embark upon a daily faith journey with Him.